LEADING POLICING IN EUROPE

An empirical study of strategic police leadership

Bryn Caless and Steve Tong

First published in Great Britain in 2017 by

Policy Press
University of Bristol
1-9 Old Park Hill
Bristol
BS2 8BB
UK
+44 (0)117 954 5940
pp-info@bristol.ac.uk
www.policypress.co.uk

North America office:
Policy Press
c/o The University of Chicago Press
1427 East 60th Street
Chicago, IL 60637, USA
t: +1 773 702 7700
f: +1 773 702 9756
sales@press.uchicago.edu
www.press.uchicago.edu

British Library Cataloguing in Publication Data
A catalogue record for this book is available from the British Library

Library of Congress Cataloging-in-Publication Data
A catalog record for this book has been requested

ISBN 978 1 44731 572 8 hardcover
ISBN 978-1-4473-1574-2 paperback
ISBN 978-1-4473-2120-0 ePub
ISBN 978-1-4473-2121-7 Mobi
ISBN 978-1-4473-1573-5 ePdf

Cover design by Qube Design Associates, Bristol
Printed and bound in Great Britain by CPI Group (UK) Ltd, Croydon, CR0 4YY
Policy Press uses environmentally responsible print partners

We dedicate this book to

Harry Peeters,

friend from the beginning

and guide throughout our European journey

Contents

List of figures and tables

Figure

Tables

Glossary

Here is a very short glossary of the most common terms, abbreviations and acronyms used in the EU. If they occur in the pages that follow, they are again explained at first use.

acquis (French) A difficult term to translate for all its widespread use in Europe. It means something like 'the heritage of accumulated knowledge' and has special resonance in policing experience. 'Policing *acquis*' can be used to suggest insider knowledge or the kinds of insight that come from long policing experience

ACPO The Association of Chief Police Officers (England and Wales); was the national voice of chief police officers until December 2014, when public funding was withdrawn. Replaced by the National Police Chiefs' Council in January 2015

agents (French) police officers in the Police Nationale

Common Market Term descriptive of the European community in the 1970s and 1980s; the commonality of trade and the formation of a 'customs union' were (and still are) features of unification in Europe

corpus juris In full, *corpus juris criminalis*, the body of criminal law. This is a commonly used term in the EU which reflects an aspiration, particularly on the part of strategic police leaders, to have an integrated criminal law operative across Europe (and probably supplemental to, rather than a replacement of, national criminal laws)

CEPOL European Police College

CSCE Conference on Security and Cooperation in Europe

democratic deficit A contested term, used to suggest that the EU is largely governed by officials and is not subject to the (rather inert) European Parliament in the same way that democratic nation-states are subject to their national parliaments (Bache et al, 2011, p. 67)

EAW European Arrest Warrant

EC European Commission: the body of European officialdom largely based in Brussels. The term was once used to describe the *European Community* (forerunner term for *EU*)

ECHR European Convention on Human Rights

ECJ European Court of Justice

ENISA The European Union Agency for Network and Information Security founded in 2009, intended to coordinate investigations into, and prevention of, cybercrime

EU European Union

Euro Currency common to most but not all EU countries

EuroGendFor European Gendarmerie Force (also EGF). The gendarmeries of Europe constitute a potent 'militarised' police presence and consist of the French *Gendarmerie*, the Italian *Carabinieri*, the Spanish *Guardia Civil*, the Portuguese *Guarda Nacional,* the Dutch *Koninklijke Maréchaussée*, the Polish *Żandarmeria*, the Lithuanian *Viešojo Saugumo Tarnybaand* and the Romanian *Jandarmeria*. The Turkish *Jandarma* was granted 'observer status' in 2009

Eurojust European Judicial Cooperation Unit

Europol European Police Office

Frontex European Agency for the management of external borders

FSB The Federal Security Service of the Russian Federation

gendarmeries A militarised form of policing developed by Napoleon from the provost role. Modern gendarmeries tend to police rural areas, undertake public order duties and royal or VIP protection

GODIAC Acronym for 'good practice for dialogue and communications', which started in 2010 and is an EU-wide initiative for understanding crowd control in political demonstrations

Gold A policing concept borrowed from the military, which designates in 'Gold', 'Silver' and 'Bronze' the respective layers of command in an incident or operation. 'Gold' is strategic police leader level

IPCB Independent Police Complaints Body

JITs Joint Investigation Teams

juge d'instruction This is the active role of a member of the judiciary in investigation of (usually) serious crime; the *juge* directs the court proceedings and questions the accused

MOPAC The Mayor's Office for Policing and Crime in London

MPA The Metropolitan Police Authority which MOPAC replaced

MPS Metropolitan Police Service

OLAF European Anti-Fraud Office

OSCE Organisation for Security and Cooperation in Europe

PCSO Police Community Support Officer; introduced in England and Wales in 2002 this is a lesser role than warranted police, confined mainly to neighbourhood patrols and dealing with non-criminal nuisance

Public prosecutor A career lawyer, this person instructs the police what to investigate, what evidence to look for and whom to question. In Scotland, the Procurator Fiscal performs a similar role

RABIT(s) Rapid Border Intervention Team(s)

Region To reinforce the anonymity of our respondents, we have used European regions rather than individual countries as markers. The regions are *Baltic:* Estonia, Latvia, Lithuania; *Benelux:* Belgium, the Netherlands, Luxembourg; *British Isles:* England, Wales, Scotland, Northern Ireland, Isle of Man, Republic of Ireland; *Nordic:* Sweden, Norway, Finland, Denmark, Iceland; *Alpine:* Austria, Switzerland, Liechtenstein, Slovenia, Germany; *Central Europe:* Poland, Czech Republic, Romania, Slovakia, Hungary; and the *Mediterranean:* Portugal, Spain, France, Monaco, Italy, Croatia, Bosnia and

Herzegovina, Montenegro, Albania, Greece, Turkey, Cyprus, Malta and the British territory of Gibraltar

rightward shift A term used to describe the increased representation of right-wing political movements in the May 2014 European elections, including groups such as the French *Front Nationale*, the Greek 'Golden Dawn' and the UK Independence Party (UKiP)

SIRENE Supplementary Information Request at the National Entry

SIS Schengen Information System

TOPSPOC CEPOL's Top Senior Police Officers' Course, run approximately annually

UN United Nations, the international forum created after the Second World War to act globally on matters of conflict, health education and so on

USSR The Union of Soviet Socialist Republics, the name for the old communist Russian Bloc, which included places now independent, such as Estonia and Georgia. The USSR extended to Germany and Berlin until its collapse in 1990

About the authors

Bryn Caless is Senior Lecturer in the School of Law, Criminal Justice and Computing at Canterbury Christ Church University, UK. He specialises in elite studies of policing and police accountability and has written *Policing at the Top* (Policy Press, 2011) on chief police officers in England and Wales. He is currently researching the role of police and crime commissioners.

Steve Tong is Director of Policing and Criminal Justice in the School of Law, Criminal Justice and Computing at Canterbury Christ Church University. He has published widely with research interests in police learning and development, professionalisation, criminal investigation and police leadership.

Acknowledgements

We heartily thank all the 108 strategic police leaders in Europe who kindly took the time to answer our questions and whose time was so precious.

In particular, we acknowledge those police leaders and their busy staff officers who assisted us at the European Police Chiefs Convention, 2012, in Europol's Headquarters, Den Haag, the Netherlands; and Bryn's four successive years of Erasmus Master's students in the Estonian Security Academy, Tallinn.

We gratefully acknowledge the help of the following:

Dr Mark Abram, Senior Research Officer, Research, Analysis and Information, College of Policing (UK);

DCI Dave Annets, Hampshire Police, UK Lead Officer to CEPOL, for so brilliantly facilitating access to European strategic police leaders, for conducting interviews on our behalf and for his ready help at the College of Policing (UK) and, above all, for his belief in the value of the project;

Ferenc Banfi, Director, CEPOL, and Deputy Director Detlef Schroeder, together with Dr Detlef Nogala, Research and Science officer, CEPOL, for their help and support;

Olivier Burgersdijk, Head of Strategy, European Cybercrime Centre, Europol, for his kind assistance and readiness to share his researches in police leadership with us;

Brian Donald, Chief of Staff to the Director, Europol for his help at the European Police Chiefs' Convention, 2012, in Europol's Headquarters, Den Haag, the Netherlands;

Canterbury Christ Church University (CCCU), particularly Professor Tony Lavender and Professor Janet Haddock-Fraser, for funding and assistance in the early empirical research phases of this work; and for the grant of study leave to Bryn Caless in the Michaelmas Term 2013, so that he could progress analysis of the data and write some of the chapters;

Kurt Eyre, Director, International Division of the College of Policing (UK), Bramshill, for his enthusiasm about our project and readiness to share his own research with us;

Dr Frank Gallagher, long-standing colleague, whose access to European, particularly French, police services is unparalleled and whose knowledge is a fathomless well;

drs Werner Gowitzke, Kriminalhauptkommissar of Duisburg Police, for his ready help in facilitating access to European strategic police leaders;

Dr Branko Lobnikar, University of Maribor, esteemed colleague from EDP days, for facilitating access in Eastern and Southern Europe;

Dr Karel Marttin, Dutch Police Academy;

Tina Maripüü and Elina Reva, Estonian Security Academy, Tallinn, for facilitating access in the Baltic States;

Drs Harry Peeters, formerly of the Dutch Police Academy, now Liaison Tutor at CCCU, for facilitating access to European chief police officers, conducting interviews, translating from three languages into English and for many years of friendship;

Dr Maurice Punch, Visiting Professor, King's College London and London School of Economics, and expert on European police, for his invaluably careful reading of initial drafts of chapters;

Dr Marisa Silvestri for reading whole draft chapters, making valuable suggestions and helping we 'pale males' to understand the female officers' viewpoints;

Dr Paul Swallow, colleague at CCCU, whose insights into European policing institutions have been most helpful and for his reading of various chapters;

Rob Wainwright, Director, Europol and Convenor of the European Police Chiefs Convention, Den Haag, the Netherlands, for his encouragement and provision of office space at the Convention;

Debbie Wells and Sheila Wraight, funding gurus, CCCU; for arranging funding for our fraught and sometimes short-notice trips to Europe to conduct interviews.

Bryn Caless offers special thanks to Dr Steve Tong, friend and colleague, who shared the research highs and lows, experienced cheerfully some of the drudgery involved in writing up the findings and statistics, and who successfully restrained Bryn from throwing a recalcitrant Belgian into the Yser Canal in 2011. And Bryn gives particular and heartfelt thanks to Clarey, wonderful helpmeet, patient listener, corrector of howlers, reader of drafts and life companion, and Maddy, who helped to keep her father rooted in cyber-reality, introduced him gently to Skype, and encouraged him to learn to share computer terminals at home, especially when hers broke.

Steve Tong would like to thank his friend and colleague, Bryn Caless, for approaching him in the first instance with the idea of examining police leadership in Europe to follow on from his work on police leaders in the United Kingdom. Bryn's determination and leadership in driving forward the research have been crucial factors in producing this book, without which it would never have reached publication.

Steve would also like to thank his family, including his wife Mel and children, Holly and Adam, for their understanding and support when he was working into the evenings and weekends. Finally his parents, Terry and Brenda, for their unconditional support for everything and anything he does.

Introduction

> Analysing empirical evidence about the police is a corrective to ideologically-based generalisations, and to (now less fashionable) postmodern assertions that we have no means of arbitrating between a kaleidoscope of competing 'discourses' and 'representations' of the police. (Malcolm Anderson, 2011, pp 1-2)

General context

For non-European readers, it may be helpful here to give a short general context for politics, policing and police leadership in Europe. We draw your attention also to the historical outline provided in Chapter One, which tries to contextualise European policing in the period immediately prior to the French Revolution of 1789 and thereafter. The Revolution and its aftermath in the Napoleonic Empire (1799-1815) did much to shape subsequent policing structures in Europe; indeed, dismantling or modifying that Napoleonic legacy may still be in progress.[1]

The European Union (EU)

Europe as a modern entity came into existence in the aftermath of the Second World War. Not only did Europe need rebuilding after the effects of war had damaged many countries' infrastructures, but there was also a strong political will to rebuild Europe along federal lines, so as to obviate the dominance of the Continent by a single European power and to reduce to a minimum the possibilities of further conflict. This is what Ian Bache and his colleagues describe as 'moves towards a consensual approach to European unity' (Bache

---

[1] The Greeks did not dismantle their Napoleonic legacy of a gendarmerie until 1974, and it might be argued that the Belgian dissolution of its gendarmerie in 2001 continued that process. As will be seen in subsequent pages, particularly in Chapter Seven, the strategic repositioning of Europe's remaining gendarmeries to meet new geopolitical challenges may be interpreted either as the final throes of the Napoleonic policing legacy, or its reinvention as something dynamic and contemporary.

et al, 2011, p. 81). Additionally, the new politics of the 'Cold War'[2] meant that the United States exercised considerable influence on post-war Europe (not forgetting its strong military presence in NATO and in West Germany). Bache et al comment on the birth of modern Europe that '[t]he signing of the Treaty of Paris in April 1951 by the governments of Belgium, France, [West] Germany, Italy, Luxembourg and the Netherlands [...] began the process commonly referred to as European integration' (Bache et al, 2011, p3).

These core members with their 'Common Market', later embraced (more or less willingly) countries on their peripheries to grow to 15 states in the European Community (EC) by the 1990s, but, after reintegration of a united Germany in 1991, the second major expansion of the renamed EU occurred in 2004, when eight 'aspirant' countries from the former Soviet Union, joined as newly fledged democracies (Cameron, 2004).[3] By 2013, with the addition of Croatia, the EU comprised 28 sovereign members, all of whom had signed up to the European Convention on Human Rights and to a series of cooperative interchanges on policing and criminal matters,[4] involving protocols, data exchange, joint staffing of the European Police Office (Europol), legal cooperation through Eurojust, and extradition through use of the European Arrest Warrant. And still a number of countries apply to join; the waiting list of applicants is growing.[5]

It is important to note that we have not confined our researches to the EU alone; indeed, we have sought comment from strategic police leaders in those non-EU countries that are active in international cooperation, including Switzerland and Norway. Although such states are not subject to EU law, they nonetheless exchange data, protocols and criminal information with the other law enforcement

---

[2] Where West was pitted against East, capitalism opposed communism in a clash of ideologies and a unified Western Europe acted as a buffer against Soviet Russia's expansion westwards.

[3] They were Estonia, the Czech Republic, Hungary, Latvia, Lithuania, Poland, Slovakia and Slovenia, together with Malta and Cyprus.

[4] Among a host of others: Criminal Law, Policing and Security comprise only a 'third pillar' of European cooperative treaties and legislation. There is a mass of agreements, protocols and understandings across a range of commercial, political, defence, trade, research, science and technology matters, which are too complex and too tedious to treat in detail here.

[5] Seven more countries wait in the wings. See: EU enlargement in 2014 and beyond: progress and challenges, *European Commission*, IP/14/1100 08/10/2014, http://europa.eu/rapid/press-release_IP-14-1100_en.htm

agencies in Europe and share international agreements with external countries such as Canada and the United States. It seemed to us daft to exclude countries that are part of the physical continent simply because they have not formally joined the EU. That said, we were unable to gain access to Belarus or to the Ukraine, or to some other 'applicant countries' and so had to draw a line somewhere.[6] What all these countries share, whether or not members of the EU, are threats to their economic and political well-being from transnational organised crime, terrorism and cybercrime.

The global criminal context

In almost the same way (and often using the same methods) as legitimate businesses have expanded their operations to become globalised concerns, so criminal enterprises have increased the scale and reach of their illegitimate operations to worldwide proportions. This suggests that we cannot regard the EU as a self-contained entity. Just as global market brands – from Coca-Cola to G4S – impact on their national economies (Gritsch, 2005), so the movement of illegal drugs, 'sex and slave' trafficking routes and the smuggling of outlawed or illegal materials impact on their law enforcement jurisdictions, as they do elsewhere in the world (Lemieux, 2010; Dean et al, 2010; Mallory, 2012). The EU is largely powerless on its own to deal with, for example, Colombian drugs cartels, but the effects of such transnational organised crime are certainly felt within Europe and preoccupy its law enforcement agencies (van den Wyngaert et al, 1993; Anderson et al, 1995; Mawby, 1999; Edwards and Gill, 2003; Mallory, 2012).

We look later (Chapter Five) at bilateral police cooperation to deal operationally with some manifestations of transnational organised crime within Europe, and note the inhibiting effects of 'pan-European' multilateralism and how national politics often determine the range and extent of force-to-force cooperation. It is not our purpose to consider global crime in any detail (there are excellent books that do that), but self-evidently, where such crime touches Europe, there are consequences for policing. For example, it is worth noting briefly that a sizeable proportion of the world's production of cocaine, heroin and other 'Class A' drugs is destined for Europe, and the importation routes intersect Europe's borders at many points. The trafficking of humans

---

[6]   This line *excluded* Iceland, Montenegro, Macedonia, Moldova, Bosnia-Hercegovina and Serbia. Some are applicants to the EU; others simply did not respond to our overtures or to those of our interlocutors.

follows similar routes (Sheptycki and Wardak, 2005; Mallory, 2012), while there is clear evidence of organised criminal groups targeting individual EU countries for robbery, theft and fraud (Siegel, 2014).

Because so much transnational organised crime originates outside Europe, there is evident need for partnerships across the world between police jurisdictions, but the reality on the ground seems to indicate a strong element of parochialism within Europe and a rather resentful partnership (probably because it is subordinate) with the United States. This demonstrates on a larger scale the general reluctance of strategic police leaders in Europe to surrender any vestige of national autonomy in law enforcement, and a parallel reluctance to engage in anything approaching 'pan-European' operational policing.[7]

In England and Wales since 2012, it has become evident that there has been a power shift from the police themselves to the police and crime commissioners, elected individuals who hold strategic police leaders to account. This has had ramifications for local policing priorities. In similar ways across Europe, policing has had to respond to the neo-liberal values now dominating social thinking, to diminished budgets and to increased austerity as a result of the economic recession, to more intrusive media commentary and to closer political attention. This power shift may not have been as abrupt as that in England and Wales, but the increased power of the media and the strength of political oversight are tangible.[8]

On a larger stage still, it might be argued that the manufacturing shifts and monetary currents that have marked the rise of China, Brazil, Russia and India (the so-called 'BRIC' countries) as new world economies, signal a long-term decline in the primacy of the United States and Europe as major actors in both crime-fighting and in global economics. If that is the case, and if power is shifting from the West

---

[7] We should note that Europol, as we explain in more detail in Chapter Five, is not a police force: it is a gatherer and analyst of criminal and other information. The nation states that make up the EU have so far proved resistant to any notion that Europol should either override their national sovereignty or be able to command their assistance, or both. Until this can happen, it is meaningless to talk of a 'European Police Force' (except perhaps in terms of a collective gendarmerie for international public order; see Chapter Seven).

[8] Some might argue that in most of Europe, care has been taken to ensure precisely that power has been moved from the police to those who oversee them: the courts and politicians. But *the exercise of force on behalf of the nation state* will always ensure that a residuum of power remains in police ownership and is detached from external influence.

generally to these emergent super-economies, we may expect that global criminality will relocate as well; targeting, as always, money, influence and power. The current flux of global political power-plays, ruinous 'foreign adventurism' by the US and UK in recent decades, the striking and prolonged failure of the United States to be the world's policeman, the 'stagflation' of the European economy, weaknesses in European banking and other capitalist fields, alongside the failure of European law enforcement agencies to act 'globally' or collectively against transnational organised crime, may together signal that the age-old global dominance of the West is coming to an end (Ferguson, 2004; Ikenberry, 2008; Pomeranz, 2009; Ferguson, 2012). At present, there is no sign that any of the new emergent world economies wants to assume the world lead in law enforcement as well (Slaughter, 2009).

Perhaps, as Maria Gritsch observes, the world is now controlled by the 'soft geo-politics' of global companies, and is no longer monopolised by strong nation states or mutually protective federations (Gritsch, 2005). If so, it cannot be long before there is a parallel criminal control operating equally globally and with pretty hard 'geo-politics', in the shadows. Law enforcement agencies, whatever their cooperative intentions and good will, may not be able to deal with that 'Dark Web' (Yar, 2013).

On 'the nature of the elite'

Elites generally seem to be fairly well understood by academics and others, but policing elites – especially those who have strategic command of policing – are much less familiar and invariably constitute a 'closed shop' to outsiders. In 2011, Bryn Caless wrote this about strategic police leaders in England and Wales: 'For all that there is scrutiny and for all that there is oversight of what he or she does, the chief officer of police remains a quite unknown and elusive factor in criminology and in the analysis of policing (Caless, 2011, p1).

It seems that his comment holds good for continental European strategic police leaders as much as for their English and Welsh counterparts. The existing studies of strategic policing in Europe are now either a little long in the tooth, or regionally based; or are part of more generalised considerations about policing,[9] while the closed shop of the police leadership elite seems to have withstood attempts to open its locked doors: indeed, there has been no empirical overview of the elite of European strategic police leaders until now. Yet it is surely important for us all to understand what sort of people make the key decisions at the top of policing in the countries of Europe?[10] Can strategic police leaders ever be genuinely independent, or are they simply subject to factors that inhibit their decision-making? What, in Gareth Rice's words, are the 'particularities of [their] power'?[11] What role do local and national politics and politicians play in policing, and how do police leaders get on with the mayors and ministers who set political parameters for them? Are there regional variations? What are the strengths and challenges in working across national borders? What other room for manoeuvre does the strategic police leader have? Does the leader have genuine discretion to act operationally or not? How accountable are strategic police officers? How did strategic leaders get to their positions and what do they think of selection processes operating at the top of the hierarchy?

This is only a selection of the questions that have surfaced during our years of involvement in the study and practice of policing and criminal justice, and from our analyses of police responses to transnational organised crime and terrorism in Europe, but those questions are the fundamental ones; many of which we try to answer in this book. When we also consider the '*acquis*'[12] of policing across Europe, and factors such as regional variations, differences in crime priorities, numbers of police forces and the many different ways in which police officers make it to the top of their profession, it is hardly surprising

---

[9] Such as studies by Anderson et al (1995), Pagon (1996), Loader and Mulcahy (2001), Merlingen and Ostrauskaite, (2006) and Meško and Maver (2010). Geoffrey Marshall argued in 1978 that 'indirect' accountability for the police was preferable to direct accountability in many ways (Marshall, 1978; Loveday, 1999), but we could argue that no police chief is ever fully independent; all his or her actions and decisions are hedged about with checks, balances and compromises.

[10] In the wider European sense, this will include countries that are not part of the EU but whose police forces cooperate with those in the Union: Norway and Switzerland are prime examples. Correspondingly, it was important for us to interview strategic police leaders from those countries (which we did).

[11] In his *Reflections on Interviewing Elites* (2010, p. 71).

[12] A useful, if somewhat vague, 'European' term: it means something like the 'accumulated weight of policing heritage' in this context.

that commentators on the police in Europe baulk at the challenge of establishing a coherent overall picture of this very complex business.

Because of this, we take Malcolm Anderson's point at the head of this Introduction to heart: no meaningful discussion of strategic police leadership in Europe and therefore of what is a highly specialist elite, can be conducted without a body of empirical evidence giving coherence and 'rich detail' to the voice of that elite. Indeed, this cannot be properly obtained without engaging with the police leaders themselves and encouraging them to speak honestly and freely about the strains and stresses of the job, offering precisely the 'discourses [and] representations' that are denied to remote external analysis. Few police leaders would willingly engage in such narratives on the record. Nearly all of those to whom we spoke asked for reassurances that what they said would be anonymous, and some repeatedly sought our firm undertaking that their names would be protected.[13] Even apparently confident elites can be tremulous when careers are at stake, it seems. But we are equally sure that the strategic police leaders were honest in their replies (why would they not be, if what they say is unattributable?) and that we were given unique access to what they think and believe. The result, we hope, is some authentic insight into the top end of European policing 'society'.[14]

Harold Lasswell and his colleagues remind us that elite groups can be mirrors of society at large:

> The manner in which the "leadership" is chosen; the breadth of the social base from which it is recruited; the way in which it exercises [...] decision-making power; the extent and nature of its accountability [...] are indicators of the degree of shared power, shared respect, shared well-being, and shared safety in a given society at a given time. (Lasswell et al, 1952, Introduction)

In other words, looking at the elites that a society produces ought to give the observer interesting insights into the values and ethos of that society. Where once birth, aristocratic privilege, land ownership

---

[13] Because they did not want publicly to be associated with their sometimes iconoclastic views and occasionally caustic comments. Our interlocutors are not 'semi-legally' anonymous in the way that a journalist's sources are, and we do not anticipate court injunctions to reveal their identities.

[14] A more detailed explanation of the Methodology of our research follows.

or industrial wealth self-evidently determined elite selection,[15] some now believe that egalitarianism dominates: skills and demonstrable merit are now primary criteria for advancement.[16] Others believe the contrary: that society still predicates its elites through opaque patronage and nepotism, 'cloning' those who will rise to the top (Vinton, 1998; Savage and Williams, 2008). A number of our interviewees indicated that cloning was active, widespread and accepted in their police forces, that they themselves had benefited from such a system and they were deeply sceptical about attempts to reform this equivalent of 'the old school tie' (Diez-Nicolás, 2005). Others pointed to a tangible equality of opportunity to rise in the ranks and some to the need for academic achievement before candidates could be considered for strategic roles. However they may be varied, there are conditions and requirements placed on those who aspire to the elite in policing – perhaps mirroring the picture in society as a whole?

About thirty years ago it ceased to be academically fashionable to examine elites as indicators of the norms and values of a larger society. Social science researchers moved away from analysing those commanding at the top of organisations to examining those 'doing the work' at all other levels. There may be a number of reasons for this drift: 'dishonest respondents' (identified by Zoë Morris, 2009), analysis of one elite does not necessarily provide insights into others (Harold Lasswell et al, 1952), elites themselves are 'a secret society' (Keller, 1991) and therefore difficult to penetrate or even understand. '[S]ophisticated but powerless' researchers (Morris, 2009; Gareth Rice, 2010) have found themselves patronised or irritably dismissed by those accustomed to deference, while the nature of the task itself is 'double-trouble' when 'conducting an in-depth interview whilst simultaneously balancing the power of an influential elite' (Welch et al, 2002; Rice, 2010). For all that, the trend may be slowly reversing again (Savage and Williams, 2008). Some good studies of power elites have appeared in the last few years,[17] but the doyenne of elite studies, Suzanne Keller, remarked that: 'studies of elites over the past several

---

[15] See Anssi Paasi's interesting essay 'Europe as a social process and discourse: considerations of place, boundaries and identity (2001), which looks at the 'narrow band' of privileged elitism in the aristocracy of 18th- and 19th-century Europe.

[16] For example, Martin O'Neill's provocative 2008 essay 'What should egalitarians believe?'; or Tang and Zhong, who wrote 'Toward a Demystification of Egalitarianism' in 2013.

[17] Such as those by Higley and Lengyel (2000); Diez-Nicolás (2005); Rhodes et al (2007); Savage and Williams (2008); Morris (2009); and Rice (2010).

decades reveal fascinating leaves but few trees, statistics aplenty but no grand new theory to illumine them' (Keller, 1991, p. 2).

We do not offer any presumptuous 'grand new theory' from the foliage of this study of a specialised elite, nor do we indulge in 'social network analysis' or 'ethnographic research' like Savage and Williams (2008), because our horizon in looking at a specialist police elite is much more modest and earthbound. Rather, we agree with Rod Rhodes and his colleagues when they say that they studied government elites 'because the decisions of the great and the good affect all our lives for good or ill' (Rhodes et al, 2007, p. 11).

The decisions of strategic police leaders, whether or not checked and balanced, whether or not modulated through a public prosecutor and subject to a rigorous criminal justice system, and whether or not refracted through a local or national political prism, affect us directly as citizens in many different ways, from our being able to move safely (or not) across Europe by motor vehicle, train or aircraft; to our confidence (or not) in the fairness and rigour of the criminal investigative processes; to reassurance about respect (or not) for ours and others' human rights; even (a very British take, this) reassurance that the use of lethal force is not a first recourse when there is disorder, despite the very evident carriage of weapons by most uniformed police on the European continent.[18]

As robbery slowly gives way to cybercrime and as community policing yields (unwillingly?) to concerted but more costly attempts to counter transnational organised crime; as terrorism generally declines but acts of individual political violence rise (for example Breivik and Adebolajo/Adebowale)[19]; and as personal freedoms are increasingly attenuated by larger societal requirements for safety and security, so we must look to the police both for our effective protection and for positive action to mitigate dangers to us. What officers do on the

---

[18]   It is the other way round in Eire, where uniformed officers are not armed routinely, but plain-clothes detectives are. In Norwegian police patrol cars, officers' weapons are locked in a secure container, not carried on the person. A patchwork of variations, this European policing: one of the authors had the dubious experience of watching French gendarmes 'Taser' a man who vaulted a barrier at Bordeaux airport in June 2014: his screams will live long in the memory. In Finland, by contrast, a police officer let one of the authors examine and hold his loaded automatic pistol, commenting that "he had never had to use it for real".

[19]   Anders Breivik carried out shootings and bombing in Norway in 2011; Adebolajo and Adebowale are the murderers of Fusilier Lee Rigby in Woolwich London in 2013.

ground is at least in part determined by the priorities and preferences of those leaders who devise policing strategy. It seems logical, therefore, to argue that if we want to understand what policing is doing, we need to look into the minds and thoughts of those at the 'high' end (Brodeur, 1983) of police forces across Europe. That, at least, is our starting point.

We asked our respondents how they became strategic police leaders and what processes were involved in their advancement. There was, predictably, a variation: approximately a third advanced through academic study, including examinations and the accretion of postgraduate qualifications, particularly in law. Others were promoted to strategic rank primarily on the basis of a track record and experience that did not necessarily prove that such candidates could function at the higher ranks. About a quarter rose to leadership ranks through internally designed police development programmes, which typically blended some academic learning with skills/competency training. A few were selected for higher office – particularly in the former Soviet-Bloc countries – because they had not been 'tainted' by the previous regime (and some of these then found it hard to sustain their positions because of a lack of experience). Some attached themselves to rising politicians and benefited from mutual back-scratching when the politicians achieved senior office. About a fifth managed to catch the eye of a senior officer, who then helped to pull up through the ranks a character he (usually) thought similar to his own. A very small number were direct appointments from outside mainstream policing, though such appointees do not usually last more than a couple of years in post.

These last advancements seemed to assume that, at least occasionally, direct and prolonged experience in policing was *not* a prerequisite for senior leadership; something vehemently argued for by veteran police officers from the British Isles to Central Europe, and from the Mediterranean to the Nordic region. Many seemed convinced that the only acceptable criteria for strategic police leadership were some combinations of experience, operational success and academic qualification. It is not always clear what relationship these factors have to each other, or what proportion each should occupy in a given individual's profile, and certainly many believe that the acquisition of generic leadership skills are not enough on their own to make someone a police leader. Prolonged experience, what is often called in Europe the '*acquis*' of policing, gave credibility they argued, particularly when commanding police forces operationally (a conception confirmed in other academic studies, see Silvestri, 2006). And yet there are some strategic police leaders we spoke to who argued just as forcefully that clarity of purpose, a vision of where policing (and even criminal justice itself) should go, and proven integrity in public office are infinitely more important at the top end of policing than the ability to investigate a homicide or command squads of riot police in public order situations.

Our own analysis, based on the responses to our question from the strategic police leaders we interviewed, suggests that well-trodden pathways to becoming a strategic leader included: selection or talent spotting, pursuing academic studies/examinations, engaging in police development and skills programmes, and being groomed by senior officers. Patronage of some kind and advancement of a favoured choice by senior officers still constitutes half of all advancements to strategic police leadership, while there is a pretty even split among the rest whether promotion is through an academic route that may entail competitive examination (and almost always requires postgraduate qualifications), or through a tailored police development programme (focusing more on experiential job competences and honing directorial skills). This debate about 'knowledge versus experience' is as old as the hills and is by no means exclusive to policing, but it does not help matters when there is no agreed competency profile for what constitutes a strategic police leader in Europe as a whole.[20]

It comes as something of a surprise that there are no pan-European criteria for what makes a strategic police leader, no profiles of an 'omni-competence' that would apply equally in Italy, Estonia, Eire or Austria. Instead, the EU appears content to leave this entirely to individual national governments to determine. It seems in some instances that even national governments play no role in establishing what criteria should apply to the selection of those who determine policing strategy; it is rather consigned to individual police forces and their existing leadership to determine who will rise and who will not (and not the least of the demerits of such a closed and unchallenged system is the glaring absence from the higher ranks of both women and representatives of minority ethnic communities in any proportionate numbers; see Vinnicombe, 2000).[21] Unsurprisingly, this leads to some uneven qualities at the top of policing in Europe, and we detected

---

[20] In spite of seminal studies of the role of competencies in Europe's other strategic leaders – see Kuperus and Rode, 2010.

[21] Though this may not be something limited to policing; the position of women in *all* occupations may be a cause for concern about fairness and equity. See, for example, *Women in Management: Current research issues* (2000), in which Susan Vinnicombe's chapter appears (cited earlier). We look at this in more detail in Chapter Four, but the issue has been with us a long time.

considerable variations in what were regarded as needful qualifications for the job.

We have already noted the experience-versus-skills debate, but another area of controversy centres on what sort of qualifications a strategic police leader should have. Many countries favour law degrees (especially in Nordic countries), while others, notably in the Mediterranean, do not specify the degree subject but insist instead on a postgraduate Master's or above. Only a few forces ask for police-related study (favourite among which is, predictably, criminology; though 'policing studies' of various kinds are beginning to appear). One interviewee insisted to us that all police leaders should have PhDs because, he said, you could be assured that the brightest available leaders were available to take charge. Police leaders had to be as clever as criminals, he argued. However, there does not appear to be any persuasive evidence to suggest that holders of doctorates make better police leaders at a strategic level. The essential point remains that neither the EC itself, nor collectives of police strategic leaders, nor CEPOL (the European Police College), nor Europol seem to think that a collective European standard for strategic police leadership is required at the moment. That makes political assertions about pan-European policing rather hollow, since operational cooperation will always be temporary and piecemeal, if strategic police leaders do not share a common approach to, and common understanding of, the nature of transnational organised crime.

It is a given in a modern democratic society that the police should be accountable for what they do, especially in the exercise of force on behalf of the nation state, and in the majority of cases this is a straightforward responsiveness either to the public through 'official' oversight mechanisms, or to the criminal law or to politicians, depending on what the nature of the accountability is. In some cases, like deaths in custody, lethal shootings or other serious complaints, recourse is made to an independent oversight body, such as an ombudsman or a specific complaints machinery, which then examines the police action and pronounces accordingly. That said, 'accountability' is actually a complex and multilayered concept that does not easily resolve itself into simple right or wrong issues (Fijnaut, 2002). In many of the former Soviet-Bloc countries, for instance, the 'default' policing model is one of democratic accountability (which we call the 'EU model', see Chapter One), but which itself is a direct reaction to many decades of subjugation to an unelected political machine and a police service that was dedicated to maintaining the governing party in office and to suppressing dissent. So accountability is a fresh, exciting and vibrant concept to these fledgling democracies in ways not always evident in 'old liberal' Western Europe. For countries in Central Europe and the Baltic regions, accountability means that for the first time, the actions of the police can be challenged and the rule of law openly supported. Many of our interviewees from these regions attested to the powerful appeal of this. The public in Central Europe and the Baltic states, however, continue to view the police with suspicion and distrust, and strategic police leaders there think it may be some years before genuine trust can be built between the police and the policed (Goldsmith, 2005; Meško and Dobovšek, 2007).

What is fascinating, but often hidden or not apparent on the surface of things, is the network of relationships and influences that elites build around themselves. This is not just a question of how people in positions of strategic power relate to each other as peers and sometimes rivals, but how they relate to associated networks and groupings, whom they seek to influence and that may influence them (Knoke, 1993; Sørenson and Torfing, 2003). In Europe, strategic police leaders have considerable influence within their respective forces, and of course with each other, whether informally through the mechanisms such as Pearls of Policing or in a more structured way through organisations such as Europol and CEPOL.[22] Outside the narrow realm of policing are other networks (forming what in 1992 Heinz and Manikas called 'structural-contextual' relationships), such as those within criminal justice and the courts, and those of both local and national politicians and ministry officials – often in the Interior Ministry or its equivalent, but, in the case of some gendarmeries, within the nation state's Defence Ministry. These wider groups have a nexus or connectivity that focuses mainly on crime and punishment or on public opinion.

At the back of all this, there are a number of filaments which stretch into the media and into the academic world and which may be classed as 'opinion-forming' (Davis, 2003). Our interviewees told us about difficulties they faced with politicians and their dislike of short-term political targets and ambitions, compared with which their longer-term relationships with public prosecutors, lawyers, judges and officials in the criminal justice system were generally more amicable and respectful (on both sides). That did not inhibit some robust police opinions on the efficacy of some judges and delight in the manipulations and stratagems that wily strategic police leaders visited upon hapless politicians.

---

[22] *Pearls of Policing* is a more or less informal European grouping of strategic police leaders, researchers and academics who meet annually under the aegis of the Dutch police. They are closed sessions; we gloss this further in Chapter One.

This closed world of hidden influence and 'clubbability' is probably where the true power of elites lies (Glasius, 2010), and strategic police leaders are by no means immune to the subtleties of the exercise of such power, particularly, it seems, in the creation of legislation and international treaties.

An extension of the networks and relationships formed by strategic police leaders across Europe is in operational cooperation. More and more, police forces are realising that they have to cooperate against international criminality, and few, if any, police forces can remain immune from border-porous activities such as drugs smuggling or people trafficking (Block, 2008). A number of our interviewees had strong opinions about the effectiveness of cross-border cooperation: many noted that they enjoyed close relationships with neighbouring forces and neighbouring police leaders, but at the same time they were impatient of what seemed to them to be a political gambit of multilateral cooperation. Often brokered by the EC through direct mechanisms, the bureaucracy of linking disparate countries for 'joint police purposes' appears to some strategic police leaders to be redundant and wasteful. They prefer to liaise and cooperate where the crime takes them, rather than embark on more umbrella structures, often involving countries with whom they have no common operational purpose (Occhipinti, 2003).

Within this, there is often expressed a blunt dislike of the role of the United States in the international arena, especially with regard to countering drugs smuggling and terrorism. The leaders we spoke to embraced willingly the requirement to work together with neighbours against multiple transnational organised crime targets, and understood the imperative to dismantle transit channels and criminal networks between countries. In places like the Meuse/Rhine region, such three- or four-way cooperation is standard (Fijnaut and Spapens, 2010). What the police leaders jibbed at, sometimes eloquently, was cooperation as a formal requirement with no operational purpose or specified criminal justice outcome; or, in the case of the United States, to be subordinate to someone else's priorities and targets.

With emergent post-Soviet states, police cooperation tends to be more cautious and formal, and many police leaders agreed that memoranda of understanding or protocols are often helpful here in paving the way to mutual cooperation. Yet behind all this, there is a distinct national determination that individual nation states will not surrender their policing autonomy to some kind of pan-European federalist police force that will have an operational and overriding role (Occhipinti, 2003). They did not claim for a moment that Europol has this kind of role or ambition, but it is evident from what the strategic police leaders say that they suspect the EC of having precisely that agenda. A federal European police force, able to investigate in, command the cooperation of, prioritise for and intervene in the affairs of an independent nation state, however attractive to politicians who want to wield power on a larger stage, is a concept too far for our interviewees, which chimes with academic research in the same area (Guille, 2010a; den Boer, in Lemieux, 2010).

The challenges that strategic police leaders face in Europe today are, at least in outline, pretty much consensual. They refer to 'the usual core of problems', which involves police action against terrorism, drugs importation and distribution, sex and human trafficking and cross-border crime. Interestingly, cybercrime is gaining a larger proportion of police attention, and our respondents noted how most of their current preoccupations with crime were simultaneously national and international. They also indicated that police structures and other factors such as their own criminal justice systems got in the way of more widespread police cooperation, commenting that bureaucracy, legislation and national police forces with narrow outlooks, too often inhibited action on a wider, pan-European stage. More fundamentally, of heightened concern to strategic police leaders across Europe is the 'hollowing out' of state policing (Crawford, 2002) and its replacement in many instances with 'pluralised' policing. Some of this 'hollowing' was signalled by a growing role played by 'private policing' companies and commercial providers of 'security'. These often globalised companies continued to obtain government contracts across Europe despite their well-documented failures to deliver.

There were regional variations in police concerns about current issues: broadly the Alpine and Central Europe regions were focused on crime types, while Benelux[23] was more focused on police structures. The Mediterranean region considered that cross-border crime was its priority, while the Baltic region put terrorism, drugs importation and human trafficking at the top of its concerns. The Nordic region flagged up cybercrime and sex trafficking among its current preoccupations, while the British Isles region thought that diminishing resources posed the greatest threat to its continued efficacy. Understandably, police cooperation was strongest with contiguous regions and weakest where there are large distances intervening.

In looking towards the future, the strategic police leaders of Europe exhibit a range of attitudes and opinions, prevalent among which

---

[23] Belgium, Netherlands and Luxembourg.

is a pessimistic, even dystopian, vision of social breakdown and the polarisation of communities. Many interviewees in Western European states drew attention to the growth of communities of new immigrants. These communities tend to huddle together both because of economic circumstances and for their self-protection.[24] What often happens then is a (largely indigenous working-class but media-fuelled) response, which demonises the immigrants as criminal or parasitically dependent on state welfare. Senior police leaders, for their part, see this polarisation between 'insider' and 'outsider' as probably leading to limited tensions and violence in inner-city areas, and possibly becoming the focus for larger-scale urban public disorder across Europe.[25]

This was less of an acute problem for strategic police leaders in Central Europe, most of whom drew attention instead to the growth in cybercrime and the likelihood that, in future at least, a significant volume of crime would be located firmly in cyberspace. This led them to call for recruits to the police having (or getting) advanced degrees in computing and software science. A number of police leaders across Europe noted that criminals themselves were exhibiting considerable adaptability to the 'net generation' and the police should show similar flexibility and responsiveness if they were to counter the criminal threat; but that means looking outside the geographical confines of the EU and engaging globally with internet service providers (ISPs) and others, to make policing in cyberspace a reality. The jurisdictional dilemma remains: individual forces can do very little. Even 'federal' organisations such as Europol exhibit frustrations at their lack of control over criminality in the 'Dark Web'. The only recourse, senior police leaders said, was to attempt to influence ISPs through the weight of public opinion – which was hard to galvanise.

A number of those interviewed (principally in Western Europe) believed that in the future, recruitment of new police officers would focus on powerfully built officers to deal with public order and riot, while more intellectual officers would police crime in cyberspace. This synthesis of two major concerns about the future – social unrest and cybercrime – was advanced seriously by some police leaders, though how such recruitment would be carried out, and how such duality

---

[24] The official EU statistics noted that in 2012 some 20 million 'third country nationals' were living in Europe, or about 4% of the whole population. See European Commission, (2012) *3rd Annual Report on Immigration and Asylum* (2011).

[25] Witness the general lurch right-wards in the European elections of May 2014, in which (*inter alia*) right-wing parties across Europe attained more seats at the expense of the federalists; see McDonald-Gibson and Lichfield, 2014.

could be justified in an egalitarian age, was not specified. A corollary of this duality of recruitment might be that Europe's gendarmeries would have the public order remit (and possibly a pan-European composition and interventionist role),[26] whereas national police forces would recruit the highly qualified specialists necessary to police cyberspace and international crime, or both. Issues here about language and federalism were not fully addressed by our interviewees – though this may have been a function of the time available in interview rather than any restriction on their forward visions. Thoughts about 'recruitment to purpose' chime with a wider consensus among police strategic leaders that in the future, there will be a general need to recruit cleverer and better qualified police officers, who can cope with the complexities of crime, including financial crime, fraud and money-laundering both in cyberspace and internationally, as well as directing the use of force in proportionate ways that support human rights, rather than threaten them. Some deplored the absence of an overarching policing plan for Europe, which would address such issues and provide some modicum of consistency, but even at Pearls of Policing and CEPOL fora, there are, apparently, few debates about a future of the kind envisaged by the strategic police leaders who spoke privately to us.

The personal views of the hundred-plus strategic police leaders who spoke to us in confidence are not normally available to the public or even to their own police forces, and this can make the elitism of Europe's police leaders an inscrutable and impenetrable phenomenon. Unpicking what they say, and according serious weight to their private views and opinions, seems to us both a sensible activity and a rewarding one. The reader may not be able to ascribe views or comments to an individual strategic police leader, or even to his or her country, but the consistency of comment, the coincidence of outlook and the commonality of theme that comes from all these anonymous data, actually do provide an insight into a 'closed' world, where considerable stresses and strains exist, where personalities are instrumental and can sometimes be destructive, and where networks and alliances are crucially important for outcomes. We would be wrong to ignore opportunities to lift this veil, even momentarily, because the decisions of those who constitute the policing elite – together with their counterparts in the criminal justice system and their politicians who create policing policy – have an impact on our lives that we should know about. Police officers in command should be answerable for what they do; and it is to the credit of the respondents in this study that they

---

[26] A prospect that we explore in detail in Chapter Seven.

gave up their time to discuss their challenges, views and responses, and that they engaged seriously with our questions. Therefore it behoves us to hear what they say, evaluate their thinking and engage with their dilemmas, analyse their visions and consider their preoccupations, so that we may better understand what they do – and understand too how we may continue to hold them properly to account.

Methodology

Our interest in conducting the research for this book followed the publication of *Policing at the Top*, a study focused on the roles, values and attitudes of chief police leaders in England and Wales by Bryn Caless (2011). Originally, we considered similar research focused only on European 'chief officers' (that is, designated command ranks), but such a project was quickly seen to be unviable given the challenges faced in securing interviews with only the topmost police officers, particularly as there is no consensus across Europe on what constitutes a 'command rank'. Rank terms vary considerably across European police forces, and translations of them into English do not always give an adequate meaning or a correct cultural resonance. For example, a 'commissioner' can be a junior inspector rank in Poland (*Nadkomisarz*), but a command rank in Belgium and France (*Commissaire divisionnaire*), and the highest police rank of all in England and Wales (Commissioner of the Metropolitan Police), while a 'brigadier' is a police sergeant in the Netherlands, but a high-ranking gendarme in Italy (*Brigadiere*) and a top police leader in Greece (*Ταξίαρχος*). By contrast, a police *Präsident* in Germany's autonomous Länder can equate in function to a *Rikspolischef* in Sweden or a *Teniente General* in the Spanish Guarda Civil, or a *Politimester* in Norway, even though they have little linguistic commonality. However, given our interest in the views of a broader range of elite senior police officers engaged with policing at a strategic or conceptual level, we decided to define our 'catchment' as '**strategic police leaders** across Europe'.

We present these **strategic police leaders** both as *elites* (a select group of 'high social, economic or political standing' or 'persons chosen by position' for a particular reason (Hochschild, 2009)) and as *leaders* (individuals initiating, directing and organising activities at a senior level). Christopher Williams (2012) challenges the issue of distinguishing between 'elites' and 'leaders', explaining that defining such terms is not clear cut and arguing that 'elites' and 'leaders' can co-exist. He also points out that leadership groups can be internally 'stratified' or 'hierarchical'. In a policing context, it can be argued that 'elites' and 'leaders' are not necessarily static, nor are stratified hierarchies always impenetrable, because roles can cross boundaries of leadership and cut transversely through groups. Similarly, the strategic leadership of the police is represented in the literature in terms of the use and manipulation of discretion, as it travels down the hierarchy from policy intention to implementation (Silvestri, 2003). This process not only creates 'internal gatekeepers' of implementation but also groups of elites lower down in the hierarchy. Therefore, *strategic police leader* seeks to embrace both 'leaders' and 'elites' under one term, at the top end of policing.

Throughout this book, the terms 'strategic' and 'senior' police leader are used interchangeably. The term 'strategic' refers to the *roles* of the officers concerned, and will inevitably provide a broader remit than 'chief officers' alone; while the more generic term 'senior' denotes the officers' *relative placement* in police hierarchies. As part of the selection process for interview, we asked potential respondents about their role and whether it involved strategic police responsibilities. In a policing context, we take 'strategic' to refer to force-level planning and management of medium- to long-term policing goals influenced by organisational objectives and available resources. This would entail leadership of large teams and involve functional or policy-orientated contributions to policing at a strategic/command level. This inevitably led us to the selection of officers in senior roles for interview or questionnaire. In a UK context, for example, this would include the 'command rank' of chief superintendent.[27] It is important to remember, as we noted earlier, that *rank equivalence* does not accurately transfer across all police systems in Europe, so selecting respondents on the basis of their roles is more useful than using an (often spurious) rank specificity. Of course, those who deliver strategic policing are usually at or near the top of their particular policing tree, and constitute a *de facto* elite. We can therefore expand the parameters of the term 'strategic leader' to include *leaders, specialists and managers, each of whom has strategic policing responsibilities at the top of the policing hierarchies within Europe.*

The research itself was concerned with capturing the private thoughts of strategic police leaders across Europe in answer to the following broad questions:

---

[27] In the *Policing at the Top* research (Caless, 2011), officers in the Association of Chief Police Officers were selected reflecting the highest levels of police management or 'top tier' leadership (chief constable, deputy chief constable and assistant chief constable).

- How do police officers progress to the most senior roles and what are their views on the process involved?
- How are police services held to account in practice?
- How effectively do police services cooperate with one another and what are the challenges to more effective cooperation?
- What are the current preoccupations with crime and criminality at the strategic level in policing?
- What are the challenges for the future of policing from the perspective of these strategic police leaders?

It was an implicit challenge to ensure that we had a sufficient sample size to be of 'representative' value and to provide a reasonable cross-section of the countries within Europe and across the regions we were exploring. We did not have a pre-established network of contacts[28] but we sought support from CEPOL, Europol and private, personal contacts with some European police services, all of which served as a means of introduction to other senior police leaders in other parts of Europe. We also used our extensive academic networks to obtain access to police forces and thence to their higher ranks. We were unable initially to be more systematic than this, and there is a sense in which our early research was somewhat piecemeal. Access improved dramatically as our intentions (and probity) became more widely known, and it was clear that many strategic police leaders were interested in what their peers had said and what themes were emerging from our research. In the latter half of 2013, we had no problems in accessing strategic police leaders, even in previously 'hard to reach' areas. In all of this, we were signally aided by CEPOL, especially its British representative.

Inevitably, there has been some subjectivity in the selection of candidates, if only on the basis of the language of communication (English) and completion of the interview/questionnaires. However, we adopted an innovative 'snowball' sampling approach, whereby the person being interviewed or questioned would be asked to recommend another person whom we could contact, using the recommender's name. This worked well, and the 'snowballing' quickly gathered momentum in 2013, especially in Central Europe, Nordic and Mediterranean regions. By this means, we were able to extend the

---

[28] Though one of the authors has extensive experience of networking (through the European Diploma in Policing) through agencies from Estonia to Slovenia and from the Netherlands to Hungary, and was able to use those contacts to obtain informal access to police forces and their leaders.

field to include representatives from every European region and from most countries within those regions.[29] This resulted, by December 2013, in 108 interviews/completed questionnaires from 29 different countries. David Bayley (1999) argues – admittedly, on a case-by-case basis – that conducting research in a foreign country can be not only problematic in terms of credible access, but also disarming to potential interviewees, since 'foreign' scholars can be regarded as less of a threat politically, as they are not active within the interviewee's ambit. Although we make no claims that this study is in any sense definitive, we have obtained a large number of interviews across a broad range of regions and can be confident that representative 'insider' opinions about strategic-level policing across Europe have been captured. CEPOL's suggestion of continued 'longitudinal' studies based in a single country across five of the regions is a logical way to carry forward this seminal research, and to put more substantial flesh on these strategic policing bones over a longer period. Whether there will be sufficient funding is a moot point: we think the research is worth doing, but will the EU?

The vexed question of language

Although a limited number of officers were interviewed by colleagues speaking in languages other than English, in the majority of cases communication between researchers and respondents was conducted almost entirely in English. Although English is widely spoken and understood among strategic police leaders, this inevitably introduced some distortion to our sample, partly because of a lack of shared cultural referents,[30] but also because such a process omitted some non-English speaking respondents, or inhibited those who wanted to take part but

---

[29] Though we acknowledge that a single interviewee probably cannot speak for the entirety of policing in his or her country: in most cases, we tried to get more than one from each police jurisdiction, but it was not always possible or practical to do so.

[30] The Sapir-Whorf hypothesis states that our perception of our world is shaped by and through our language (Anderson and Lightfoot, 2002). For example, research by Guy Deutscher showed that our colour perception is entirely a function of our colour vocabulary, which varies across linguistic frontiers (Deutscher, 2010, chapters 1 and 6).

whose command of English was weak.[31] Completed questionnaires ranged from pages of comprehensive feedback and forensic argument to (occasional) very limited and basic, almost monosyllabic, responses. This was probably due to available time, the individual's enthusiasm about the themes contained within the research questions, as well as the respondent's English language abilities. We had carefully considered various strategies around employing interpreters, but on balance thought that introducing additional (non-policing) barriers to gaining trust with participants, as well as concerns about the cultural accuracy of transcriptions (not to mention the expense of needing translators in at least seven languages), were formidable barriers. So, although colleagues kindly translated a handful of the interviews they had conducted for us, we decided against using interpreters in principle. Given time, space and an unlimited budget, we might think differently.[32]

Problems of comparison

Cross-cultural studies reveal substantial challenges around comparative research of this kind. Research into educational leadership in China by Wing-Wah Law warns against stereotyping the differences between Chinese and Western culture and tells us not to underestimate the impact of an increasingly 'interconnected and independent world'. At the same time, we should not overestimate the influence of Anglo-American intellectual and cultural frameworks; national cultures can perfectly well shape their own leaders and elites (Law, 2012).

In policing across Europe, there has been a primary influence of democratic forms of policing but there have been changes too around pluralisation (including 'private policing' from multinational

---

[31] This was marked among a few strategic police leaders whom we approached at Europol's European Police Chiefs' Convention in Den Haag, 2011. This was a misconception: since they could follow proceedings there, they could have coped with our questions perfectly well (Harris, 2013).

[32] Indeed, as we note above, CEPOL opines that the way forward for this kind of research into policing elites in Europe might be undertaken through longitudinal studies in individual countries, by local researchers. This would establish very detailed understanding of the strategic police leadership role in many different structures and in native languages, but would still face the expensive problem of translation into a common language (probably English, though French and Spanish are also possible) and, of course, it would take years to do, and would need careful oversight and coordination to stay on track. We detect no EU appetite for such exciting research.

companies), budget cuts and resource constraints, 'professionalisation' of aspects of policing, such as the investigation of homicide, and major restructuring – from the nationalisation of police services and realignment of role (EuroGendFor or the European Gendarmerie Force), through to devolving policing powers (Wright, 2001; Stevens, 2013; Padurariu, 2014). With different states reflecting a variety of characteristics around the historical development of policing services, political regimes supporting or opposing federal policing approaches, supportive or indifferent relationships with bordering nations and varying levels of tolerance and demonisation of 'the other' in relation to European and non-European immigration, the cultural diversity across Europe is interconnected but highly complex (Bayley, 1999; Findlay, 2008). These different police and political foundations present a picture of constant flux within and between states, like tectonic plates which are increasingly overlapping, volatile and influenced by global changes. This pattern reflects the 'convergence' and 'divergence' debate in policing (den Boer, 1999), but it is still disconnected in terms of, respectively, criminal law, criminal justice systems and federally operational policing agencies. From a research perspective, the impossibility of trying to understand all the practitioner, linguistic, jurisdictional, political, parochial and cultural distinctions in strategic policing across some 35 nation states, leads us to the conclusion that we should celebrate such diversity, not deplore it. It may be some time before we have uniformity in strategic police leadership across Europe, if ever.

Data collection

The data collection method adopted for this research was based on interviews and questionnaires supported by a literature review.[33] In order to get a wide range of responses, and to access remote or busy strategic police leaders, we used questionnaires, while also seeking to establish in-depth personal interviews with available participants.

---

[33] We have read as widely as our limited command of other European languages allows; studying some things in the original German, French or Italian, even some Swedish, but mostly relying on published translations or the good offices of other authors to render their research and commentary in English. We hope that our Bibliography demonstrates the range, number and variety of texts and data that we have accessed, though we acknowledge, very readily, its imperfections. We have tried to be 'good Europeans' but know that CEPOL's proposed longitudinal study would make up for our personal shortfalls, and would introduce greater linguistic capability.

When considering an 'interview strategy' we did not believe that using interviews alone would generate a large number of responses, mainly because of time constraints on senior police leaders and the availability of funding to visit them. We decided to adopt a dual strategy of using interviews (face-to-face and telephone interviews)[34] where we could, and using emailed questionnaires where direct access was problematic or likely to be delayed. In the event, the two methods were pretty evenly matched: out of our sample of 108, there were 49 interviews and 59 questionnaires. The interviews followed the same script as the questionnaires but were semi-structured in delivery and wide-ranging in content, while the questionnaires were structured, unprompted and more limited in range. Confidentiality was inevitably important to all participants and attempts to gain interviews were particularly difficult during conferences when officers were often preoccupied by the agenda and conference schedules were tight (and some may not have wanted to be seen talking to researchers). However, participants were happy to respond to requests for interviews or to complete questionnaires when approached individually by researchers or through recommendation by another participant or professional colleague. No 'blanket' email approaches were made; all respondents were approached specifically because of their professional backgrounds and roles, usually invoking the name of a colleague as introduction or as evidence of our *bona fides*. We believe this carefully targeted approach to be the correct one, and the method most likely to yield results. Untargeted or unspecific attempts to gather data are pretty much blunt tools that police officers can easily ignore or deflect: the rejection of an individualised approach was less likely, though of course it did happen.[35] It appears from many respondents that the themes of leadership, selection, development, European cooperation and police accountability were issues they were keen to contribute to, and their

---

[34] Skype was considered but was largely unavailable to police officers in situ during our research between 2011 and 2013. One of the authors has since used Skype extensively in other research (2014–15) to interview police and crime commissioners (PCCs) in England and Wales. The PCCs use the system easily; chief police officers by comparison are much more reluctant and appear to equate Skyping with being interviewed on television.

[35] There were five direct refusals for interview, and about 30% of questionnaires sent remain unanswered. We cannot be more specific, as questionnaires were often distributed at seminars and collegiate meetings at which strategic police leaders were present and at which we were invited to speak. Exact numbers of questionnaires disseminated were not recorded at the time, which was a failing we will live with.

views on crime and criminality were equally forthcoming. Our sample of 108 strategic police leaders was made up of 24 females (23%) and 84 males (77%); the average age of respondents was 51 years; and 10% of the sample were either on the point of retiring or would be retiring within two years.

Anonymity

Anonymity was crucial to this research. As you read through the book, you will see that direct quotations are used extensively, but not sourced individually. We have tried to follow Robert Reiner's (1991, p. 45) example, in attempting to 'create a picture' of the strategic leaders' perspectives using their own words, but we do not provide identifying detail of the background of our respondents and will not reveal their ranks or national origins. Christopher Williams (2012) has noted that 'elite' and 'powerful' research participants should be afforded just the same protection and ethical standards as any other respondents, acknowledging their equal vulnerability.[36] In order to provide requisite anonymity, we decided to present direct quotations and any associated analysis through **regions** rather than distinct countries. On one research level, this has implications since both our analysis and citation become 'regionally dispersed', but these were necessary compromises to gain our respondents' cooperation and to ensure protection of their identities. Each nation has a distinct and identifiable social, economic and political history that creates a unique contemporary context with associated governance, policing and global challenges. It follows that, if we undertook to keep the identities secret of those who spoke to us, we would not want inadvertently to expose them by invoking factors unique to their own nation state.

Origin by region

In consequence, countries are in standard regional groupings based on socioeconomic and geographic associations:

- Baltic: Estonia, Latvia and Lithuania (5);[37]
- Benelux: Belgium, the Netherlands and Luxembourg (11);

---

[36] While confidential interviews of the powerful can sometimes reveal controversial things, continued access to them is important to organisational learning and *not* compromising access for future researchers is paramount.

[37] The figures in brackets represent the 'regional' number who spoke to us.

- British Isles: England, Wales, Scotland, Northern Ireland and the Isle of Man, and the Republic of Ireland (10);
- Nordic: Sweden, Norway, Finland, Denmark, Iceland (20);
- Alpine: Austria, Switzerland, Liechtenstein, Slovenia, Germany (18);
- Central Europe: Poland, Czech Republic, Romania, Slovakia, Hungary (22);
- the Mediterranean: Portugal, Spain, France, Monaco, Italy, Croatia, Bosnia and Herzegovina, Montenegro, Albania, Greece, Turkey, Cyprus, Malta and the British territory of Gibraltar (22).[38]

Although some countries in the sample are not members of the European Union, they are part of geographical Europe and its general policing context and we cheerfully acknowledge that we are using the term 'Europe' in its broadest context.

---

[38] In such classifications, Slovenia often appears as 'Mediterranean' as well as 'Alpine'. To avoid double-counting, we have included Slovenia only in the Alpine region.

ONE

European policing in context

The Abbé de Saint-Pierre suggested an association of all the states of Europe to maintain perpetual peace among themselves. Is this association practicable, and supposing that it were established, would it be likely to last? (Jean-Jacques Rousseau, *Emile: or On Education*, 1762)

Until relatively recently, policing operated primarily in a local dimension. While there were always exceptions, crime tended to be generated from within a limited area; most police officers almost never came into contact with colleagues from distant jurisdictions; and knowledge about policing was generally based on local experiences. (Casey, 2007, p. 244)

The 'local dimension' that John Casey mentions in the quotation above is still very much a part of modern community and locally delivered policing in districts all over Europe, but increasingly, local crime has an international dimension. Among other things, we are concerned in this book to examine what Casey calls 'distant jurisdictions' in European strategic policing, yet even such a 'continental' approach might be regarded as parochial, especially by the Americas and the Far East in terms of, say, drugs smuggling or people trafficking. Nonetheless we are aware, as is Casey, that the average *senior* officer 'routinely' works in areas involving terrorism, cybercrime and human trafficking (Casey, 2007). The boundaries have to be drawn somewhere, and, as we explained in the Introduction, our concern is strategic police leadership in the modern European law enforcement context, because while there may be many studies of the police tactical interdiction of crime,[1] and while there may be analyses of how 'policing' has reacted to social change,[2] there are no contemporary studies that look in detail at strategic police leadership across Europe.[3]

This chapter is partly a historical overview of the evolution of policing in Europe, partly a literature review of contemporary thinking about European policing and partly, but most importantly, the provision of a context for the views of those who spoke to us about contemporary strategic policing concerns. The most obvious example that encapsulates all three concerns is in rethinking the role of Europe's gendarmeries (Hovens and van Elk, 2011, *passim*; and Chapter Seven).

How did Europe come to have a sense of its own security? Are its police services evolving into something approximating to a federalised 'nation state'? What is entailed in terms of prevention and interdiction of crime on a federal scale? The concept of a 'nation state' (analysed by Max Weber[4]) and the need for that state to monopolise the directed use of force through its armies and through its police is, partly at least, a response to the requirement of the state to safeguard law and order. Vivien Schmidt (2004) has argued the intellectual contrary: this readiness to compare the whole of the EU to the Weberian notion of

---

[1]   Such as: Bigo, D. and Guild, E. (eds) (2005), *Controlling frontiers: free movement into and within Europe*, London: Ashgate Publishing Ltd; den Boer, M., Hillebrand, C. and Nölke, A. (2008), Legitimacy under Pressure: The European Web of Counter-Terrorism Networks, *Journal of Common Market Studies*, 46, pp. 101-124; and Feltes, T. (2002), Community-oriented policing in Germany: training and education, *Policing: An International Journal of Police Strategies and Management*, Vol. 25, No. 1, pp. 48-59.

[2]   For example: Dimovné, E. (2004), Hungarian police reform, *Transforming police in Central and Eastern Europe*, 17, Münster: Lit Verlag, pp. 1992-96; or Falkner, G. (ed.) (2011), *The EU's Decision Traps*, Oxford: Oxford University Press; or Hovens, J. and Van Elk, G. (2011), *Gendarmeries and the Challenges of the 21st Century*, Koninklijke Marechaussée, Den Haag, Netherlands.

[3]   Though there are some specific studies which examine current police leadership, structural reform and police roles in restricted geographical scope, such as Caparini and Marenin (2004), Schafer (2010), Bingöl (2011), Ferreira (2011), Anderson (2011), van Buuren (2012) and Donnelly, D. (2013) – see the Bibliography. J.-P. Brodeur's final book, *The Policing Web* (2010), examines police types, styles and how 'militarized' they are and has a sweep and range that we found informative, but he did not empirically analyse European police leadership.

[4]   See Beetham, 1974, Chapter Five, for example.

the 'nation state' is based on a false premise and confuses the issue, she says. Instead, she asserts, the EU should be conceived of as a 'regional state' in which: 'the creative tensions between the Union and its member states ensures both ever-increasing regional integration and ever-continuing national differentiation' (Schmidt, 2004, p. 4).

This sounds like very special pleading, in which unity is encouraged but diversity persists: it is both having your cake and eating it. Schmidt's interpretation of the EU as a 'regional state' cannot be realised as long as there is a 'democratic deficit' in the EU, where the European Parliament is relatively weak and ineffectual within the organisation's institutional balances (Bache et al, 2011, pp. 68-69). Essentially the EU 'still lacks the popular authority of national assemblies' (Bache et al, 2011, p. 69) and this deprives it of any legitimate mandate to *impose* security or to *require* member states to subordinate national interests to what may be termed 'Europeanisation'.[5] What works for the notion of the single nation state in Weberian terms may not translate to the 'supra-national' very easily, particularly if it involves a federal monopoly of the use of force. Instead, any sense of the EU's security, and its determination that transnational crime must be matched by transnational policing, derives from what Claudio Radaelli calls 'clustered convergence' (Radaelli, 2006, cited in Bache et al, 2011, pp. 66-67) in which: 'states with similar characteristics or preferences in a given domain respond in similar ways to particular pressures or opportunities' (Radaelli, 2006, cited in Bache et al, 2011, p. 66).

The convergent interests of states for collective *security* is perhaps more familiar and accessible as an idea and, in the past, has provided the basis of countless temporary alliances and pragmatic cooperation within Europe, so that Radaelli is not so much describing a new process as enunciating the realpolitik of 'Europeanisation', in which mutual help between states offers mutual security to those states.[6] That said, the position of the police as providers, or guardians, of mutual security within the 'clustered convergence' is largely the outcome of social and political changes in Europe in the latter part of the 18th century and an evolution through the 19th and 20th centuries, punctuated in the

---

[5] 'Europeanisation' as a concept dates back to the 1990s, where Ladrech (1994, p. 69) tried to define it. Radaelli took it further in 2006. The best current summary is in Bache et al (2011), pp. 58-66.

[6] See also Radaelli, C.M. (2012) 'Europeanization: the challenge of establishing causality', in T. Exadaktylos and C.M. Radaelli (eds) *Research Design in European Studies: Establishing Causality in Europeanization*, Basingstoke: Palgrave Macmillan, pp. 1-16.

latter by the cataclysmic social and geopolitical changes consequent upon the two world wars (Anderson et al, 1995).

Catherine Denys (2010) admirably analyses the transition in Europe from 1740 to 1750, when the old 'citizens' militias', in place since mediaeval times, were deliberately changed to 'professional, militarized watchmen', and she shows that this development was widespread in the second half of the 18th century (Denys, 2010, pp. 334–36). The quasi-voluntary night-time 'Watch' in turn gave way to the creation of an armed, paid, disciplined force, somewhat like the military itself. In Britain, however, such a body was anathema and smacked of 'continental practices', interfering as it did with the hallowed middle-class tradition of individual liberty from state interference – whatever the sacrifice in personal security. It took nearly another hundred years before Sir Robert Peel's civilian 'new police' in 1829, and even this was promoted as a direct reaction against the prevailing French police model[7] imposed by Napoleon on much of the rest of Europe from 1799 (Hurd, 2007). These polarisations continued for the next 150 years, even though their origins were partly the result of simplistic demonising and partly a means of justifying or excusing reforms. We need to look in more detail at these 'models' of policing across Europe, where three hundred years of history and wide regional/social variations have produced different models at different times.

---

[7] Strictly, the brainchild of Joseph Fouché (?1763–1820), radical and revolutionary who came to prominence during the 'Terror' which followed the French Revolution of 1789. Fouché was appointed formally as Minister of Police by Napoleon in 1799 and he intermittently presided over state policing and organised espionage for the next 10 years or so, though seemingly perpetually dismissed and reinstated. He was a born intriguer, turning against Napoleon when the latter made himself Consul for life and at one point (1810), he conspired with the British to overthrow Napoleon, but by then Fouché's power was waning. His name is a byword for repressive police action on behalf of the state, and his 'reign' was largely regarded in Britain with repugnance. His career is also a classic study of constant betrayal and political expediency (see, for example, studies by Fouché and Cole, 1971; Lignereux, 2002; and Gildea, 2003). Fouché was supposedly the inspiration behind the character of Inspector Javert in Victor Hugo's 1862 novel *Les Misérables*, as Fouché's successor, Vidocq, was apparently the model for the protagonist, Jean Valjean. Malcolm Anderson has a fascinating discussion of both men in his masterly work on the police and gendarmerie in France: *In Thrall to Political Change*, 2011, pp. 24–30.

Policing models in Europe

Essentially, six kinds of policing have evolved in Europe since 1750:

- the 'continental' model (also called the 'Napoleonic' model), which often included both armed national police and paramilitary gendarmeries;
- an 'Anglo-Saxon' model, which created an unarmed civilian police, locally accountable in the UK;
- the Royal Irish Constabulary or 'colonial' model, an armed militia/ gendarmerie upon which British (and other European) colonial policing was subsequently based;
- a repressive model of secret political policing as practised by, inter alia, the KGB (the Soviet Russian secret police or the Committee for State Security), the Gestapo and the Stasi respectively between 1933 and 1990;
- a 'dispersed' or decentralised policing model which re-emerged in West Germany after 1945 and in a united Germany after 1990; and
- a 'transition to democracy' or 'EU' model, which was adopted by many of the former Soviet-Bloc countries following independence from the USSR after 1990 and which consolidated respect for human rights (Koci, 1996; Caparini and Marenin, 2004).

There are variants on these basic models; for example, the Belgian national police model, which disestablished its Napoleonic gendarmerie in 2001; the new Scottish national model of one unitary force replacing eight disseminated forces in 2013; and the changes in the structure of the Dutch police from a 'proliferated' (25-region) autonomous model to a 'centralised hub and regionalised spokes' of 1 plus 10, also in 2013 (Hoogewoning et al, 2015); as well as innumerable minor national interpretations of the central concept of 'police', all illustrating the variety and national individuality in European policing today.

Catherine Denys warns us against simplistic notions of 'linear history', in which we erroneously assume that there is a causal link between events in time, such that one circumstance appears to emerge naturally from another. For instance, it would be wrong to suppose simply that the notion of 'police as *preventive*' progressively gave way from 1750 onwards to 'police as *suppressive*'. No such steady linear development occurred, partly because in continental Europe there was no consensus on what was meant by 'police' and partly because the convulsion of the French Revolution in 1789 short-circuited anything approximating to evolution. In Germany, the notion of 'police science'

(*Polizeiwissenschaft*), first given coherence by the economist Johann Justi in about 1756, was actually intended to underpin a primary duty of the police to secure economic advantage (Backhaus, 2008).[8] This contrasts with the emphasis in pre-revolutionary France, for example, where the concept of 'police as preventive' was largely defined and debated by the legal profession. This was not a rarefied subject, obscurely discussed only by academics or lawyers. As Denys shows, there was considerable and widespread debate about policing among the intelligentsia of Europe in the latter half of the 18th century: 'during the Enlightenment, the improvement of policing became an issue of everyday debate' (Denys, 2010, p. 342). The 'common discourse about policing' (Denys, 2010, p. 341) gave rise to considerable proliferation of policing practices and in the compositions of the groups charged with maintaining law and order – often former soldiers, led and managed by 'minor notables' (Denys, 2010, p. 340). This in turn led to discussions about who was in charge. The French (or more strictly, Parisian) model for what we might now call a strategic police leader, was the *lieutenant général de police*, who created from 1667 'a Parisian police force that was as effective as it was formidable' (Denys, 2010, p. 337).[9] This initiative was imitated elsewhere in Europe, with varying degrees of competence, often stimulated by a reigning monarch with a keen eye on his internal security, such as in Lisbon (the 'Intendant General') in 1760; Madrid ('Superintendent-General of police') in 1782; Milan ('Director of police') in 1787; matched in May of the same year by the installation of Ferdinand Rapédius de Berg as 'Director of General Policing in the Netherlands' (Denys, 2010, p. 337).

The same processes of innovation, experiment and reform, headed by a police leader who was responsible for strategy and direction, can be found 'from Milan and Paris to Brussels and Naples' (Denys, 2010, p. 342), showing that the debate about what policing was and who should lead it was widespread, characterised by a lively, informed interest that modern Eurocrats might envy. However, the French Revolution of

---

[8]   This concept of 'police' included aspects of town planning, monitoring of the price of goods – particularly foodstuffs – and public health. The *police* enacted *policy* – which incorporated theories about the spread of disease by vapours and 'night miasmas' (Emsley, 2007; Backhaus, 2008). 'Police science' was middle European rather than specifically German, though Justi first gave it theoretical respectability.

[9]   Denys cites Williams (1979) and others in refuting this notion of an all-powerful police chief in Paris, because it seems that a degree of mythologizing attaches to the plaudits that the first *chef de police*, Gabriel Nicolas de la Reynie, and his successors have received. See Denys, 2010, p. 337, but see also Stead, 1983.

1789 and its aftermath swept much of this elegant and enlightened discussion to one side in an unsubtle bid for dominance – and it is to that brutal new order that we must now look.

The 'continental' or 'Napoleonic' model of policing

The 'continental' or 'Napoleonic' model of policing is so expressive of modern Western European policing in one way or another that we are apt to forget that it had its origins in the convulsions of the late 18th century's revolutionary fervour.

Rob Mawby noted that the politicised nature of French policing today can be traced back to a French Revolution tripartite police system of militaristic gendarmes, a larger force of National Police that had a remit for gathering intelligence on suspect citizens (Mawby, 1990) and a localised municipal force that largely operated in towns under the control of the mayor.

This model brackets *security* (through the imposition of order) and *surveillance*, and it was widely exported by Napoleon as he successively conquered and occupied countries in Europe during the wars of 1799–1815. It moved policing at a stroke from the passively preventive to the actively suppressive, principally because the new order in France saw itself as surrounded by enemies, both external and internal. Mawby argues that this model, where the police act largely as political agencies, perpetuates a reactive force that is separate from the public (Mawby, 1990, p. 34). To be fair, communitarianism was never the purpose either of the gendarmerie (mostly controlling the countryside and the roads) or of the *police nationale* (largely urban and counter-insurgent) when they were formed. 'The public' was not a recognised entity; rather, mass protest by the mob – such as the 'storming' of the Bastille or demonstrating for bread – was deeply feared by the ruling elite, whether monarchy, military or the 'Committee of Public Safety'.[10] Even in Napoleon's time, despite the external appearance of uniform support for his rule, large groups of *refractaires* (young men dodging conscription) roamed the countryside and there was always the threat from counter-revolutionaries in the Vendée (Joes, 2006; Anderson,

---

[10]   The 'Comité de salut public' was the tool of the '*Terreur*' from 1793 to 1794. It had replaced the Committee for General Defence, and not only aimed to secure France's external borders, but also to eradicate any opposition within France. A parallel may be seen in the 'soviets' or 'workers' councils' in revolutionary Russia in 1917-18, which were quickly subordinated to the larger national 'Soviet' that brought the Bolsheviks to power.

2011), such as the so-called 'White Bourbons', or there were aimless, drunken groups in the cities, searching for an outlet to blood lust (Forrest, 2012, p. 51).

Napoleon was by no means alone in wanting to control such anarchistic tendencies on the part of the citizenry; Wellington also feared the mob (such as his swearing in of thousands of Special Constables to deal with the Chartists, in their marches in London in 1849), as did Metternich in Austria ('the year of revolutions', 1848). Such uneasiness was long a part of governance. Accordingly, a principal role of the police in both France and in conquered Europe, either as *agents* (officers in the Police Nationale) or as *gendarmes*, was to snuff out any tendency to large-scale disorder or (counter) revolution. Robert Gildea suggests that the thrust to create order stemmed from Napoleon's own dominant personality:

> what characterised the Napoleonic regime above all was the strong executive under the control of a single charismatic figure who appointed and dismissed ministers, generals, prefects, and bishops, commanded armies, directed foreign policy, saw to the codification of laws and reorganised the systems of education, worship and administration. (Gildea, 2003, p. 38)

Indeed, a 2012 study of Napoleon by Michael Broers proposes a 'new history'; one that assesses his legacy and effect rather than his battles and conquests, noting the persistence of his influence not only in the model of policing but also in the 'Code Napoléon' structures of civil and criminal law, as the *Code* became 'the essence of the common law of Europe' (Broers et al, 2012, p. 2).[11] The petty kingdoms, principalities, dukedoms and monarchies had the opportunity to revert to their own *anciens régimes* after Napoleon's defeat at Waterloo in 1815 and peace returned to Europe. But they did not all revert, and that suggests that they saw merit in the new policing system, and something fundamentally stable about the *Code* which countries wanted to keep; not least of which was a delivery to the state's rulers of the order and control that they needed to remain in power. Sceptics might suggest

---

[11] But Broers and his colleagues are also right to remind us that Europe was not some empty *tabula rasa* passively awaiting the arrival of Napoleon and all his administrative and judicial retinue to impose their systems upon a series of blank pages. There were already civil structures, criminal laws, justice systems and police functions in individual European states, long before French was heard in their streets.

that retention of the 'continental model' can be ascribed in part to inertia, or to a passive acceptance of leaving what works, intact; but in Italy, the Netherlands, Belgium, France, Spain, Greece and Portugal, there are to this day discernible traces of the Napoleonic *Code*, its legal structures and vestiges of its policing model (Gildea, 2003; Broers et al, 2012). That suggests strongly that the model was actively adopted and sustained, not passively endured (Emsley, 2007, pp. 89-91). Maurice Punch has noted[12] that Napoleon was 'an inveterate tidier', who brought organisation and clarity to previously unorganised systems and to uncodified and disparate laws, across a Europe consisting of 'a jumble of near autonomous principalities'.

The French policing model was retained in Holland up to the 1850s, when the modern Dutch constitution was being formulated, because even democratic politicians did not want a police that was too independent. Like other countries of Europe formerly occupied by the French, the Dutch authorities wanted to keep control of the police (spread across the ministries of internal affairs and justice), as well as of a gendarmerie answerable to the minister of defence, just in case.

Enduring characteristics: evolving features of policing in Europe

The first characteristic of this model is a fundamental also of orthodox military command: it is *the centralisation of the use of force*. The 'strong' state gathers together under its aegis the means to control, direct, strike and destroy, as well as all the reins of communication, command and control, so that there is central direction, central coordination and pyramidal bureaucracy (operated 'top down', see Thoral, 2012, p. 59), while at the same time there is inhibition of any parochial tendencies to vary from the norm. It is a template for central control. What Napoleon wanted was instant responsiveness to his commands (Broers, 2012), and that cannot easily be obtained under a pluralist, dispersed system, since fast responses require high levels of discipline and uniformity, which themselves cannot admit of inconsistency or local autonomy. As a result, there is much less likelihood of muddled incompetence or inconsistency at a local level, but there is also the potential that such a regime could collapse exponentially if its charismatic leader is removed (as happened notably with Napoleon, Hitler and Pol Pot, for example). The state leaders of the early 19th century in Europe – often Napoleon's

---

[12] Maurice Punch, Visiting Professor at LSE, is joint author of *What Matters in Policing?* (2015) and has long been an authority on European (particularly Dutch) policing, in a communication to the authors in May 2013.

family members and, later, restored monarchs and nobility – all wanted order and method, suppression of dissent, uniformity of administration and effective state surveillance and that is what the structural system of the continental policing model provided (Rapport, 2012, pp. 88-99). Clive Emsley remarks that:

> French bayonets and Napoleonic administration imposed [...] structures of bureaucratic repression and more effective, permanent policing across much of Europe. (Emsley, 2007, p. 103)

Second, the police forces of such centralised states are highly militarised. The historical reason for this is probably twofold: one is that military force effectively (if sometimes heavy-handedly) counters disorder in most guises from street protest to armed insurrection; and the second is that militarism lends itself most effectively to centralised command.[13] The interchangeability from soldier to police officer was a natural or pragmatic response to conditions in the field (Campbell and Campbell, 2010). Even though Emsley asserts that '[s]oldiers fight battles, police control the populace' (Emsley, 2007), it was sometimes immaterial which was which; since gendarmes could fight sustained battles[14] and soldiers (sometimes less brutally than national police) could control a

---

[13] It is worth pointing out that this is no longer military orthodoxy. Now, 'delegated command' coincides with 'devolved operations' in most combat situations. This is predicated partly on better and nearly instantaneous communication – conspicuously lacking in the early 19th century – and partly on the often greater effectiveness of contextual judgement on the spot. Moving massed armies on a chessboard battlefield effectively ended with the armoured manoeuvres between Hitler's *Wehrmacht* and the Soviet Red Army at Kursk in 1943, and has never been seen since. Under Napoleon in 1799-1815, and for a hundred years more, the military convention was large-scale action in geographically compact areas (for ease of communication), modulated through centralised command. See Paret et al, 1986; Duggan, 2002; Fremont-Barnes, 2010. The best modern book on military command theory is McCann, C. and Pigeau, R. (eds) (2000), *The human in command: Exploring the modern military experience*, which was based on a NATO workshop in Jamaica in 1998.

[14] Such as in Italy in 1943, when Italy changed sides, and the Carabinieri fought against the Germans (see, for example, Paoletti, C. (2008), *A Military History of Italy*, Westport, CT: Greenwood Publishing Group.

population.[15] Nonetheless, the predominant model became one where militarised police, and the military exercising a policing function, considerably overlapped and interchanged their roles (see Cole, 1999; Campbell and Campbell, 2010; and van der Burg and Lok, 2012, pp. 106-07). There is also the example elsewhere in the world of the 'peace-keeping role' of UN soldiers, often indistinguishable in function from their police counterparts. Proliferation of different kinds of police still characterise parts of Europe today, with regional police in Catalonia and the Basque country, for example, or the *Guardia di Finanzia* (Fiscal Police) in Italy, or the reintroduction of the municipal police in France.[16]

The third element in this model was an extensive system of espionage directed against threats to the continuation of the state; laying the foundations for a 'political police'. What began as a defensive response to external threat soon matured into a fully fledged espionage system, which monitored the general citizenry rather than defined security threats. Insensibly, the apparatus became the tool of the governing power, wielded to suppress *any* opposition, whether that governing power was (successively) Robespierre, the Directory, Napoleon or the restored Bourbon monarchy. Napoleon's extensive espionage and informant system, developed by Fouché and expanded by Vedocq,[17] was exported to the conquered countries of Europe as well as widely deployed in France itself. It was a system in which: 'the sister would denounce her brother, the son his father, and friends suspected each other of being a traitor' (van der Burg and Lok, 2012, p107; quoting *Schets der gevolgen van den invloed der Franchen op Nederland, sedert het jaar 1795* (Amsterdam, 1814)).[18] The result was 'a tradition of suspicion of police powers throughout the continent' (Tupman and Tupman, 1999, p. 25).

In the turbulent politics of Revolutionary and then Napoleonic France, and subsequently much of Europe, firm government often meant the exercise of arbitrary, suppressive power. Yet most people would have settled for a quiet life in an ordered society. In practice,

---

[15] An example is the French military occupation of the unfederated states of Germany during the Napoleonic Wars, see John Childs' (2011) Barracks and Conscription: Civil-Military Relations in Europe from 1500, *EGO (European History on line)*, http://tinyurl.com/p7cako

[16] Maurice Punch, 2013, in a communication to the authors.

[17] See Anderson, 2011, pp. 24-30.

[18] We (freely) translate this as: 'Outline of the effects of the French influence in the Netherlands since 1795'.

this entailed a severe curtailment of individual freedoms in the pursuit of the security of the state. This is probably why many countries continued with the policing system imported by Napoleon, long after he had gone to exile and death; what he proffered was not perfect, but it worked: pragmatism will usually prevail over idealism.

The 'Anglo-Saxon' model: the opposite of the 'continental' model

The Anglo-Saxon policing model was claimed by its proponents to be diametrically different from Napoleon's centralised, repressive, militarised and surveillance-hungry policing, and they argued that the British system was conceived from the outset to be a model for civilian policing, with a uniform that was distinctly unmilitary, a decentralised structure and a modicum of independence from the governing power.

That does not necessarily mean that loud insistence about the differences between the Anglo-Saxon model and the continental model is accurate. Emsley noted that the English perception:

> of their own liberty and their hostility to things French made them wary of any institution that smacked of a military presence or a political surveillance of the population (Emsley, 2008, p. 67)

But the initial British requirement that a police force should not be a gendarmerie (unless in Ireland, Canada or the colonies, see later in this chapter), and that routinised internal espionage by the state police should not happen systemically, does not mean that the two systems are diametric opposites. Claims that the English system is comprehensively decentralised do not always stand up to scrutiny, any more than the insistence that the 'new police' was purely civilian is entirely accurate. Emsley notes that the original intention was to make the 'new police' look very different from the army:

> New policemen did not look military. They wore top hats and blue uniform long-tailed coats; both very different from the plumed shakoes and scarlet, short-tailed coats of the British infantry. (Emsley, 2008, p. 68)

Even so, such police officers 'belonged to a hierarchical, drilled and fiercely disciplined organisation' (Emsley, 2008, p. 69), whose role was as 'an instrument for controlling and disciplining a burgeoning and increasingly self-confident and non-deferential working class' (Emsley, 2008, p. 66).

In many ways, this echoes the function of their opposite numbers in France and in the rest of Europe, where preservation of law and order, so that trade could flourish and citizens live peaceable lives, was a principal function of policing as far as the governing classes were concerned. For all that, those who supported the introduction of the 'new police' in England wanted them to be at a remove from the 'system of espionage' that 'was the essential role of the police in France' under Napoleon, and unlike 'the armed, military police institution that patrolled the main roads - the **gendarmerie**' (Emsley, 2008, p. 68, his emphasis).

Another means of ensuring that the English system did not resemble the one in France – and by extension, the rest of Europe – was to establish English police forces as shire- or county-based independent organisations from the late 1850s. Even that is not as straightforward as comparative apologists would have us believe, because the system of inspection of police, also established in the 1850s, and the powerful leverage exerted through the Home Office's contribution to police budgets, ensures that some degree of centralisation is always present, if not always evident.

Other features of the Anglo-Saxon model of policing remain stable and familiar; one of the most obvious of which, in keeping with a civilianised police, is that police officers in England, Wales and Scotland are not armed: 'The ordinary police constable carried a wooden baton as his only normal armament' (Emsley, 2008, p. 68).

The truncheon has since given way to the extendable baton and the pepper spray, but even when in possession of these items, a modern British police officer cannot be said to be armed.[19] The routine carrying of a lethal weapon, whether sidearm or semi-automatic carbine, is still comparatively rare in Britain, other than at major airports or in Downing Street. The marketisation of the 'unarmed' British police suggests that somehow there is a moral point being made about deeply peaceable British society compared with violently lawless European

---

[19] 'Ordinary' British police officers do not carry Tasers routinely. These are carried, in addition to guns, as a 'less-than-lethal' option by trained firearms officers, who usually require express authority from a strategic police leader to deploy.

society and, of course, there is no truth in either extreme.[20] Many European police officers told us that they served out entire careers without once drawing their personal weapons for self-protection, let alone discharging them with lethal force; whereas arming of British police at 'firearms incidents' is now so common as to be unremarkable and there are around three or four instances per year in the UK of officers discharging weapons, about half of them with fatal effect.[21] As usual, the truth lies somewhere between the two poles of the heavily armed and not armed at all. Peter ('Tank') Waddington gives us a salutary reminder that: 'the nature of policing, including the role that weapons play, cannot be divorced from the context in which policing takes place' (Waddington, 1999, p. 152).

That context determines whether or not overt arms are carried and whether policing is 'by consent' or whether there is resistance to state power at the popular level. Rob Mawby remarks that:

> [Given] the extent to which the police exhibit paramilitary or militaristic qualities defined across a range of criteria, including for example armaments, training elements, uniform, rank structure, tactical deployment, formal links with the armed services, ministerial responsibility, disciplinary code and living arrangements, we may conclude that while the English police exhibit less [sic] of these qualities than the police of, say, France or Italy, there have been marked shifts in recent years. (Mawby, 1999, p. 18)

Mawby, like den Boer (1999), believes that there is a gradual convergence between the Anglo–Saxon and the Napoleonic (continental) systems, but this may confuse identity of purpose with identity of structure. 'Tank' Waddington reminds us of the origins of the continental model and how Britain differed crucially from it:

---

[20] In a BBC report by Jon Kelly in September 2012, Peter Waddington noted that all major police forces in Europe, as well as the US, Canada and Australia, routinely carry firearms. The exceptions are Britain, the Irish Republic and New Zealand. In Norway, police officers carry firearms in their cars but not on their person. Kelly's article is available at: www.bbc.co.uk/news/magazine-19641398

[21] For example, in the period 2009-12, officers opened fire 18 times – nine fatally. See, for example: www.channel4.com/news/police-fatal-shooting-trigger-happy-fact-check, January 2014 (data originated from the Home Office).

> Policing throughout Europe was a creature of the strong
> state of absolute monarchies, autocratic empires and
> latterly, dictatorships [...] Britain avoided much of the
> turmoil that afflicted continental Europe [...] because its
> political institutions successfully incorporated the emerging
> industrialized working class into social, economic and
> political institutions. (Waddington, 1999, p. 153)

Waddington's 'incorporated' might be read as a neutralising of working-class protest and resistance, born of a prevalent fear of the mob by the 'political institutions'. It was not that Britain could not produce a militarised police; rather, the British chose for themselves a broadly localised police, responding not to state *diktat* but to local magistracy, which grounded their civil police in both community and local law. Only such a compromise could satisfy the vociferous demand for personal freedom by the middle-class libertarian who simultaneously wanted the working classes kept in their place. Yet, for all that, the continental model in countries like the Netherlands and Belgium has distinct parallels with the devolved model, as equally 'grounded [...] in both community and local law' (Waddington, 1999, p. 153). The truncheon was often enough in Britain to deal with the unarmed criminal or unarmed protester, but we would do well to remember Waddington's cautionary note about 'the patina of sentiment': 'The unarmed constabulary was not nearly as vulnerable as it appeared' (Waddington, 1999, p. 155).

When managing major public disorder or armed threat, police forces can call on the military[22] (as the Metropolitan Police did at the Sidney Street Siege of 1911, the Royal Ulster Constabulary did in Northern Ireland 1968-97 or the Metropolitan Police Service (MPS) did at the Iranian Embassy Siege of 1980). Some forces are capable of carrying out effective armed interventions with their own squads, such as the MPS's CO19[23]) and forces have a range of options in between, including anti-riot equipment, Tasers and 'kettling' (confining crowds

---

[22] As aid to the civil power (Military Aid to the Civil Power), both in siege or terrorist situations, and in terms of major emergencies.

[23] Police armed intervention units are *not* equivalent to military intervention units such as the SAS or SBS. The latter military are trained to neutralise by the effective focus of lethal firepower, while the police aim, or should aim, for resolution with the minimum of lethal force.

to specific locations until they can be dispersed).[24] By contrast, there have been instances in Europe when armed police or military forces resorted to the use of powerful or high-velocity weapons because there were no alternatives. The debate about 'less-than-lethal' weapons for use by police has intensified in recent years, and not just in Britain. Peter Rowe points out that countries signed up to the European Convention on Human Rights (ECHR) were liable to prosecution if their police or armed forces did not have a range of options to deal with disorder or protest:

> [The European Court of Human Rights] has found States to be liable [of causing death unnecessarily], largely due to the inadequacy of any alternative strategy to using high-powered firearms against demonstrators or suspected terrorists. In **Gulec v. Turkey** (1998) the Court concluded that 'the gendarmes used a very powerful weapon (firing from an armored [sic] vehicle) because they apparently did not have truncheons, riot shields, water cannon, rubber bullets or tear gas. (Rowe, 2002, p. 61)

It is relevant that resort to lethal weapons generally has only one outcome, whereas resort to a range of non-lethal weapons or options can at least offer results that are not fatal. In this, the principle of arming the police only when justified or necessary has a resonance that the routine arming of police does not.

This may hold in the management of internal disorder, but probably does not when there are external threats (such as international terrorism) or when there is a situation, such as rioting occasioned by external events (as seen in Cyprus in March 2013, for example), which falls between internal and external security. In such an event, argues Derek Lutterbeck, gendarmeries are carving themselves a role where their armed intervention or interdiction can straddle internal and external security alike, plugging any gap that might arise between

---

[24] Only the Police Service of Northern Ireland routinely has access to water cannon or lachrymose (CS) gas to deal with rioting. These are not yet options for the British mainland, though some MPS officers have been trained after the riots in English cities during summer 2011. See a report in *Police Oracle*, 22 May 2013, www.policeoracle.com/news/Uniformed+Operations/2013/May/22/Water-cannon-in-G8-training-programme_65520.html. The Mayor of London, Boris Johnson, controversially purchased two water cannons in 2014, against the express wishes of the Home Secretary; see O'Neill and Elliot (2014).

using the army and using the police (Lutterbeck, 2004). Such flexibility appeals to governments, because they can then claim that the force they deploy, having fallen short of deploying soldiers, is proportionate. It is, incidentally, a political positioning by gendarmeries of uncharacteristic sophistication, which may in turn suggest that they are evolving their roles just as much as state police forces are.[25] One strategic police leader commented:

> 'A gendarmerie prevents what is called the "Fouché spirit" of unchallenged police power, and it also prevents the military mistake of the "Caesar spirit" which is absolute power for the Army. Governments in democracies (and elsewhere too I guess) need to be assured that they will not be toppled in a coup by any side which can use force.' (Interviewee B104)

The 'colonial' model of policing

We turn now to two linked models; one with which the British pacified, or more strictly suppressed, the population of Ireland from about 1750, and one deployed with subsequent utility in the growing British Empire overseas.

Waddington notes that: 'Ireland was the first colony to be policed and it continued to influence the conduct of colonial policing throughout the era of the British Empire' (Waddington, 1999, p. 154). But there were refinements even within such a system, since: 'European colonists were served by civil police while the native population was often subjected to more oppressive paramilitary treatment' (Waddington, 1999, p. 153).

The colonial model, then, was designed to hold a population in subjection, and this was policing more akin to the Napoleonic or continental model, since it was not predicated on any form of democratic consensus (Sinclair and Williams, 2007). The indigenous people did not want to be policed by invading colonists, therefore the police system operated on behalf of the occupying power in suppressing dissent and ensuring, at best, a sullen compliance. This was by no means a policing model restricted to the colonising British; Bankole Cole has pointed out that repressive colonial police forces were utilised by the French, Belgians, Germans, Dutch, Spanish and Portuguese, more or less all as 'a by-product of the global expansion of capitalism

---

[25] A point expanded in the gendarme leaders' own words in Chapter Seven.

in the nineteenth century' (Cole, 1999, p. 89). Cole goes on to make a distinction between colonies 'that were annexed for the purpose of settlement' and those 'pacified' colonies that were 'annexed mainly for the purpose of trade'. Cole also suggests, like Waddington, that a civilian policing structure was normally used for the settlement, while a paramilitarised model was used in those places conquered for trade (see also studies by Brogden, 1987; and Deflem, 1994).

The Irish Constabulary policing model was a military gendarmerie in form and appearance. Tobias (1975) described the appearance of the (Royal) Irish Constabulary as 'quasi-military' with its dark green uniform with black buttons and insignia, deliberately reminiscent of The Rifle Regiment (the 95th).[26] Its purpose, like a conventional continental gendarmerie, was to bring law and order to the countryside (towns, by contrast, were largely managed by municipal police), to control large demonstrations – increasingly, in the 19th century, for 'Home Rule' and independence from Britain – and to protect the property of the (largely absentee) British landowners in the countryside from the anger of their exploited and often hungry tenantry (Palmer, 1988). From the beginning, then, the Irish Constabulary was intended to suppress political *and* economic unrest. It was this twin role that was exported to the rest of the British Empire, but it was not always a rigid model imposed on a rebellious populace.

The model when operated in Canada was very much favoured by settlers and fur traders. Originally the gendarmerie was named the North-West Canadian Mounted Police; later it became the Royal Canadian Mounted Police, which now enjoys a federal role in policing across Canada. Herlihy notes that the Royal Newfoundland Constabulary in independent Newfoundland, as well as the Victoria Police Force in Australia, were originally modelled on the Irish Constabulary, but they soon developed or acquired their own local characteristics (Herlihy, 1997, p. 88). Such forces for law and order in rural parts were reassuring to the new settlers; not only did these

---

[26] The original Corps of Riflemen was formed in 1800, and brought into the British 'line' as the 95th Rifles, serving in the Peninsular War with distinction. The Royal Green Jackets (previously a generic title for Rifle regiments) was itself an amalgamation in 1966 of The Oxfordshire and Buckinghamshire Light Infantry (43rd and 52nd), The Kings Royal Rifle Corps and The Rifle Brigade. The 95th and the Royal Green Jackets were finally amalgamated with other Light Division regiments to form the five-battalion-strong The Rifles in 2007. Good historical accounts are in Mark Urban's *Rifles*, 2003, and John Kincaid's 2009 study *Adventures in the Rifle Brigade*.

armed police protect them from attack by locals, but also ensured that 'rights to property' and land occupation were upheld at a time of anarchy and lawlessness in the wilder parts of the Empire. The practice of using armed police persisted whether the model was for settlement or for exploitation of trade.

Perhaps one further characteristic of the gendarmerie / colonial force model worth noting is that it made extensive use of local informants, wherever it was based. The Irish Constabulary was able to break up hostile groups in Ireland because it had penetrated groups like the Fenians and the Irish Republican Brotherhood (Herlihy, 1997; Borgonovo, 2007); while the colonial versions of the model, particularly in Africa and India, used tribal, caste or internecine rivalries to maintain a largely effective surveillance on native populations (Deflem, 1994; Das and Verma, 1998; Cole, 1999). In this aspect of its work, which Cole describes as the 'political system of divide and rule' (Cole, 1999, p. 95), the colonial police model replicates what Napoleon's gendarmes did in European rural areas.[27] Knowing why and when the local population felt restless, was key to the effective policing of a subjugated people, whether Irish peasants, First Nation Canadians, African tribes, Australian Aboriginals, New Zealand Maoris or Indian 'natives'. The common factor in the application of this colonial model of policing was that it could be seen to work effectively on behalf of those in control, and, initially anyway, there were few voices raised against a consciously racist and repressive policing intended for those who were not British or European (Brogden, 1987; Palmer, 1988).

This may be why many former colonies, both British and those deriving from other European states, have armed, centralist, quasi-militarist police forces which, as Cole reminds us, are good at law enforcement and the maintenance of internal security, but which have 'no effective review mechanisms to enable the public to call their police forces to account' (Cole, 1999, p. 99). Gendarmeries on the Napoleonic model were adopted in countries like Chile and Mexico as a legacy of Spanish occupation, and 'in many cases, the control of the police has simply changed hands from one authoritarian government to another' (Cole, 1999, p. 98).

---

[27] As well as the French *Police Nationale's* more systematic espionage system in the towns and cities.

Policing as political repression: the Gestapo, the KGB and the Stasi[28]

Absolutist governments want to suppress any form of dissent or disobedience, and such regimes, whether communist or fascist, are characterised by extensive routine monitoring of the population and a readiness to utilise a deeply repressive secret-police system to serve the political aims of those in charge. What we might call the 'Gestapo/KGB/Stasi' model of absolutist policing used methods that included torture and kidnapping, as well as secret murder and unlawful imprisonment. What is more, the secret police did all these things with the connivance of their ruling political party and on a massive scale. Few other regimes, even that of the Russian *Okhrana* under the Tsar,[29] were as ruthless, single-minded and unaccountable as the Gestapo/KGB/Stasi.

The Stasi

The East Germany state security police, the Stasi, is estimated to have used 500,000 paid informants, which, at its height in the 1980s, represented one spy for every 166 citizens. Joe Koehler put this proportion in a quaintly domestic context: 'at least one Stasi informer was present in any party of ten or twelve dinner guests' (Koehler, 1999, p. 9).

By comparison, it is estimated[30] that the KGB had about the same number of full-time agents to oversee 280 million Russian people, and the Gestapo had something like one secret police officer to every 2,000 citizens. Nonetheless, the point is clear enough: surveillance of the citizenry and close monitoring for dissent or disaffection is hugely manpower-intensive. All the secret police systems in absolutist regimes are grossly swollen and mundanely bureaucratic: perhaps the biggest shock for East Germans, following the collapse of the communist regime in 1990, was to discover (in the copious files that the Stasi

---

[28] The Stasi in East Germany is used as an example; there were repressive police in all the countries in the Soviet Bloc, including Poland, Hungary and the former Czechoslovakia.

[29] See Fischer's 1999 account of the Paris operations of the Tsar's secret police at the turn of the 20th century; or Zuckerman, 1996.

[30] By Koehler, in his colourful (1999), *Stasi: the untold story of the East German Secret Police*, p. 8.

held on individuals) who had informed on whom.[31] From Catholic priests to university professors, from children to spouses, the Stasi cast its net aggressively wide; yet this lack of discrimination contained the origins of its weakness. Jan Gieseke argues that the Stasi was a failure because its massive documentation was purposeless; it did not inculcate support for the East German communist regime. It simply held the lid on a boiling pot for decades, but its demise in 1990 was so rapid that many were taken by surprise (Gieseke, 2006).

The KGB

The Stasi modelled itself on the Russian state security apparatus, the KGB, even to imitating its sword and shield symbol.[32] But the KGB itself did not spring from nothing, ready-made as a repressive arm of the Soviet state. There is a long tradition in Russian history of a security apparatus to protect those in power and to deal with dissent, from the *Oprichnina* founded in 1565 by Ivan the Terrible, through the 'Third Section' and later the *Okhrana* of the Tsars, the *Cheka* and OGPU (Joint State Political Directorate) of the Bolsheviks, the NKVD (People's Secretariat for Internal Affairs) of Stalin and the KGB of the modern era (Andrew and Gordievsky, 1990, pp. 1- 42). Often, the security apparatus of the day did not survive the death or disgrace of its leaders, but each gave way to a new machinery. It seems there has never been a time when the Russian people were not under scrutiny by the state, whatever the combination of initials or names of the organisations doing the monitoring (Knight, 2003). Indeed, the remit for the work of Tsar Nicholas I's 'Third Section' of 1826 could serve equally well in describing the domestic function of the KGB:

> The major preoccupation of the Third Section was what the KGB later called 'ideological subversion': political dissent in all its forms. Like the KGB [...], in order to keep track of

---

[31] See Jan Gieseke's meticulous 2006 monograph, *Der Mielke-Konzern: Die Geschichte der Stasi, 1945-1990*, Munich: Deutsche Verlags-Anstalt.

[32] KGB, *Komitet gosudarstvennoy bezopasnosti*, the Committee for State Security, was formed after the death of Stalin in 1954, surviving until 1991 when it was replaced by the **FSB** (see Andrew and Gordievsky, 1990). All Soviet-Bloc countries had secret police systems modelled more or less on the KGB; consequently this has given a legacy of fear to many countries now in the EU and emerging from the shadows cast by such regimes.

dissent, it believed it necessary to monitor public opinion (Andrew and Gordievsky, 1990, p. 2)

The Third Section head also had command of the Corps of Gendarmes, 'several thousand strong, charged with safeguarding state security' (Andrew and Gordievsky, 1990, p. 2), though its strength was much smaller than the later KGB. The Criminal Law of 1845 institutionalised political crime, which remained more or less until 1988, making it a crime to 'question the existing political order' (Andrew and Gordievsky, 1990, p. 3). Thus, it is possible to assert that: 'Tsarism bequeathed to Bolshevism both a political culture and a legal system in which only the state had rights' (Andrew and Gordievsky, 1990, p. 3).

'Pussy Riot' in 2012, along with other dissident groups and journalists in Putin's Russia, might argue that nothing much has changed. The KGB by the late 1960s had become a massive state bureaucracy, focused on the need to suppress dissent wherever it might be found (Knight, 2003). In the wake of the 'Prague Spring' (*Pražské jaro*) of 1968, when Czechoslovakia's leader, Alexandr Dubček, sought very limited reforms, the Soviet Union set up a 'Fifth Directorate' within the KGB whose remit was:

> to study and crack down on dissent of all forms. Specialised departments [...] were responsible for the surveillance of intellectuals, students, nationalists from ethnic minorities, religious believers and Jews. (Andrew and Gordievsky, 1990, p. 406)

It was this legacy of absolute control and surveillance that the former communist states sought to discard from 1990. It is why they adopted the ECHR (the European Convention on Human Rights) and passed it into law in their respective countries, and why they sought a democratic policing model.[33]

Fittingly, perhaps, the end of the KGB as an instrument of state power came when its chairman, Vladimir Kryuchkov, attempted a *coup d'état* in August 1991 against President Mikhail Gorbachev and failed (Knight, 2003). The end of one era embraced the beginning of another, and the FSB (Federal Security Service of the Russian Federation) took over from the KGB, with no indication that it is

---

[33] But see also Rawlinson, 2010, and Ruggiero, 2014, on the range and extent of organised crime in Russia and Eastern Europe.

any more tolerant of dissent than its predecessors (Bacon and Renz, 2003; Rawlinson, 2010).[34]

The Gestapo

The role of the Gestapo as part of the repressive state security system in Nazi Germany and throughout Occupied Europe from 1940 to 1945 is too well known to merit much repetition here, especially as it has become a byword for a sinister secret police, answerable only to its highly placed political masters.

A characteristic of the Gestapo function was that it was without judicial oversight; but it made considerable use of the People's Courts (*Volksgericht*), which connived at weak evidence, allowed confessions under torture and ignored even feeble defence pleas. For all that, research by Robert Gellately among others, has shown that the lauded effectiveness of the Gestapo relied for about 80% of its information on denunciations of people by their fellow citizens (Gellately, 1991, pp. 135-7). Some of the myth-making about the Gestapo's ubiquity and the reach and range of its surveillance, may have been promulgated by those who wished to hide their own involvement in denouncing their neighbours, teachers and relatives for a variety of motives (Gellately, 1988; Butler, 2006/2012).

The mythology was in fact helpful to the Gestapo, as the assumptions about its being all-powerful and all-knowing belied its often limited and reactive function.[35] Indeed, research material that is only now being made available online shows that Gestapo offices in places such

---

[34] The State Security Bureau (FSB) carries on the grand Russian tradition of crassly repressive state clumsiness, like the arrest and imprisonment of 'Pussy Riot' in 2012 (three women singing a song against Vladimir Putin in Moscow's Cathedral) or the heavy-handed response to Greenpeace protests at Russian oil-drilling in the Arctic in 2013, when some 30 foreign protesters were held in prison for weeks. The FSB was instrumental in fomenting unrest in the Crimea in 2014 and was probably behind the violent protests in East Ukraine during 2014, see Sandford, 2014.

[35] Gellately, for example, showed that local Gestapo offices were often undermanned and overburdened in Nazi Germany. The dual role of the Gestapo in hunting down Jews and suppressing the Resistance in Occupied Europe could not have been undertaken except with the active cooperation of local police units; aided, as always, by spates of denunciation (Gellately, 1988 and 1991).

as Vienna had prescribed procedures like any police bureaucracy[36] and that the range of possible offences and targets with which the officials had to deal was large. They included (*inter alia*): labour movements, the Protestant Church, border issues, individual resistance activity, the Roman Catholic Church and other denominations, Jewish men and women, prisoners of war and civilian forced labourers, repatriates from Russia and economic matters (*Dokumentationsarchiv des Österreichischen Widerstands* (DOW), 2013).[37] The Gestapo was rightly designated as a criminal organisation after the war, but new research is showing that it gathered information just as unsystematically as the KGB and the Stasi, and could be just as inept at processing it (DOW, 2013).

We need to understand the historical significance to Europe of these repressive secret police systems. The reaction in Germany to the role of the Gestapo has brought about a reversion to the decentralised *Länder* or provincial structure (Wallace, 1994), while the former communist member states of the EU have as emphatically rejected their own legacies of unaccountable extra-judicial policing (Meško and Dobovšek, 2007). Knowing where such countries have come from, and what they endured, gives us insight into what their leaders now profess as policing ideals, however unexceptionable those ideals may appear to some jaded Western European eyes.

States in transition: the German 'decentralised' model

Just as the persistence of the colonial model is a product of historical currents, so the decentralised model of policing in modern Germany is a product of its own historical past (Wallace, 1994). Germany needed to evolve a new model of policing in the post–Second World War years, particularly since the hurried imposition of policing by the Allied occupying armies from 1945 to 1947 was fragmented and ill-assorted (Ziemke, 1975). West Germany's recourse was to turn back to its autonomous *Länder*, within which each would have its own independent police force. How does this model work?

All police forces in modern Germany are subordinate to the respective *Länder* ministers of the interior. Not all the *Ländespolitzei*

---

[36] See *Daily Reports of the Gestapo Headquarters in Vienna 1938-1945*, edited by Brigitte Bailer and Wolfgang Form, www.degruyter.com/staticfiles/pdfs/produktpraesentationen/Daily%20Reports%20of%20the%20Gestapo%20Headquarters%20in%20Vienna%201938-1945.pdf

[37] *Daily Reports of the Gestapo Headquarters in Vienna 1938-1945*, Dokumentationsarchiv des Österreichischen Widerstands (DOW), 2013 database.

are structured in the same way, but the general form is that the headquarters of the regional police, known as the *Präsidium* in most *Länder*, directly answers to the regional interior ministry (Reinke, 2009). The Präsidium (Office of the Präsident) directs the police across the region, and this includes specialist units, including traffic. *Direktionen*, or district police commands serving the equivalent of large towns, come under the Präsidium, and local units (*Inspektionen*) are subordinate to the *Direktionen*. Feltes et al describe the relationships between *Inspektionen* and their communities in the *Länder* as robust and productive, and there has been a development of 'security partnerships' between the *Direktionen* and representatives of citizen organisations, businesses and private institutions (Feltes et al, 2013).

Most of this 'devolved policing' had originated in the princedoms and duchies before Germany was united in 1871, and each police force evolved with minor differences (Deflem, 1996). Indeed, in the immediate pre-war years (1933-39), the Gestapo under Hermann Goering operated only in Prussia, and it was not until Hitler made Heinrich Himmler head of all policing in the Nazi Reich, that the Gestapo model was imposed from the centre on the rest of Germany and became a truly 'national' model (Browder, 1996). Thus, while the immediate historical legacy may be of a repressive secret police under central command, the historic pattern in Germany is actually quite different. West Germany's adoption of the *Länder* police system (alleged by Tupman and Tupman to have been imposed at American insistence[38]) actually recreates the dispersed policing model which had existed before unification in 1871, and which had lasted until the end of the Weimar Republic in 1933 (Deflem, 1996). Only two major forms of federal policing were developed after the war; one was

---

[38] Tupman and Tupman, 1999, p. 7: 'forced on the Germans in 1945 by the Americans'. If true, it was a reversion to a familiar and time-honoured model, and one that would require little 'force' to impose.

for protection of Germany's borders and the other was in criminal investigation.[39]

Much may be made of the autonomy of the *Länder* in Germany, and indeed, the administration of criminal justice, the police, the courts and mayors all seem to function effectively at a local level.[40] This arrangement is pushing at an open door, because research among Germans showed a greater desire for localised community policing than for any federated form (see Feltes, 2002). Sir Christopher Meyer, HM Ambassador to Germany, expressed the pattern of devolution in Germany like this, in 1997: 'Germany has astonishing variety and regional differences. It is like having 18 Scotlands, plus the complexity of proportional representation'.[41]

Where the *Länder* do encounter problems is not in immediate cross-border cooperation but where there are no contiguous borders between regions. Since criminals either take no account of the borders, or deliberately exploit differences between *Länder* for their own illegitimate purposes, the need for a federal mechanism of some kind, however cosmetic, quickly became apparent. The *Bundeskriminalamt* (BKA) investigative force is a grudgingly tolerated manifestation of that federalism. It is rather the degree of separation between police forces and the fierceness with which any centralised control is resisted at the *Länder* level that gives the German model its real resonance (Brodeur, 1995; Feltes et al, 2013). It is not like the Dutch 'hub and spokes' model of police command coordinated from the centre (introduced in 2013), nor the Italian regional command with its federal overlay (introduced in 1971), nor is it the indefensibly cumbersome English and Welsh 'shire county' model of 1964, consisting of 'forty three robber barons'

---

[39] A federal uniformed police force (the *Bundespolitzei*) replaced a more makeshift 'Border Force' (the *Bundesgrenzschutz*), but it took on its full role only in 2005; while the investigative force (the *Bundeskriminalamt* or BKA) has had a federated role since formation in 1951 – a little like that of the FBI in the United States. See the BKA web page at http://preview.tinyurl.com/oho8qlm. Meanwhile, communist East Germany was developing its own monolithic state model of policing, the **Stasi**, modelled naturally enough on the Soviet Union but with distinctly repressive echoes of the Gestapo. The general collapse of communism from 1989 and that of East Germany in particular in 1991, led to the abolition of the Stasi. Instead the newly united Germany established the *Länder* model of policing for the whole country, progress towards which was initially slow (Harlan, 1997).

[40] See, for example, explanations on the Deutsche Bundestag's homepage: http://preview.tinyurl.com/nosbwj5

[41] In his valedictory to the Secretary of State; see Parris and Bryson, 2011, p. 45.

(Caless, 2011, p. 108).[42] The German model is genuinely devolved, and if that incurs some duplication, extra expense and some political posturing, then both the *Länder* and the German people themselves think it is worth it.

The eastern/central 'EU' model: transition to democracy

It may be premature to discuss the nature of policing in those states that formerly came under the aegis of the Soviet Union,[43] until it has fully matured. However, a generation has elapsed since European states to the east and north asserted their independence and it is more than 10 years since they became fully operational members of the EU (2004), and therefore part of Europol, Schengen, the ECHR, Maastricht and all the other familiar features of pan-European policing.

The 'EU police model' is broadly derivative of Western European policing, and aims to be democratic, largely separated from state power, responsive to political will but not to an individual party, located firmly within the rule of law, directed by and integrated with the office of public prosecutor, and tries to be transparent, responsive and communitarian. That at least is the theory as far as former Soviet-Bloc states are concerned, although Tupman and Tupman warned that: 'The lack of any tradition of serving a community or populace presents a major problem today for the ex-communist police organisations' (Tupman and Tupman, 1999, p. 20).

There is a historical legacy in all this, stemming from the hostilities engendered between East and West during the Cold War and the general unease in Western Europe at the East's apparently slavish obedience to Soviet hegemony. Yet, when the Union of Soviet Socialist Republics (USSR) collapsed between 1989 and 1991, the states that bordered Western Europe declared their independence and freedom, losing no time in moving into alignment with the West. Plans for the reform of their police systems followed almost as quickly, though states did not always seem certain which precise model they wanted

---

[42] Caless is quoting a chief police officer (his Interviewee 67).

[43] Communist Russia and its satellites from around 1946-91 were known in the West as the Union of Soviet Socialist Republics (USSR) or the 'Soviet Bloc'. Those countries under direct Russian military control were also known as the 'Warsaw Pact'. See McCormick, T. (1998), *Rethinking the cold war*, [edited by A. Hunter], Philadelphia: Temple University Press; and Selvage, D. (2001), The Warsaw Pact and Nuclear Non-proliferation, *Cold War International History Project Working Paper 32*, Washington, DC: US Government.

to adopt in the 'new world' of a federated Europe. Christopher Paun, for example,[44] noted the 'shall we/shan't we?' vacillation of Poland:

> Poland [chose] to decentralize its police in 1991, [...] then re-centralized [...] in 1995 [...] again decentralized in 1999 and [has] made further adjustments to the combined central-decentral control of [its] police since 2002 (Paun, 2007, p. 8)

Such dithering is rare; Hungary debated a decentralisation of its police but opted in the end to 'keep it centralized' (Paun, 2007), most others remained as they were.[45] In general, the newly independent states that emerged in 1991-92 (aside from East Germany, which was reabsorbed into the rest of Germany), wanted to create their own democratic police systems, free from party control, responsive to the people, communitarian and transparent but largely centralised in structure and overseen in function and finance by a political department, usually a ministry of the interior or its equivalent (Shelley, 1999). Lauri Tabur, using his own country as an example, claims that 'Estonia is a good example for future police reforms in post-totalitarian states' (Tabur, 2013).[46] These necessary reforms could not be done overnight. One of the prerequisites to join the EU is adoption of the ECHR, which eschews any repressive secret police practice. That requirement meant a purge of police departments in the newly independent states, replacing the previous political appointees with 'clean skins' at most levels, but particularly at the top. This has sometimes proven easier to want than to do, and some of the former Soviet-Bloc countries are still engaged in removing final links with the old regime (Bridger and Pine, 2013; Meško et al, 2013). The balance was to get rid of the apparatchiks but at the same time not 'dilute' the police of all experience and leadership. However, in the top echelons, new blood, untainted by association, is now firmly in charge, though Stojanka Mirčeva and Rade Rajkovčevski are right to remind us that 'the reform of the police [in Central and Eastern Europe] is an ongoing process and activity', so we may expect

---

[44] Paun refers in this context to Haberfeld, M. (2002), *Critical issues in police training*, Upper Saddle River, NJ: Pearson Education.

[45] Except Bosnia and Herzegovina, which followed Poland down the decentralised route (Paun, 2007, p. 8).

[46] Tabur, who directs the Estonian Police Academy, goes on to note that 'one of the priorities in developing the police is making its duties and tasks understandable to people', (Tabur, 2013, p. 81).

emergent police forces adopting a broadly 'EU' policing model to be in transition for some time yet (Mirčeva and Rajkovčevski, 2013).

Louise Shelley points to other problems entailed in trying to establish a model for Central and Eastern Europe to fit the new requirements of policing in a democratic country (Shelley, 1999, pp. 78-85). The old USSR system ruthlessly suppressed all minority movements together with any overt nationalism; since independence – most notably in former Yugoslavia – minority groups and groups with distinct ethnic identities have been making their presence felt and heard, and this has posed problems for some of the new police forces. Others, such as the Baltic States, have found some difficulties in policing the residual Russian national populations who thrived under the Soviet-Bloc regime but which now claim to be disadvantaged minorities (Tabur, 2013). More importantly across the new member states of the EU, is the general attitude of their public towards the police: there are deep levels of distrust and fear, which may take decades to overcome. The ordinary people in the former Soviet-Bloc countries have such legacies of the brutal suppression of dissent that resentment and fear may take a long time to be replaced with genuine community-based policing and trust of the police.

The states themselves realised what the 'package' was to enter the EU, and none appeared to demur at the principles of democracy, accountability, the rule of law and a policing system that was subject to all those things; this is the model that new member states of the EU want to establish and consolidate. Although old-established Western European states may occasionally feel unease at doing policing business with former communist countries, the integration within EU policing mechanisms, from the European Police College (CEPOL) to 'Pearls in Policing',[47] has proceeded quickly and comprehensively. The transformed structure and staffing of police departments among new EU members is virtually complete, and integration within the European policing mechanisms is well established. But the relationship between police and public in the individual countries is still in its infancy.

---

[47] 'Pearls in Policing' is a regular, well-attended, invitation-only forum for discussion about strategic policing issues hosted by the Dutch Police Academy, featuring university academics as well as strategic police leaders from all over Europe. Its detractors commonly refer to it as 'Pearls before Swine' (see the Bible, Gospel according to St Matthew, chapter 7, verse 6). See http://tinyurl.com/m3aupxk

Summary

There are six basic policing models, some historical, some evolutionary, which co-exist across Europe. These range from the Napoleonic or continental model and its stubbornly proclaimed opposite, the Anglo-Saxon model, through exported models of gendarmerie for colonial 'pacification' and a repressive extrajudicial secret police, to a genuinely devolved model of policing in modern Germany and the generically democratic police model adopted by the former Soviet-Bloc countries that joined the EU more than 10 years ago. In such circumstances, the EU has to be a broad church; it would be pointless attempting to prescribe what the policing system ought to be in any member state, because that member state's criminal justice system has evolved alongside its police and both would need equal reform and equal integration. This would be an integrative step too far in the current climate.

The best, perhaps, that the EU can hope for is that individual member states continue to rub along, evolve and adapt, that convergence continues, albeit with its customary glacial slowness, and that the overarching mechanisms which the European Council has put in place since 1990 – namely Europol, Eurojust, Joint Investigation Teams, CEPOL, Schengen, SIRENE, the Lisbon Treaty and other cooperative mechanisms – will supply any gaps between countries' systems in policing.[48] The real opportunity probably lies in the sense of shared strategic purpose at the top of policing, and it is to this that we now turn, to try to get some sense of whether or not recruitment to the upper echelons of policing has consistency, strategic vision and shared values.

---

[48] The Cross Channel Intelligence and Security Conference is an example of a non-governmental police cooperative arrangement that has been running for years; see Gallagher, 1998.

TWO

Getting to the top:
the selection and appointment of
strategic police leaders in Europe

Quel vicaire de village ne voudrait pas être Pape? (Which parish priest would not like to be Pope?) (Voltaire, *Lettres Philosophiques*, 1733)

The conundrum of selecting suitable candidates to take over from the existing elite has preoccupied leaders for centuries. Katie Jacobs, quoting Stephen Dando, operating partner at Bain Capital, noted:

> Succession matters hugely [...] whether you like it or not, senior roles matter disproportionately, and senior external appointments are notoriously risky: the absence of a succession plan means you raise the risk for your organisation significantly. (Jacobs, 2012, p. 1)

This refers to the perennial problem that it is difficult to attract suitable candidates for strategic leadership roles (whether in business generally or in policing). The risk of getting it wrong is large, and many organisations attest to wrong appointments at the top, with the result that business goes astray and the organisation founders.

Abysmal leadership of the Royal Bank of Scotland and the Co-operative Bank are recent UK examples, while Silvio Berlusconi's embarrassing indecision in Italy, the collapse of SeaFrance, the bankruptcy of Swissair, the Icelandic Bank (*Kaupþing*) collapse 2008–11, the 2010 sovereign debt crisis in Greece, or the failure of Malev (Hungarian) Airlines, are parallel examples from the rest of Europe.[1] Peter Neyroud argues that, in the British police:

---

[1] See, for example, the 'briefing' article (no byline) (2012) 'Les Misérables' (on European entrepreneurial leaders) in *The Economist*, 28 July, www.economist.com/node/21559618

[t]oo often in the discussions that we have had with leaders across the service from a range of different roles and ranks, it has been quite apparent that the requirements of each leadership role are unclear and that in itself appears to contribute to the sense that through-career talent management of the service is not succeeding. (Neyroud, 2011a, p. 115)

Yet adequate succession planning, finding the right kind of leader to take the organisation forward, remains a key objective in strategic planning. Jay Conger and Robert Fuller noted that:

Succession management systems should focus intensively on linchpin positions—jobs that are essential to the long-term health of the organization. They're typically difficult to fill, they are rarely individual-contributor positions, and they usually reside in established areas of the business and those critical for the future. (Conger and Fuller, 2003, p. 80 (p. 4 of online version))

Succession planning in police forces matters just as much as in commercial business, but it is an area beset with organisational difficulties across Europe. Such difficulties include:

- identifying successor candidates;
- a lack of consensus on the qualities of those who should lead;
- female officers too often being excluded or obstructed by gender-biased processes;
- too few representatives of minority ethnic groups in the upper echelons of the police;[2]
- no consistent and systematic process for existing chiefs objectively to identify and develop their potential successors;
- an ever-present danger of 'cloning' – that is, developing people who mirror the attributes of those already in charge, rather than developing those who do not, although the latter may have equal potential to lead.

This is not just a human resources conundrum (Jacobs, 2012), nor is it something limited only to private industry (Conger and Fuller, 2003).

---

[2] See Chapter Four, where both gender and minority ethnic representation are discussed.

'Succession planning' as *a means continuously to develop the best available talent* is a puzzle for businesses and public service organisations alike, and the police have no monopoly over how best to pick people to become strategic leaders.

Indeed, it is not always possible to obtain the necessary calibre of leader from among the ranks of the police alone, as was acknowledged by the (London) Metropolitan Police in 2007. Remarking that '[t] op class leaders are thin on the ground', the Metropolitan Police Authority's (MPA's) Coordinating and Policing Committee produced a report in February 2008, which noted that: 'very shortly we will have to introduce a scheme that recruits the best talent from a variety of backgrounds' (Metropolitan Police Authority, 2008, replaced in 2011 by the London Mayor's Office for Policing And Crime (MOPAC)).[3]

The notion that at least some of the senior ranks in policing could be filled from outside the profession was repeated in a report prepared for the British government in 2012 by Tom Winsor (who went on to become the first 'civilian' HM Chief Inspector of Constabulary), in which he recommended that recruitment from outside the police could be applicable to ranks at inspector and above, but particularly recruiting directly into the command ranks 'persons of exceptional achievement and ability who have been assessed as having the potential to be senior police officers' (Winsor, 2012, p. 20). This suggestion, while popular at governmental level, has yet to find many open sponsors among senior practitioners.[4] The ingrained and time-honoured supposition in British policing (and in some parts of Europe) that strategic police leaders must serve as constables and rise progressively through the ranks, will be difficult to eradicate; particularly because those in charge have risen that way, and seem to have little incentive to modify the system, however acute the problem of finding a sufficient pool of talent to replace them. Winsor, typically and iconoclastically, went further and

---

[3]   This was in the initial context of the MPS/MPA/MOPAC's frustration with the England and Wales *High Performance Development Scheme*, a fast-track system for promising police officers that nonetheless did not offer enough places to satisfy demand. Characteristically, the MPS (with the MPA's full agreement) chose its own route, and began to look outside policing for potential leaders (MPA, 2008).

[4]   When Bryn Caless put the proposition of direct recruitment to ACPO (strategic police leaders) in his 2009-10 survey of chief police officers in England and Wales, the response against the notion was vociferous but smaller (just) at 48% than the 51% who broadly favoured the idea. These were anonymous responses; it is likely that the public position of individual ACPO officers would be hostile to direct entry (Caless, 2011, p. 186).

suggested that: 'Chief constable vacancies should be open to officers with experience in chief officer equivalent roles in countries with common law jurisdiction that practise policing by consent' (Winsor, 2012, Part 2, p. 21).

The processes to enable direct entry variously at inspector, superintendent and strategic police leader (chief superintendent and Association of Chief Police Officers (ACPO)) ranks came into force in October 2014[5] and appear to suggest that *any* non-British strategic police leader could command forces in England and Wales, if he or she has experience of similar kinds of policing. In practice, this probably means the US, Canada or Australia,[6] but might not exclude, for example, strategic police leaders from the Netherlands or Germany or any other EU country who can meet the 'common law jurisdiction' criteria and match with these a fluency in English. There is no suggestion yet, from the EU or anywhere else, of any reciprocal agreement where UK strategic police leaders could lead forces in other member states, but there is some possibility that, with a *corpus juris criminalis*[7] and harmonised criminal justice systems, this might become a reality in the long-term future.

It is not clear whether the importation of leadership talent from outside policing is simply desirable in view of what talent is internally available, or whether the need is urgent because of the inability of the existing selection procedures to supply the right kinds of leaders for the European policing future. The problem is probably even more acute

---

[5] Initial recruitment is at superintendent level from business leaders and the like, with others coming from the British military into inspector ranks (to command firearms teams, for example), but no one really knows what the longer-term effect of open recruitment will be in the UK or elsewhere in Europe. At the time of writing, no non-police officer has been appointed since about 1966 as a strategic police leader in the UK (though one did lead the Civil Nuclear Constabulary from 2009 to 2012 – but was seen as a special case). A cohort of 9 began in September 2014 and is expected to conclude in 2016, having had modular learning programmes and practical embedding and role studying in a police force. It may be five further years before any direct recruit makes strategic police leader (ACPO) rank.

[6] Neyroud (2011a) indicates that in the UK there is already substantial interest in bringing together police leaders from the United States, Australia, New Zealand and Canada on international policing programmes. Whether they then command individual police forces is still open to debate, however.

[7] A common body of criminal law; as we explore in Chapter Seven, this is something of a chimera in European criminal justice, where agreement by all member states on what constitute the top 10 or 15 criminal offences is yet to be reached.

than that: police leadership is 'a contested concept' (Caless, 2011). Rob Adlam puts the problem squarely:

> No systematic analysis [has been] offered concerning the ways in which police leadership is
>   a) like all other manifestations of leadership,
>   b) like some other types of leadership (e.g. public service), and
>   c) like no other form of leadership (in virtue of its specific tasks and functions) (Adlam, 2003, p. 40, cited in Caless, 2011, p. 81)

In other words, is there something we can point to and call *police leadership*, which is different in kind and degree, or nature, from any other kind of leadership? If there is not, then does that mean that generic notions of leadership apply to the police as much as they do elsewhere? The British ACPO has developed, with the skills for justice sector, a set of 12 competences for strategic police leaders, upon which their performances are assessed. For ease of reference, the 12 competences[8] are:

- Strategic perspective
- Openness to change
- Negotiating and influencing
- Maximising potential
- Respect for diversity
- Team working
- Community and customer focus
- Effective communication
- Problem solving
- Planning and organising
- Personal responsibility
- Resilience.

It is worth noting that more than half of these competences are prescribed for *all* police officers at *all* ranks, as 'behavioural competences' in England and Wales,[9] yet it is evident that none is specific to policing;

---

[8] See ACPO/Skills for Justice, 2003.

[9] Specifically, the seven 'behavioural competences' are: respect for diversity, team working, community and customer focus, effective communication, problem solving, personal responsibility, and resilience (see Caless, 2011, p. 83).

indeed, these competences would be unremarkable in any boardroom, top team or cabinet anywhere in the world. The competences are simply what might be expected of any strategic leader, whether in public service or in commercial activity.[10] This leaves us where we began: there appears to be no consensus that there are leadership abilities that are found only in policing. However, we could point to factors – outside these dully generic competences – such as those dealing with armed criminality, leading public service responses to civil emergencies and understanding the physical threats to prominent public figures and ensuring their protection, not found (or not found in totality) outside policing.[11] They have yet to find their way into any list of competences, despite 'Gold' command being a fundamental of strategic police leadership. Hoogewoning et al noted dryly that:

> the [European] police chief does not have some simply-defined and unquestioned task but is responsible for a diffuse range of tasks that are continually under scrutiny and debate while also being held to account for handling major incidents, operations and investigations (Hoogewoning et al, 2015, p. 19)

The 'diffuse range of tasks' necessarily includes operational decision-making whether the task is in Poland or Portugal, the Baltic or the Balearics, and the commonality here surely is in the (transferable?) ability of the strategic police leader to make the right decision in the right circumstances to ensure the right outcome? We might quibble over the precise meaning(s) of 'right' in this mantra, but operational success is, or should be, easier to quantify than something like crime prioritisation or the abstractions of permeable borders. It is an obligatory skill in policing to make the best operational decision; one that does not excessively intrude on or put at risk a criminal justice outcome. Officers who have come up through the ranks assert that they possess this skill, whereas someone appointed to command from outside the police does not. Hoogewoning et al observe that, in this respect:

---

[10] A point made in detail by Caless (2011, Chapter 3, pp. 83-97), who analyses the competences at length before concluding that none is specific to, or unique within, policing.

[11] Occasionally they might be found in the military, which has a different conception of leadership, working on the 'ex duco' (I lead out; the root of the word 'education') principle and believing that leadership is not just hunger for command but rather a front-end response to events which engages everyone in team effort.

> Policing [is] a *unique* service with exceptional duties, functions and powers and consequently [needs] to embrace the fundamental responsibility of accounting to government, oversight agencies, the media and the public. [There is] ... persistent pressure on senior officers to display both leadership and its corollary, accountability. (Hoogewoning et al, 2015, p. 12)

In other words, an exceptional task requires an exceptional set of skills in the leader, and those skills 'cannot be seen as merely an instrumental attribute that can be routinely injected through a standard course' (Hoogewoning et al, 2015, p. 12). Policing is not selling houses or banking services, and any read-across to corporate leadership is not always persuasive: 'Senior police officers are not the same as managers scrutinizing spread-sheets in the executive suite at the top of the corporate sky-scraper' (Hoogewoning et al, 2015, p. 7).

Nonetheless, there is an assumption throughout Europe that the skills required for police command can be learned or developed; all that is needed is the right 'model', said some of our interviewees. What sort of model did they mean?

Scoping police leadership competences

A 'Pearls in Policing' initiative in May 2013 involved more than a hundred strategic police leaders from all over the world, including many from Europe, to discuss the nature of police leadership and what it entailed. When the discussion concluded, there were more than 60 specifications for a strategic police leader's desired competences. The Europol representative, Olivier Burgersdijk, assisted in the design of a core competency model, which eventually encapsulated nearly all the elements that had been discussed.[12]

Olivier Burgersdijk and Michael Outram noted that:

---

[12] The authors are grateful to Olivier Burgersdijk for sharing with them these research initiatives and for kindly making available his own analyses and modelling. This is a huge project that will continue to develop on a global basis; the two things that concern us are: a) whether the model *can* be used in the European context; and b) whether it *will*. Europol and CEPOL both support the work done by Burgersdijk et al, but that, alas, is neither the same as having it adopted across Europe as the working model for strategic police leadership development programmes nor the same as using the model to inform internal (national) selection procedures.

> Ensuring a good fit between senior executive leadership in police forces and the future operating environment requires a re-focus on how the qualifications, behaviours and competences, on which leadership selection and development are based, can assist police organisations achieve such a fit. (Burgersdijk and Outram, 2013, p. 1)

They suggested further that recognised attributes from the business world are equally applicable to policing in general terms:

If leadership is defined as *the ability to optimise policing services through rapidly mobilising intellect and resources*, then the range of organisational attributes that can affect the swiftness with which adjustments can be realised become important, including change readiness and implementation approaches. (Burgersdijk and Outram, 2013, p. 6)

They go on to suggest that:

> [...] senior executive leaders can influence culture, and through effective leadership, also create competencies such as agility. Furthermore, [...] these organisational attributes going forward may provide a basis for monitoring and reporting on the effectiveness of senior executive [police] leadership at the team level. (Burgersdijk and Outram, 2013, p. 7)

Further researches and discussions in June 2013 resulted in a police leadership competency model, consisting of four key areas, centred on policing's 'core values', as illustrated in Figure 2.1.

Figure 2.1: The 'Core values and key areas' police leadership model

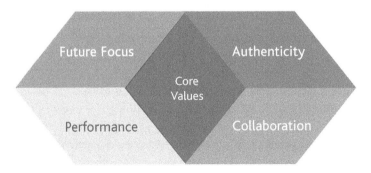

Source: Chalk and Burgersdijk, 2013; reproduced with the kind permission of Olivier Burgersdijk

This model was first presented in a paper by Kevin Chalk and Olivier Burgersdijk in June 2013 towards the conclusion of the Pearls in Policing Conference, where it reportedly received general approbation from the strategic police leaders present. Chalk and Burgersdijk suggest that: 'For police leadership; integrity, courage and diversity are deemed as the most essential **core values** to be applied and promoted' (2013, p. 2, our bold emphasis).

These 'values' emerged from the wide-ranging discussions at the Pearls in Policing Conference, and Chalk and Burgersdijk go on to specify what the other 'key areas' consist of:

- **Future focus:** [t]he primary obligation of leaders is to prepare their organisations for challenges ahead
- **Authenticity:** [police] [l]eaders must be trustworthy and believable. More importantly still, they need to be seen as having those attributes by others
- **Performance:** [t]he bottom line for performance is that it can only be assessed on the basis of results
- **Collaboration:** [p]artnerships and strategic alliances are emerging as perhaps the next great trend in policing (adapted from Chalk and Burgersdijk, 2013, pp. 1-3)

While this is not a specifically European model, it was further presented to the European Police Chiefs' Conference in September 2013. The model is still developing at the time of writing and more work remains to be done, but it is the first articulation of general core values and competences for strategic police leaders globally, and has resonance for those who are examining such leadership in Europe:

> Instead of trying to develop a [theory of leadership] in numerous competencies, this model assists in focusing on the most essential fields of competence. It is not so much about the individual competencies, but rather about how several competencies together contribute to a leader's

ability to perform. (adapted from Chalk and Burgersdijk, 2013, p. 4)[13]

Nonetheless, the central reservation that we have applied to the British competences for strategic police leaders, applies equally to the Chalk and Burgersdijk model: *none of these 'key areas' as depicted is exclusive to policing.* They are generic to leadership and useful in demarcating those areas in which police strategic leaders are expected to show skills, ability and achievement, but they are *applied* to policing rather than exclusive to it. The comment of a strategic police leader in this context is apt. He notes that his experience 'about being led' is what motivated him to become a strategic police leader, aiming 'to avoid the mistakes' that he had experienced from police leaders above him during his career. Only later did he understand that there were specific leadership skills that he had to acquire:

> 'my years in the job (more than twenty) have taught me a great deal about being led – much less about leading. To start with, I wanted to avoid the mistakes that leaders had made with me; only after this did I add on leadership skills.' (Interviewee BI 100)

It would seem that we are as far as ever from determining if there is a tangible activity called 'police leadership'; apparently we must be content with 'leadership for policing', which could equally be 'leadership for Fire and Rescue' or 'leadership for public service'. Both the British ACPO and the Chalk and Burgersdijk models have real virtues, and they can act as indications of the behaviours that strategic police leaders should generally exhibit. It is notable that the latter model emerged from a police conference that specifically debated what a police strategic leader must be able to do. The essential fact,

---

[13] The model, though, does not make a distinction between the characteristics of leadership that an *individual* might exhibit (ability to conduct a fluid operation, marshal resources to need, make effective operational decisions, set clear investigative parameters, and so on) and what the system provides in terms of corporacy, strategic appreciation, fluency of exposition, expression and understanding, acting *primus inter pares* (first among equals) and all the other *group* characteristics that are developed by mechanisms such as the Strategic Command Course.★

★ One of the authors was invited to address a Police Foundation seminar in February 2015 on police leadership. The perennial question of whether there is something which is police leadership and no other is still being debated actively.

however, is unchanged: the leadership competences as articulated can apply outside policing as well as within it. There is nothing pinpointed that happens only in police leadership and not anywhere else; nothing that reflects what Maurice Punch and his colleagues described as the 'unique' in policing – 'that operational decision-making which risks human life' (Hoogewoning et al, 2015). As long as the *operational level* with its complexities is missing from the core strategic competences, there will be something opaque and unspecified at the heart of police leadership.[14]

General leadership development in the police

By contrast with the Pearls in Policing initiative, which tried to get at the essence of what police leadership encompasses, the training and development of strategic police leaders in Europe, as exemplified in the courses run as 'TOPSPOC'[15] by CEPOL, does not tie itself down to definitions of leadership, or even appear to deal with 'police leadership' as a learning concept. Instead, the TOPSPOC courses, for high-level strategic police leaders across Europe, tend to concentrate on factors such as common interests in investigation, information exchange, networking, sharing policing problems, disseminating best practice and other matters. The following was the course summary for TOPSPOC in 2014:

> The Police College of Finland in Tampere hosted the CEPOL course 60/2014 Top Senior Police Officers Course: The Stockholm Programme Realisation, Module 1 on 9–14 March 2014. 32 participants from 25 EU Member States and Associated Countries, together with EU institutional representatives, took part on the first module of the programme.

The general programme was described in these terms:

> The TOPSPOC course is part of a four-module programme that aims to bring top senior police officers together to work at a strategic level to create a more open and secure Europe serving and protecting the citizen. The course is specifically dedicated to facilitate the strategic, professional and personal development of the participants from EU

---

[14] TOPSPOC descriptors: http://tinyurl.com/kxfvkea

[15] TOPSPOC is the acronym for **T**op **S**enior **P**olice **O**fficers' **C**ourse.

Member States, Associated Countries, Interpol, Europol and Frontex. (TOPSPOC 2014 Programme description)

This was amplified in the course outline for 2013:

This course takes place in four modules spread throughout the year. Modules cover different aspects of international police cooperation, linked to the Stockholm programme,[16] and internal security strategy. (CEPOL, 2013)

The second module of the 2014 programme was hosted by Italy in May, in the course of which delegates studied four subject areas:

- **Management systems**: Corporate Social Responsibility and its relevance in a law enforcement environment;
- **Leadership**: police leadership in borderless Europe;
- **Realisation of the Stockholm Programme**: impacts and influences on policing culture;
- **The unified delivery of a police service**: the strategic use of intelligence-led policing to police our communities. (TOPSPOC, 2014)[17]

What we may conclude from studying the CEPOL literature and talking to participants in TOPSPOC[18] is that even though the concept

---

[16] The 'Stockholm Programme' describes itself as a 'roadmap for European Union (EU) work in the area of justice, freedom and security for the period 2010-14'. See the Europa website at: http://europa.eu/legislation_summaries/human_rights/fundamental_rights_within_european_union/jl0034_en.htm

[17] TOPSPOC programme, www.cepol.europa.eu/media/blog/20140731/cepol-course-612014-top-senior-police-officers-stockholm-programme-realisation

[18] We noted the following from CEPOL's 2014 website: 'TOPSPOC is to end in 2014. In 2015 a pilot course shall [sic] be delivered by CEPOL as a comprehensive training portfolio supporting EU law enforcement leadership' (http://tinyurl.com/m7guce9). There are no further details on what this leadership 'training portfolio' will look like and for whom it is intended. What we can be certain about is that whatever CEPOL produces will be subordinate to individual member states' selection, appointment and development of their own internal candidates. Additionally, a thematic search of CEPOL's website did not uncover 'leadership' as a learning category; and a similar search of forthcoming CEPOL programmes failed to elicit any detail about the proposed 'pilot course' for 'law enforcement leadership' (http://tinyurl.com/kg7oob8; searches conducted on 23 October 2014).

of police leadership is considered and studied (as we see above), nonetheless this is not the same as teaching people to lead. It is a generic programme, like all the others, not a leadership development programme for potential or actual European strategic police leaders. It appears to be implicit that such development is best left internally to the member states to bring on their own leaders. There may be shared assumptions about what police leadership is, but, other than the ACPO list of competences, and the current modelling presented by the Pearls in Policing team to the 2013 European Police Chiefs' Conference, these assumptions have not been articulated nor subject to development (or challenge). As a result, we probably should not be looking for already existing harmonisation or consistent practice in leadership development across Europe, but rather to diversity of method and quite narrow national/local requirements in the selection of strategic police leaders.

The selection systems used in Europe

With this in mind, it is time to look at the questions we posed to the strategic police leaders whom we interviewed:

- How did you become a strategic police leader?
- Did you want to be one?

We noted from their replies that uniformity does not exist even within some countries, let alone between different ones. For example, one strategic police leader commented that:

> 'There is no formal selection system; you are picked to become a [strategic police leader] on the recommendation of two senior and serving [strategic police leaders] so as to avoid any suggestion of bias or favouritism.' (Interviewee A7)

This suggests that such a selection system is both inherently haphazard and actually *is* dependent on subjective opinion rather than avoiding 'any suggestion of [...] favouritism'. An interviewee from a different region noted that there was both more rigour and more formality in his country's selection system, which is heavily predicated on the individual's desire to move upwards:

'You need to have an academic profile; usually a Master's degree. You need to have served at least nine years before you can be considered for command rank. Once you have chosen to go for chief officer, you need to pass an assessment centre and a series of interviews, preceded by an examination. Every year we have about 40 vacancies for chief officer and usually there are 150 candidates, so there is no guarantee that anyone will succeed in any given year.' (Interviewee M14)

The odds against success here appear to be at least 3:1, and multiplied in each successive year, so that there has to be both determination and some element of luck in play for the candidates who make it to selection for, and membership of, the policing elite in interviewee M14's country. The assessment and selection processes appear to be both formal and rigorous, but we cannot make an objective judgement unless or until the whole apparatus involved is made more transparent. Such 'closed' systems, involving strategic police leader selection processes that are not subject to external validation, appear to be common across Europe. Indeed, some of the selection systems for strategic leadership positions in policing seem to entail political considerations and judgements that may be made more on the basis of what may work politically than on whether the candidate shows outstanding leadership potential:

'When I was first appointed some years ago, there was a "red/green" coalition running the province, and the Greens had the right to appoint the chief police officer. I had a discussion with the political minister that took 10 minutes. On that basis, I was appointed and have served ever since. I like to believe that my candidature had been carefully scrutinised beforehand, but I doubt it.' (Interviewee A27)

Another officer believed that his potential to become a strategic police leader was spotted early and he was given selected opportunities to show his capabilities in successive postings:

'I was selected after I had done my degree as a person who had some potential and I believe that my old Chief was watching carefully for opportunities for me and so I had the chance to do jobs which were of high profile and which gave me skills.' (Interviewee N9)

By contrast, a police leader from a different region decided that it would be tactically better to plot his own route to the top, by careful observation and working out what the talent spotters were looking for. He deliberately cultivated the 'right profile' for advancement:

> 'I wanted to become a top cop when I observed more closely those who had become strategic police officers. No mystery to this; I could do it. I worked on my profile (getting useful jobs which brought me to notice; making noticeable contributions at meetings, supporting chief officers in their work). I saw education as vital in making the right profile and worked hard at this, as well as using every opportunity to show how fast I had learned. I also needed to show strategic grasp and gave strategy papers to my boss (which made him look good and which made him realise I could make strategic police leader too).' (Interviewee M15)

This set of tactics would certainly bring the officer to notice, and even to a senior officer's recommendation of the officer for higher rank, but that is not the same thing as eliding a national selection process, in which the candidate presumably needs to impress others than his boss. Norman Dixon reminds us that some of the characteristics involved in succeeding to high office are not always savoury:

> [...] those personality characteristics which take people to the top and establish them as all powerful decision-makers tend to include the very nastiest of human traits – extremes of egocentricity, insincerity, dishonesty, corruptibility, cynicism, and on occasion ruthless murderous hostility towards anyone who threatens their position. (Dixon, 1994, p. 307)

This suggests that perhaps strategic police leaders are as keen as anyone else to show their more favourable sides to enquirers, and keep out of sight the 'nasty' aspects to their characters, which got them to the top in the first place. The officer who so carefully plans his route to the top, and notes what markers will show his progress, may unconsciously be exhibiting the same characteristics that Dixon saw.

Another police leader agreed that getting the 'right profile' was important, but believed that it was not possible to do this alone. The successful candidate needs someone in power to support his or her candidacy, though the consequences of not succeeding, or not delivering once given an opportunity, are severe:

> 'Networking is very important, because if you impress the right people with your skills or your determination, then they will ask for you for a task and then help you to rise if you are successful. That is the point: if you fail, you will have no backers or support. This game is all about winning.' (Interviewee M16)

Nonetheless, occasionally one finds a strategic police leader whose ambition knows no limitation and who is entirely focused on becoming 'the best of the best':

> 'I have always wanted to be at the top, no matter what profession – best doctor, best engineer – so why should it be different because I'm a cop? I joined with that intention and I would have left if I had not been promoted progressively. I have always kept the five top strategic jobs in view.' (Interviewee A26)

Such a concentration on the positions of power within an organisation can lead to distinct unease on the part of those already there:

> 'I look sometimes at the calibre of the people below me in the strategic role and I admit that they make me nervous: they are so intent on grabbing the job above, that one of my colleagues suggested we leave sealed instruction for lawyers to investigate our untimely deaths! More seriously, I can't remember ever being that ambitious: it must get in the way of doing your job properly if you are constantly looking for chinks in the armour of those above you. Such persons need to get a life.' (Interviewee N79)

This urge to attain to strategic command, Punch surmises, might also lead to the development of unsavoury characteristics once in office: 'Even worse, if that is possible, than the traits which take them to the top are those which they acquire upon arrival – pomposity, paranoia and megalomaniac delusions of grandeur' (Hoogewoning et al, 2015, p. 9, citing Dixon, 1994, p. 232).

This is not exclusive to policing. Looking for the 'chinks in the armour' of those above has probably preoccupied subordinates for many hundreds of years; deliberately exploiting such vulnerabilities may well be a companion activity, which spills over into the portfolio of leadership skills. Ruthlessness of ambition is not normally cited as a desirable trait, and is not taught as a leadership competence on those programmes that aspire to delivering the 'complete leader'. For all that, it exists and is identifiable. By almost perverse contrast, others have noted that criteria for promotion sometimes include some element of 'reflective' self-learning, or, in the case of promotion to the strategic police leadership ranks, the demonstration of academic capacity:

> 'In my country, you cannot be promoted to a chief officer rank unless you attend the staff college to study leadership, understand strategic planning and critically explore the relationship between the police and the judiciary.' (Interviewee Ba13)

Many of the semi-structured selection processes for strategic police leadership entail attendance on a higher education (HE) programme of some kind; the Strategic Command Course in the UK for example (which used to include study at the University of Cambridge's Institute of Criminology), or the virtually mandatory Master's in the Nordic Region, or CEPOL's TOPSPOC (as mentioned earlier in this chapter), though it is not always clear what such attendance provides in terms of enhanced leadership potential, unless it is the ability to demonstrate advanced learning, engage in the expression of ideas and experience the rigour of academic thinking (Neyroud, 2011a). These are all worthy things to have, but they are not guarantees of effective strategic police leadership. Yet so common is this academic route that one might quite reasonably term it to be a normative precursor to promotion to strategic command rank (see, for example, Punch and Lee, 2004). Sometimes the process involved in obtaining selection and then clearing the various hurdles can seem mechanistic:

> 'I entered university and studied law [...] and joined the police on graduation directly as a manager. I did not have to serve as a rank-and-file officer and did not go on the beat. Despite this I was able to move quickly up the ranks to senior positions and then, with my [postgraduate qualification] almost completed, I was selected to be a chief officer.' (Interviewee C61)

Another officer noted that the days of succeeding solely through patronage were gone, at least in his country. Joining the race to the top might entail personal investment:

> 'There is much competition to secure a place to study, and this requires agreement from your boss and from the Ministry of the Interior, as well as time allowed to do the study, some of your own money to support the learning, arrangements to cover your absence: you have really got to want it badly. And I guess I did. Also I have a baccalaureate in law, so I can practise as a lawyer if I need to do this. It is the first qualification of high rank and the Master's programme is now another. It means that you cannot now become a top cop because of who supports you alone. You have to show a brain too.' (Interviewee C71)

Of the 108 strategic police leaders whom we have interviewed, 97 mentioned that they had either attended university to study for a first degree or a Master's or had embarked on a postgraduate study programme (to places like the John Jay Police College in New York, or the FBI programme in Quantico, or in national 'police' universities). Table 2.1 gives a more detailed analysis.

Table 2.1: Higher education qualifications for strategic police leaders

First degree	Second degree	Postgraduate or HE study programmes	Total
38	26	33	97 (90% of interviewees)

Though simply indicative, our data suggest that not only is higher education (at Level 4 and above) a factor in determining who will come to notice for advancement, and that most of those embarking on an upward path will ensure that they have relevant qualifications, but also that attendance on such programmes is likely to show the individual's determination and intellectual ability as well as leading to contact with existing strategic police leaders and therefore to significant opportunities for networking.[19] This is of a piece with some research undertaken in 1992 on two Canadian police forces, which concluded that there is a tendency in police forces to regard higher education and the possession of degrees as indicative of a person's aptitude for high office (Buckley et al, 1992). No one claims that a degree or an HE Diploma are of themselves requirements for promotion to strategic police leadership positions, but possessing them undoubtedly helps, as our interviewees attest.

A further example of the 'academic precursor' is evident in this account:

> 'I was promoted and this time it was clear that they were serious about me making chief officer rank, so I went to do a Master's degree and then got on the Selection Programme, which is linked with a university. When that was done, I was promoted to a "first chief's" job.' (Interviewee N9)

This experience is echoed by another interviewee:

> 'I attended the Police University to do my Master's, having been selected as one of the few candidates for the Higher Duty, partly because of my academic record but also because of my profile within policing work in my region. I had entered with a degree … so it was not hard to present myself as a candidate for command.' (Interviewee A65)

Other candidates in other regions appear to have had their track record as police officers taken into account as the primary indicator of fitness to command, rather than academic qualifications in their own right. They were accordingly recognised and rewarded as a result of their specialist knowledge. For others, the selection process and the often prolonged 'apprenticeship' to become a strategic police leader, proved rather more wearisome and much less direct:

> 'Fortunately, history coincided with my ambition, and the liberalisation that followed the collapse of the USSR enabled me to show myself and begin the long climb. My advancement at first was quite fast. It slowed, of course, as I got higher and that was when I did most of my additional

---

[19] We have not assumed that those who did not specify their academic attainments had none.

study and travelled in Europe and further abroad. But it took a lot of energy and a lot of stamina to keep going; I was very tired when I finally made it to leader.' (Interviewee C50)

Others found the whole business of finding replacements and successors at the top of policing to consist of labyrinthine informal and subjective 'conversations':

'[...] there is firstly an informal conversation between the aspirant individual and the senior administrator of the promotion process to see if there is a "type match". A formal route follows, but you can probably already sense if the individual is capable of promotion or not. It is important that you are asked. Then there is a conversation between the senior police administrator, the chief public prosecutor and a mayor or perhaps more than one mayor. Afterwards a further conversation takes place with a staff delegation and separately with the governing Council. These conversations are to examine the profile of the candidate chief officer and there could already be strong recommendations and a file of information on each aspirant. There will also be 360 degree assessments. The candidate must also have indicated a preference for promotion in order to be considered. Following all this, a panel comprising the chief public prosecutor, a strategic police leader and an administrator will sit to judge the candidates for strategic office, taking into account all that there is on file, in assessment and as a result of previous deliberations.' (Interviewee M37)

We might describe this as a (very) prolonged euphemism for merely subjective selection, but other respondents have commented that such a process can also be given a political overlay. If we add that the various systems are not transparent, externally validated or scrutinised, then it is unlikely that selection processes to strategic police leader in most of Europe would include an unconventional thinker.

In light of all this, we can make some basic analysis from our data of the principal ways in which our respondents became strategic police leaders.

Becoming a strategic police leader: process

The interviewees were questioned about what was involved in the process of their selection to become strategic police leaders. Was it through:

- a talent-spotting process;
- advanced study or competition in examinations;
- a specific police development programme that looked to supply succession;
- a process that included grooming by their 'patrons' in the ranks above?

We might tentatively conclude from our data that formal learning is an important criterion. Nonetheless, personal opinion, judgement and subjective assessment of potential still play prominent roles. Currently, the systems of selection are seemingly influenced by competitive examination or a development programme on the one hand and by talent spotting and 'grooming' by seniors on the other. As Interviewee M37 noted earlier, 'you can probably already sense if the individual is capable of promotion or not', which may be reflected by the significant minority of candidates still primarily selected in this way. The opinions of others may carry considerable influence, particularly if the individual concerned had not previously given much thought to advancement to high rank:

> 'As I slowly went up the ranks ... the possibility of becoming a chief began steadily to appeal to me. This was especially so when I saw people I joined with, rushing on past me into high rank and that stung a bit. Anyway, I'd done the usual crop of courses, and so I gave way to my bosses' argument that I could do a strategic job. They were right!' (Interviewee BI 73)

Becoming a strategic police leader: motivation and ambition

The opportunities to become a strategic police leader vary from region to region in Europe, but generally competition for posts is intense, and the individual has to show both ambition and persistence in seeking promotion to strategic police leadership. The summary data (from

Table 2.2: Were you ambitious to become a strategic police leader?

Yes	No	Only when I saw the quality of those above me
79 (73%)	**17** (15%)	**12** (12%)

108 responses) in Table 2.2 suggest that a primary motivator for the strategic police leader is personal ambition and a desire to command. Nearly three quarters of respondents (73%) admitted that they were driven by a desire to rise. Only 15% claimed that they were not ambitious to become a strategic police leader, though even here there may be some further detail to be had, since some leaders had ambition belatedly awakened in them by others. In parallel with this is the 12% who were moved to become chief officers when they concluded that they would do better than the bosses they had experienced.

Sometimes it might be meeting strategic police leaders from other countries that first brings the possibility of further advancement to the individual's attention:

> 'It was when I was in the National Investigation Bureau dealing with international crime that I first met people of my age from other countries who were already chief officers, and here was me doing what I was told in the Bureau like a little meek person. So I thought: "Look! You are intelligent, you have a degree, you have investigation experience and you know what is needed to do this job, so why are you *taking* orders and not *giving* them?"' (Interviewee N54; interviewee's own emphasis)

This sudden realisation that one has the capability to go further in the police is a touchstone for many, and interviewees across Europe agreed that it was often comments by others – or the fact that one had been overtaken by younger people – that acted as the spur to apply to rise, or which planted the seed of ambition that later germinated. This officer's comment is typical of many that we have heard:

> 'I don't think that I thought much about being a chief officer until I [obtained a new post], and this led to lots of contacts with people from other departments and with politicians. Someone told me that I should try for a chief's role, because I had a good grasp of strategy and the general governmental picture which policing was a part of. Then

I thought, I can do this just as well as some of the people who are there; and it was true.' (Interviewee C50)

Some strategic leaders acknowledge that the rapidity with which they have risen may engender resentment or envy from others left behind, but one or two dismiss this as an inevitable corollary of advancement to strategic rank:

> 'Of course, there is a lot of resentment from those who are plodding upwards at their much younger and better-qualified colleagues going past them, and I have personally felt this sometimes, but I don't care. I've made it, not them.' (Interviewee C61)

Others, from the European member states that formerly came under the control of the Russian-dominated 'communist federations', had a different tactic or approach to becoming a strategic leader. This often called for careful positioning early on in their police careers, so that they were not 'contaminated' by association with a discredited regime. It is worth looking at one such account in some detail:

> 'I joined the police from the Army. At that time, (before independence) the roles of the police and the army overlapped greatly, especially in controlling violence and disorder among our ethnic minority groups. I very soon saw what was happening in geopolitics – the old communist federations were breaking up and the notion of "perestroika"[20] was gaining ground – so I was careful to position myself so that I was not contaminated by connection with the old system. I applied to move to Border Policing and by the time independence came fully in 1992, I was one of those young officers that the new government recognised and wanted to rely on.' (Interviewee M63)

This officer, unlike his predecessors in office, had no patron or sponsor to rely on to help him upwards, only his own urge to improve policing

---

[20] The word is Russian and means 'restructuring'. It was much used by the former Soviet leader Mikhail Gorbachev, when discussing what the USSR had to do to modernise itself. Some commentators have argued that *perestroika* occasioned the break-up of the old Soviet Union in 1989-91. See Brown, 2007, p. 336, for example.

from the top. His rise was nonetheless very swift, even by modern standards – and practically breakneck speed compared with the old patronage-dominant communist system:

> 'I worked in the Internal Affairs and this was a good time to be there and to be seen, because after a bit more time I was promoted to become a strategic police leader.
>
> I joined the police to rise to the top; I was quite deliberate about this. You do not go into an organisation to be mediocre and stay at a low level, do you? I was [relatively young] when I first made chief and that was not too early for me, as I had all my military experience too.' (Interviewee M63)

What we have here is an alliance between motivation and opportunity. The political leaders of the new democracies, themselves often victims of persecution or harassment by their previous communist rulers, were determined to ensure that no vestige of the old corrupt and venal system remained. If that meant promoting comparatively young people to lead the police, then so be it. The unavoidable outcome of such a deliberate policy, though, was a diminution of experience and 'street credibility' among the top strategic leaders. A number of untried people were exposed somewhat in strategic leadership positions, where they were sometimes taken advantage of by their more experienced subordinates:

> 'The senior ranks looked at us and resented us like hell but they knew that their own days were probably numbered. So what did they have to lose? I was pushed to make bad decisions based on bad advice at the very beginning, and for a time it was doubtful if I would remain. But I realised what was happening, changed my advisers and made many of my own decisions against what they had said. It turned out to be a wise thing to do, in the event.' (Interviewee C72)

It took time for the new strategic police leaders in the former communist countries to acquire the necessary experience:

> 'You have to know that it has taken more than ten years for my country to be admitted to the European Union and during that time, almost, I joined the police from the military and before that I was at university, so actually, I have been a strategic police leader for quite a short time. Yes, I

wanted to be one, and this is why I made the transfer. All the time I worked closely with the Ministry of the Interior to become in a position to influence and rise. But I am not a political person; I am for order and peace after all the years of occupation by foreign powers.' (Interviewee C6)

Another officer found that merely removing the communists from public service was not enough. Sometimes, those who replaced them were not competent (often because of inexperience), or did not quickly enough meet the requirements of the new politicians in charge. The result in some cases was another seismic disturbance of those at the top:

'I actually had no ambition to be a strategic police leader and was content to do my job as crime investigator, but then we had a huge reorganisation when the Minister of the Interior got rid of whole layers of the new officers at the top, and I was one of those who was [promptly] promoted to become a chief police officer, mostly because I had been competent in what I had done and because I was not associated with the regime which had just fallen. So I lacked experience of command which I had to make up very quickly. But I did not join with the ruthless intention to rise to the top, like some of my older colleagues.' (Interviewee C71)

A more experienced officer of gendarmerie from a non-communist country noted that, although you might be motivated to 'run your own show', actually the exercise of pure power is elusive and at this strategic level of command, it is more about the ability to compromise and integrate than about taking independent action:

'I did not join the gendarmerie to remain an aspirant,[21] but to rise at least to field rank[22] and if possible beyond to independent general command.[23] Yes, I wanted to lead, but every officer should seek this and look for opportunity to run his own show. All the same, no command is truly

---

[21] The lowest officer rank, equivalent in the UK to second lieutenant or cadet officer. The term comes, ironically, from a word meaning those new officers who want to rise in the ranks, and 'aspire' to higher office: an 'aspirant' without ambition is almost a contradiction in terms.

[22] That is, command of operations, usually major or its equivalent and above.

[23] At the rank of brigadier-general (lowest 'general' rank) or its equivalent.

independent because you have to integrate with others and respond to political imperatives, so often your room for autonomous movement is quite restricted. That does not mean that I did not want to be the person giving the orders rather than receiving them!' (Interviewee M88)

Although it may be the case that some candidates for strategic command were jolted into applying through some sort of epiphany, plenty seem to enter policing with a distinct vision of where they wanted to go:

'Oh yes; no point at all in entering police to stay as a mere agent.[24] I wanted to be at certain grades by certain times: … I achieved this [strategic leadership rank] with time in hand, you might say.' (Interviewee Ba13)

Not everyone enters the police with such an exact and pressing timetable of advancement. Indeed, some can suddenly come to the realisation that life is passing them by, when they notice younger people overtaking them in the rankings and thereupon decide that they have to join the race, or be permanently by-passed:

'I was a front-line commanding officer until I was 40 years old and I suppose I was a long time on the road. I saw others going past me as I found it harder and harder to stay fit and focused, and so I thought "I have to stop this now and become a boss"; so I did.' (Interviewee M14)

Others stumbled across the notion and showed no urgency until provoked by colleagues to consider the possibilities:

'I did not think of becoming a chief officer until I was on secondment in Italy and then a friend pointed out to me that I thought strategically all the time and that therefore I would make a good director of security. This started me thinking and then I decided that I could do it.' (Interviewee A7)

This next strategic police leader noted laconically that he had his ambition to rise to command awoken in him after 10 years' service, and

---

[24] The term 'agent', generally used in national (state) police forces, equates to a constable or the lowest rank on entry to the police.

he has given himself a simple criterion to justify aiming at promotion to the rank above him:

> 'It took me 10 years to develop the ambition of being a chief police officer. I started realising that I would get more influence and more satisfaction by getting higher ranked, and every time I got promoted I looked to the person one step above me and asked myself the question: "Could I do better?" and so far the answer has been: yes.' (Interviewee N41)

Another leader used what he calls 'double-insured' routes to the top of policing; one was by using continuing professional successes – in his case as a detective – and the second by using a 'political route', where his successive promotions were endorsed (whether tacitly or actively is not entirely clear) by members of his political party. He is blasé about these parallel means to rise:

> 'My reputation became high in criminal justice because I was known as persistent and very interested in the application of science to criminal investigation. There were some successes of significance, but I cannot detail them now, or this would identify me too much. I also had a political route where I influenced and informed a number of political figures in my party to regard me with favour. It's OK to be double-insured like this, and so with the backing of the courts and the mayoralty, and the good opinion of my superiors, I made strategic rank.' (Interviewee M92)

Most aspirants to strategic leadership positions, in the words of Interviewee C71 (quoted earlier), 'have really got to want it badly' and will not let petty obstacles obstruct them in their drive for advancement:

> 'I always intended resolutely to rise to the top of policing, though I am not an arrogant person. My parents taught me to expect nothing but the best and so I set myself to be the best and become the top police officer in my country. This I have done.' (Interviewee Ba5)

A British Isles strategic police leader was open in interview about what motivated him to aim at command rank. He claimed that all he was doing was what all 'control-freak' police officers do when faced with problems or some situation needing intervention – he took charge:

> 'From the first moment I entered policing I wanted to be in a position to command. I don't think that this was arrogance so much as a desire to take control. Every strategic police leader is, to one degree or another, a control-freak and I was no exception. It's just in my case I wanted it from the beginning.' (Interviewee BI 100)

Some leaders had the ambition to reach the top even before joining the police:

> 'Almost from the cradle; well, I certainly had a legal/law enforcement career in mind when I was at school and university. It coalesced into policing only later and with mature reflection, but I never wanted to remain a patrol cop. It was rise to chief officer or leave really. Does that sound arrogant? It should sound purposeful, because I knew what I had to do to get there.' (Interviewee M28)

This interviewee, like the one cited before him, disclaims arrogance yet there seems to be a hint in what they say that they are excusing the trait of pride in themselves at the same time as they recognise it. Another interviewee (like others, setting himself a timetable of advancement) surpassed even his own expectations:

> 'I joined the police from compulsory military service. I was mature and able to make reasoned judgements. I told myself that I wanted to be in charge of strategic policing [by my 40s], so you could say that I was focused on being a chief, yes.' (Interviewee A60)

But, to balance the accounts of relentless ambition given above, one strategic police leader claimed to know what really matters in his life:

> 'I expect to become a top officer in my next posting, but I would not kill to get it. It isn't my ultimate goal and I prefer a proper, balanced family life to the lonely intensity of naked ambition.' (Interviewee Ba13)

There is an endearing mix of the balanced and the aspirational about this statement. On one hand, the leader expects to become a 'top officer' but on the other he celebrates the attaining of a work/life balance. It could be indeed be self-delusory to 'have it all', and this leads us to consider those officers whose ambitions to reach strategic rank may have been formed by accident or chance. Some grew into it as they gained experience in policing, others seem surprised to find themselves running a police force. Here is a typical response:

> 'I did not join the police with a plan to become a chief officer but as opportunity succeeded opportunity then a route to the top became clearer and was within my grasp; so I began to consider the possibilities of command.' (Interviewee A12)

And from another in the same region, a laconic acknowledgement that his eventual choice was a good one:

> 'I didn't particularly choose policing as a career – more that it chose me, I think, as I had done a law degree and a judge told me that the police needed people like me if they were to develop and improve, and that he would recommend me if I applied. So I did, and progress was rapid. Once I was in, I was ambitious to do well and to become the best.' (Interviewee A26)

Another strategic police leader commented that what stimulated his interest in strategic command:

> '... was actually a chance remark. I was moaning as usual about the calibre of the people above me, when a friend said "Well, why don't you do something about it? Why don't you become a chief and make it better for the rest of us?" So that really was when I first began planning to become a strategic police leader.' (Interviewee BI 31)

Another comment, where the officer believes that he 'stumbled' into policing, is notable for its self-deprecation:

> 'I didn't even plan to be a police officer let alone a chief one! You could say that I stumbled into policing by accident almost, as I was looking for something to do after university

and I had planned to travel for a year before settling, so I needed money and joined the National Police to do that. Now more than 20 years on, I still want that year of travel around the world.' (Interviewee N52)

A last word on this may be given to the same strategic police leader (N52), who also remarked that 'it is my duty now to spot talent in others and encourage it to grow', but, he cautions, not everyone really wants it, and you can tell a genuine leader's potential from some distance:

'My experience is that only a few actually want to go far, and you can see that in them, it is a sort of hunger to take responsibility and a readiness to try new things. When you find it, it is very exciting for you and for the person, to watch them fly.' (Interviewee N52)

Summary

It seems that patronage still plays a prominent part in the selection and appointment of strategic police leaders, and there is strong emerging evidence from interviewees' testimony that the selection systems across Europe continue to rely on such leaders being spotted early and nurtured by existing chiefs. This raises in turn questions about potential for 'cloning' and whether movement between or across national systems will ever be practicable while the selection and appointment of strategic police leaders is based on relatively narrow national criteria. So too, many strategic police leaders are critical of their selection processes, believing them to be opaque and unstructured, while others deplore the lack of development once appointed to a command and beyond. By contrast, some believe that the selection process has become too managerial and that there are too many chiefs for the task.

There is no consistent pattern across Europe to suggest that strategic police leaders follow predictable paths to the top, nor indeed that experiences of the selection system and promotion processes are translatable between regions, or even that any sharing exists between countries within a region. There are common experiences, of course: the influence of parents upon the choices that people make, the opinions of others in suggesting that further promotion is achievable, the track record and experience which leads people to think that they could do as well as those further up, and the educational or study programmes which indicate that showing a brain (Interviewee C71) is important in demonstrating the intellectual capacity to perform at the strategic level.

All the same, the narrow confines of the national systems are geared towards raising people internally; they are not part of any wider plan or process. Until there is interchangeability between countries and interoperable postings of strategic leaders, this will probably persist.[25] Nonetheless, if the EU is to succeed in its 'pan-European' policing ideal, and if it is to be capable of countering transnational organised crime (as it declares it will[26]), then at least thought has to be given to how this might be achieved, what such a process might look like, who would deliver it and what learning outcomes will be entailed. It would presumably fall to CEPOL, whether alone or as part of Europol, to think outside this particular box – and the suggestion of a CEPOL 'leadership pilot' in 2015 may perhaps be the first faltering step towards a pan-European police leadership programme. Any work here is likely to include Burgersdijk and Outram's 2013 model, and this in turn may develop the 'key area competences' into specific development and learning programmes for strategic police leaders, delivered by CEPOL (or by CEPOL's proxy).

At the same time, a very relevant point is raised by Hoogewoning et al (2015), when they argue that not only is policing unique among leadership professions in demanding practical experience, but it is also precisely that practical experience which entails, more often than not, an effective outcome in operational decision-making. All strategic police leaders share the necessity to make operational decisions, but they do not all arrive at that point in the same way. Bringing into policing from outside people who will function in strategic command without, as it were, 'having fired a shot in anger', gives us pause. It

---

[25] One of the authors helped to develop a European (postgraduate) Diploma in Policing in cooperation with Kent Police, NPIA (National Policing Improvement Agency, replaced by the College of Policing in 2013) (International Division, Bramshill), Canterbury Christ Church University, the University of Maribor in Slovenia, the Estonian Police and Security Academy and the Dutch Police Academy, from 2001 to 2007. However, despite generous support from the Leonardo Da Vinci Fund, there was reluctance among the rest of the member states to embrace this opportunity for 'pan-Europeanism'. There was instead an exponential attack of cold feet.

[26] *EU Commission Staff Working Document* (2013, p. 7), for example, which says: 'Activities of criminals are getting more complex, diverse and international. Large scale criminal and terrorist networks pose a significant threat to the internal security of the EU and its citizens.'

is what makes the requirement at least to start talking about 'pan-European strategic police command' an important matter for the EU to address. However, we do not anticipate swift action on this, any more than we anticipate definable timeframes for other developments in 'supra-national' policing, or adequate provisions for the selection and development of women and members of ethnic minority groups as strategic police leaders in a much more systematic way (see Chapter Four). The political will has to come first.

Despite its desire to appear unified, and for all its talk about 'European policing', the EU is in fact not monolithic, or even monothematic, when it comes to selecting and promoting police officers to strategic leadership positions. The identification of potential, the careful grooming for high office, the selection processes, the placement in strategic roles and development once in those roles, is defaulted to, and is entirely a matter for, national governments. As might be expected, there is no consistency between member states on selection methods, assessments, core competences, candidate profiles, experiential pathways or academic/vocational qualifications. Often, there is little consistency in such processes between separate forces within a single member state (for example, between selection for a gendarmerie or for a national police agency). This should not surprise us too much – as we will see graphically in Chapter Five – nationalism characterises the external presentation of member states' police and no EU political or strategic oversight body has ever proposed a coherent plan to change this. Does it matter?

In our judgement, it matters very much, but not simplistically as an abstract desire to obtain consistency and order for their own sakes. It matters because 'chiefs' need to talk to each other, to plan strategies together and to adopt consistent positions (for example on terrorism) that will be seamlessly interchangeable between member states. They say that they do this in conferences and strategic meetings, of course, and they certainly do it bilaterally in joint investigations, but they do not do it consistently or routinely at a strategic multilateral level, or with *the leadership of the police in Europe* as a criterion. Not only that, but true interoperable command – for example in the interdiction of major transnational crime – cannot function as well as it might when the strategic leadership structure of one member state is at variance with, or markedly different from, another's.[27] We saw vestiges of this in Chapter One, with the glacially slow convergence of criminal justice systems and overlapping police models. Where some police forces value academic qualifications as a precursor to strategic command, where others demand instead a strong practical track record, where others demand a blend of the two but then have no requirement for candidates to speak two or more European languages fluently, and where there is no agreement anywhere on what constitute operational 'competences' or any objective assessment of the ability to make crucial operational decisions – then this bewildering proliferation of multivariate 'police leaders' will persist.

What is lacking, it seems to us, is a coherent plan for the leadership of policing in Europe. No one seems to know what strategic police leadership is supposed to look like, how we get to it, how we evaluate it (assuming that somehow we do get there), or even what sort of people should become police leaders.[28] We have enquired, without success, of the European Commission about its publications, plans for publications and upcoming strategic discussions about law enforcement and police leadership. There is no EC blueprint we are aware of that plans for diversity in European policing (or even for diversity in society as a whole[29]), nor apparently is there a published strategy or template that gives us a vision of where the EU would want strategic

---

[27] As was articulated by Rob Wainwright, Director of Europol, and reported on the front page of *The Times*, 2 October 2013. Mr Wainwright is reported to have remarked, of the noises in Britain about withdrawing from Europol, that 'there was growing international anxiety that Britain – a pioneer in police cooperation to tackle cross-border gangsters – was pulling back as the criminal threat became more global'. Wainwright went on to describe withdrawal as 'an unmitigated disaster for the UK police community'. It would not go unnoticed either in the rest of Europe, which was his larger point. See O'Neill, S. (2013), Director warns of 'unmitigated disaster' if Britain quits Europol, *The Times*, 3 October, pp. 1-2, http://tinyurl.com/pp4x32t

[28] As one of the authors discussed extensively in February 2015 with the College of Policing and others.

[29] Though the EU has come up with a plan for placing women in top business jobs across Europe. The rather opaque document which announced this has not received much airing in the media. See 'Cracking Europe's Glass Ceiling: European Parliament backs Commission's Women on Boards proposal', Brussels, 20 November 2013, http://tinyurl.com/lzpv98k

police leadership to be in, say, 10 or 20 years' time.[30] In July 2014, a new European Commissioner for Justice, Martine Reicherts, was appointed, and on taking office, she declared:

> 'The Charter of Fundamental Rights has been applied across all areas of EU activity, and proposals to safeguard the rights of citizens in criminal proceedings, the protection of personal data and gender equality in public companies have underlined the EU's commitment to its citizens.' (Reicherts, 2014)

However, no sign was given of plans for any overarching law enforcement strategy that addresses those 'criminal proceedings', or any comment on the role of the police in criminal justice or any replies to any of the questions raised in this chapter about European police leadership, selection strategies, harmonisation of processes and commonality or coherence in strategic police leadership.[31]

When the prevailing status quo simply lets things drift without even addressing the issues, such lassitude is building problems for another generation of police officers to solve.

---

[30] A Google search in July 2013 resulted in over 1 million entries and references; few of them European. We found one site that concerned itself with 'Debates (without vote) [...] for: Common European Asylum System, EU Counter-Terrorism Strategy – Discussion paper, Draft Council conclusions on the provision of information on rights to victims of trafficking in human beings' which are laudable themes, but do not constitute strategic policy; see http://tinyurl.com/k88vtfv. Yet the potential clearly exists, because there is an EU strategy to counter drugs, which runs from 2013 to 2020 (see http://tinyurl.com/kqkdlbv), and a cybercrime strategy (see www.europol.europa.eu/ec3).

[31] Martine Reicherts from Luxembourg, replacing Viviane Reding on 18 July 2014, http://tinyurl.com/llwpawy

THREE

Accountability

> I repeat that all power is a trust; that we are accountable
> for its exercise; that from the people, and for the people all
> springs, and all must exist. (Disraeli, B. (1826), *Vivian Grey*,
> Book VI, Chapter 7, London: Henry Colburn)

Most strategic police leaders accept being held to account for what they do as an integral part of living in a pluralist, liberal Europe (Marshall, 1978; Loader, 2000); but it is not always apparent to the public in how many complex ways and in what respects that accountability is manifested:

> 'I am answerable in a number of ways: professionally, I
> answer to the deputy police commissioner; politically
> I answer to regional mayors, in the law I answer to the
> courts and in terms of local policing targets for my region,
> I should answer to the people, but in reality I answer to the
> journalists of newspaper and television.' (Interviewee N79)

Encapsulated in this wry observation by an experienced strategic police leader are the elements that we shall consider in this chapter: the complexity of accountability; the offices, people or organisations to which the police are accountable; and the nature of the relationship with the media that the strategic police leader endures or enjoys, coupled with a detailed presentation of his or her responses to political direction. As we shall see, the responses vary across Europe, with rather world-weary observations from the member states in Western Europe contrasted with the sometimes tremulous but also resolute reactions from those who have recently emerged from the Soviet communist hegemony. These are by no means monothematic responses: most strategic police leaders in interview took time and care to formulate their replies. This was not a matter of choosing their words carefully to present a bland public image, but rather that they wanted to present a commitment to democratic principles, while at the same time noting ambiguities and complexities within the fact of accountability. It did not appear to us to be lip service:

'I am judged by the Chief Director and he is judged by the Minister of Home Affairs. So if I mess up, so does he and the Minister can look foolish too. Therefore, great care is taken to make sure that we don't mess up. I am under no illusion – if things go wrong on my watch, I shall be sacrificed very ruthlessly and quickly.' (Interviewee C81)

There is much at stake in this accountability business, and police leaders take it seriously. So they should. The United Nations (UN) is in no doubt that accountability in policing is integral to the proper working of a democracy and that the police act as an important constitutional safeguard within that process:

[Accountability] aims to prevent the police from misusing their powers, to prevent political authorities from misusing their control over the police, and most importantly, to enhance public confidence and (re-)establish police legitimacy. Accountable policing means that the police accept being questioned about their decisions and actions and accept the consequences of being found guilty of misconduct, including sanctions and having to compensate victims. (Osse and Dossett, 2011, p. 8)

It is not entirely clear from this, the 2011 *UN handbook on police accountability, oversight and integrity*, how it is possible to 'prevent political authorities from misusing their control over the police', but the police themselves acknowledge that the variety of ways in which they themselves are answerable probably insulates society from political abuse:

'The people know if you are truthful and really on their side, but they have had to put up for so long with politicians and police saying "things are like this" and they, the people know that this is bullshit, they *know* things are not at all as the chiefs and MPs describe them. So if you can get the public to trust you, you can be accountable to them.' (Interviewee M16; speaker's emphasis)

However, the UN handbook goes on usefully to spell out what the various components of police accountability are and how they balance each other. The UN calls this 'a conglomerate of processes', in which 'different actors share responsibility' (Osse and Dossett, 2011, pp. 12-13). The UN intends its handbook to be applicable globally, not just in Europe, but the essence of the accountability here is that it means different things in different contexts (Marshall, 1978), and that the consequences of derogation or failure vary proportionally as well. The role of an ombudsman, for example, is to provide independent 'civilian' oversight of the police.[1] In 2009, the Council of Europe published the views of its Commissioner for Human Rights, 'concerning Independent and Effective Determination of Complaints against the Police', which reiterated the principles of the European Convention on Human Rights.[2] The document, rather quaintly called an 'Opinion', is fundamentally important in establishing Europe-wide police accountability. Paragraphs 18 and 19 are of particular relevance:

> 18. Adherence to the rule of law applies to the police in the same way that it applies to every member of the public. [...] Police ethics and adherence to professional standards serve to ensure that the delivery of police services is of the highest quality. There can be no police impunity for ill-treatment or misconduct.
>
> 19. As police powers have increased so too has the expectation that police services will conform to principles of democracy, accountability and respect for human rights; namely, as written in the Preamble to the United Nations *Code of Conduct for Law Enforcement Officials* – 'every law enforcement agency should be representative of and responsive and accountable to the community as a whole'. (European Union Commissioner for Human Rights, 2009)

Of course, this is not only about complaints against the police and the upholding of the law, but also about the wider principle that, because police officers are given powers denied to the ordinary citizen,

---

[1] Monica den Boer and Roel Fernhout produced a detailed and insightful paper in 2008 examining the roles of the ombudsmen and their equivalents in Europe. den Boer and Fernhout conclude that more research needs to be undertaken into the effectiveness of the role, but 'an ideal police oversight mechanism consists of an independent specialised Police Ombudsman with a broad mandate and sole competence and responsibility for police complaints, preceded by a well-structured mandatory internal complaint procedure with an advisory independent complaint commission' (den Boer and Fernhout, 2008, p. 33).

[2] See http://tinyurl.com/k2v7o4m. This *Opinion* is an important document in the regularisation of police accountability across Europe.

including the legitimation of the use of violence ('reasonable force'), their standards of conduct should be proportionate to the exercise of those powers. The *Opinion* puts it like this:

> In the interest of independent, impartial and effective delivery of policing services, and to protect against political interference, the police are granted a wide degree of discretion in the performance of their duties.
>
> For the purpose of performing their duties, the law provides the police with coercive powers and the police may use reasonable force when lawfully exercising their powers. (European Union Commissioner for Human Rights, 2009, paragraphs 15 and 16)

Where there is complaint, an Independent Police Complaints Body (IPCB) is designated to investigate and determine outcomes. The form of the IPCB may be in the person of an 'ombudsman' (as in, for example, Spain, the Czech Republic or Bulgaria, or embodied in Finland's Chancellor of Justice) or a complaints body (like the Independent Police Complaints Commission in the UK or the Standing Police Monitoring Committee in Belgium (the 'Comité P'), or France's Commission Nationale de Déontologie de la Sécurité[3]), each more or less independent of the police:

> The institutional design of IPCBs established in a number of jurisdictions in Europe [...] has taken the form of specialised ombudsman institutions or, alternatively, standing commission structures. The appointment of a Police Ombudsman or a Police Complaints Commission, comprising a number of commissioners co-ordinated by a Chairman, are each capable of overseeing a fair, independent and effective complaints system. (European Union Commissioner for Human Rights, 2009, paragraph 35)

It is by no means proven that these systems are effective safeguards (Loader, 2002) or that they reinforce police accountability or may become (as sometimes seen elsewhere in EU institutions) a bureaucratic obstacle to change (Marshall, 1978). Certainly, signing up to the

---

[3] A fairly comprehensive list of police oversight organisations in Europe can be found in den Boer and Fernhout, 2008, pp. 8-10.

creation of a police ombudsman or a formally constituted police complaints body is now required of all member states in the EU, including candidate members and new joiners, though Ian Loader has critiqued the tendency of political institutions in Europe to be complacent about how effectively such mechanisms actually do hold the police to account (Loader, 2002).

The multiplicity of ways in which the police are made accountable reflects the complexity of policing itself, but can also point to a deep-seated suspicion of police practices that have tarnished the police and engendered distrust. den Boer and Fernhout note the former as something not always recognised by commentators:

> Police oversight or police accountability is a very complex matter, given the several layers of accountability that apply, as well as the many different tasks that are performed by operational police agencies. (den Boer and Fernhout, 2008, p. 3)

So it is that in the UN handbook we encounter 'accountability' for the police glued on to their internal processes (including independent inspection),[4] as well as external processes such as state oversight functions, including the criminal law and the criminal justice system. It is not surprising, therefore, that police leaders occasionally feel beleaguered:

> 'There are times when I feel that the eyes of the whole world are on me and what I do, and on my staff and their actions. I know that is not the actual fact but it feels so. Every action, every word, every initiative, every justification, every media appearance: all are looked at as carefully as if I was in a lawcourt giving evidence. The words are weighed, my appearance assessed and my demeanour examined, and the fact that I am a woman is always mentioned. I am not paranoid I hope, but I really do not know what other job has this kind of focus. I don't much like it; but what can you do?' (Interviewee M78)

---

[4] As with the inspector-general role in some European states or with HM Inspectorate of Constabulary in England and Wales. Notably, such inspection regimes are almost always composed of serving or former police officers.

den Boer and Fernhout draw attention to the complications that arise when overseeing more than one police force, or when 'policing' is diversified across a number of functions:

> European countries show a very diverse pattern when it concerns the organization of their accountability systems in general, as well as their police organizations [...] For instance, while a country like The Netherlands has a single but de-concentrated police force which is organized in [...] semi-autonomous police regions, Italy has at least five police forces that play a significant role in the public arena, each of them falling under a different political authority as well as jurisdiction. (den Boer and Fernhout, 2008, pp. 3-4)

Few countries have a single police force. Eire, Scotland and Sweden are examples of countries with one unified national force, but most member states have proliferations of police, national police as well as gendarmeries, or, as in the British Isles, a 'model' that embraces simultaneously 43 decentralised police forces in England, a separate transport police, the Police Service of Northern Ireland, a unified national force in Scotland and a specific armed force that guards nuclear installations.[5] Another example is Portugal, which, while it does not have the proliferated model of the British Isles, nonetheless has a multiple one. Principally consisting of two main agencies, the national police (*Polícia de Segurança Pública*) and the National Guard gendarmerie (*Guarda Nacional Republicana*), the Portuguese police system includes traffic policing, the coastguard and a 'Fiscal Action Unit' that replaced the separate Finance Police in 1993. Such multiple functions and multiple reporting chains (across Europe, the 'national police' generally report to the Ministry of the Interior or its equivalent, while the 'gendarmeries' usually report to the Minister of Defence or equivalent)[6] make accountability within the governance system a complex business. We should not assume, in any of the discussions that follow, that we are dealing with a single entity, accountable in

---

[5]   The Civil Nuclear Constabulary that was, until 2012, headed by the first 'civilian' chief constable appointed from outside the British police service.

[6]   Since 2002, the *Gendarmerie* in France has reported to the Ministry of the Interior on policing matters, but remains part of the Army for defence purposes; while in the Netherlands, the *Maréchaussée* reports to Interior, Justice or Defence depending on the function. General 'repositioning' of gendarmeries is discussed in Chapter Seven.

simple ways up a single chain of command: the reality is much more convoluted and consequently harder to monitor and assess.

At a conference on police accountability in 2001, the veteran Dutch academic Cyrille Fijnaut noted that the proliferation of police organisations became really complicated when one considered the range and variety of policing across the European Union, where the permutations already existing in single member states were multiplied at least 10 times. There was therefore no meaningful sense in which we could talk about 'the police' and by that term embrace every detail of every manifestation of public policing in Europe.[7] Fijnaut and his fellow contributors (Fijnaut, 2002) agreed that more research is needed on the nature of police accountability, particularly at the 'transnational' level, but this remains today an area that is still under-researched and not as well understood as it should be, nor is the larger societal or organisational structure examined in any detail by contemporary commentators or analysts. The addition to the European Union of 11 more member countries (bringing with them at least one or two more permutations on the policing structure), since Fijnaut edited his one-off edition of *Policing and Society* in 2002, has complicated further an already confused scene.[8] We could add from our own modest forays into this territory, that 'police accountability' would certainly be enhanced if the *whole* criminal justice system were similarly explored and mapped.

The people of Europe cannot reasonably insist that the police are accountable to them if they do not also ask for at least some responsiveness to their concerns from the wider justice machinery. Research funding, political will and media interest in such proposals seem to be minimal, for reasons that are not entirely clear, though they probably include a lack of visibility of criminal justice systems across Europe and the insistence on a strict division between the executive and the judiciary in order to prevent any political party in power from domination or control of the independent legal system.[9] The public is perhaps not as engaged with the more obscure faces of

---

[7] Despite moves to 'Europeanise' some policing elements, such as the European Guard Force for gendarmeries, or border agencies.

[8] We refer to a wider Europe than the members of the EU (Croatia became the 28th member in July 2013), and we include Norway and Switzerland as integral within the policing 'chain' of nations. There may even be a case eventually for including other non-members such as (West?) Ukraine, Belarus and Iceland.

[9] As happened for example in Nazi Germany 1933–45 and in the 1930s 'show trials' in Stalin's Russia, when the courts were complicit with their tyrannical rulers.

criminal justice as it is with its daily experience of policing, and across Europe, general ignorance persists about the nature of oversight of the criminal justice process. The police shrug and get on with the job, but occasionally it rankles that they are the ones under the spotlight and not judges or lawyers:

> 'I don't mind what I do being [monitored][10] by anyone and everyone, provided a) they know what they are talking about and are not out to prove some mad conspiracy theory and b) it is not just the police who are so regarded. We need to look at the way the judges operate, how public prosecutors reach their decisions and how they superintend police investigations. In fact, the whole [criminal justice] system in a democracy should be answerable to the people, but at the moment it's us and only us. Even the prison system isn't looked at in the same way we are, and God knows it should be.' (Interviewee N57)

Not all would agree with the findings of a group called Altus Global Alliance, which carried out a limited survey in 2006 and concluded that:

> [p]olice services are becoming more professional, more effective in dealing with crime, and more respectful in their treatment of civilians. As part of these changes, police are becoming more accountable for all three dimensions of their performances: professionalism, effectiveness, and respect. In the member states of the Council of Europe, police are being held accountable to the state, from which it [sic] derives its policies and powers. (Altus Global Alliance, 2006, p. 6)[11]

Empirical evidence for such a sea change in the 'professionalism, effectiveness and respect' of the police is not plentiful, and tends to the anecdotal or small sample range; nevertheless, it seems to be the

---

[10] The word the interviewee used was 'surveilled', which has no rendering as an active verb in English.

[11] This 'survey', which was limited in scope and range, consisted of data gathered in an exercise called *Police Station Visitors' Week in Europe*. Nearly 300 'civilians' visited in total 75 police stations in Belgium, Germany, Hungary, Latvia, the Netherlands, Russia and the United Kingdom in autumn 2006.

case that the police forces of Europe, and the strategic police leaders who command them, are more aware now than in the past of the need to be responsive to oversight, and there is some emerging evidence that they are more professional in their dealings with those whose job it is to challenge what the police do. Research published in 2000 by Andrew Goldsmith and Colleen Lewis detected a trend emerging in which complaints about the police, in accordance with new business practices in Europe, were resolved more informally than in the past, and that strategic police leaders were increasingly instrumental in obtaining such resolutions (Goldsmith and Lewis, 2000, pp. 4–5). It follows then that negotiation and diplomacy have to figure largely among leaders' skill sets in policing – as they do, of course, among chief executives everywhere. In 2007, Christopher Stone argued that police accountability is increasing in many parts of the world, partly as an inherent element of democracy, as countries embrace the concept (often, as in the former Soviet Bloc, as part of their independence), but also because, by their actions, police forces bring such scrutiny upon themselves (Stone, 2007).

A more general point to make is that there are too many instances when the police, left to themselves, betray the trust that the public normally vests in them. This is not a matter of the police being indistinguishably part of the political arm (as it was with the Stasi or the KGB, see Chapter One), but more a matter where social cohesion itself may be compromised by police officers abusing or misusing their powers. We know from comments made by strategic police leaders in the former communist states of the Baltic and Eastern Europe that one of their most difficult long-term tasks is establishing or recreating public trust in the police after decades of abuse.[12]

Examples of police scandals across Europe within the last twenty or so years include:

- the inept investigation of the murder of Stephen Lawrence in London in 1993, which led to the Metropolitan Police being labelled in 1999 as 'institutionally racist' by the Inquiry Chairman, Sir William Macpherson;[13]

---

[12] See Chapters One and Six.

[13] Followed in 2013 by allegations that the Metropolitan Police covertly monitored Stephen Lawrence's family, apparently to try to discredit them and thus blunt their criticism of the police; see Richard Stone's *Hidden stories of the Stephen Lawrence Inquiry*, 2013, Bristol: Policy Press.

- the infamous Marc Dutroux paedophile case in 2004 in Belgium (Punch, 2005), which exposed the inefficiencies of the police investigations and lack of communication between Belgian police forces and regions;[14]
- the calls for greater scrutiny of the police following the actions of the Special Unit for Police Affairs of the Norwegian Police in 2007 (four officers were responsible for more than half of the complaints against the Unit);
- the casual killing of a student by Greek police in 2008;
- the Romanian police corruption scandal of 2010, in which criminal files were purposely destroyed; instances of police brutality in Macedonia in 2011, which provoked widespread public dismay;
- the Irish Garda's 'bugging' in 2013 of the offices of the country's independent police watchdog (Dalby, 2014).

This series of events is what Maurice Punch, in another context, called 'rotten orchards' to signify something rather larger and more serious than the usual attempts by politicians or senior police leaders to explain away police corruption or ineptness as 'rotten apples' that can be simply eradicated (Punch, 2003).

The natural urge to clean up this form of corruption (on the part of the public but also, it has to be acknowledged, on the part of honest police officers who do not want to be tainted by corruption, incompetence or brutality), has in many cases led to legislation, the installation of oversight systems, the formal accountability of police leaders, and the involvement of academic commentators in devising systems that hold the police to account, such as the UN handbook and the EU Commissioner's *Opinion*, mentioned earlier. Few, if any, of these additional measures and safeguards would have been needed if the police had not exceeded or abused their powers in the first place, and it could be argued cogently, if a little selectively, that the police get the accountability measures they deserve.

All this serves to intensify, in some strategic police leaders, an aggrieved defensiveness:

'there must always be a secret conspiracy, there must be
bad cops hiding behind a smooth face, there must be

---

14   See, for example, the accounts of ineptitude and petty jealousies by the various police agencies in Belgium in Sabine Dardenne's astonishingly moving account of her ordeal at the hands of Marc Dutroux (Dardenne, 2005, especially pp. 137-138). A good academic analysis is by Punch (2005).

reasons for actions that you are not telling us, there must be something behind your statements that we don't know.' (Interviewee A65)

Gorazd Meško in a paper about police professionalism in Slovenia in 2007, remarked on what accountability means, or should mean, to police officers in the newly democratic states in Eastern Europe that had recently shaken off decades of Russian domination. There is resonance too in what he says for police leaders in the rest of Europe, who should be encouraging such positive responsiveness to oversight in their forces:

> The police can be trusted, but not unconditionally and external accountability is crucial. In a democratic society, the police have a duty to explain themselves when challenged or asked about their conduct. *They have to accept the reality that others will judge their performance and have a right to do so.* Accountability and civilian supervision should not only function to discipline the police after misconduct on their part; but also serve to guard against the normalisation of small-scale abuses [...] within the police role. (Meško, 2007, p. 30, fn 14; our emphasis)

It is timely, therefore, to consider what this means to the sceptical police officer in the 'old' democracies in Western Europe, where accepting 'the reality that others will judge their performance and have a right to do so' is sometimes regarded with rather more jaundiced eyes:

> 'As you rise, you are subject more and more to external (that is, non-police) scrutiny and assessment and that assessment is increasingly political too. Assessment of me is largely by the minister of justice, the policing minister and chief of the criminal court [translations of speaker's own terms] a sort of triangulation on my abilities. The further you go up, the further you have to crash and burn, so you need to be surefooted at this level. That does not mean that the people holding you to account have any notion whatever of how hard the job is or how you often have to run to stand still. Those who judge me would not themselves stand up to much scrutiny.' (Interviewee N21)

Meško's point, though, is well made: if oversight and challenge are not robust, then the police may develop a creeping culture of cutting corners in procedure, racial and other kinds of stereotyping, stopping and searching without justification, refusing to explain their actions, avoiding responsibility and arbitrarily exercising power for its own sake. Strategic police leaders should be on the alert for such abuses of power in their staff and in themselves, and should not merely default to this kind of exculpatory self-justification:

> 'I'm sick of being on the defensive about what I do and what policing is. We clean up the streets, we sort out the messes that people make of their lives and of each other, we are the last resort when things go wrong. And what happens? We get accused of being heavy-handed when we separate opposing and warring factions; we're investigated when we react to provocation or shoot some mad bugger who has just slaughtered his family, we are subject to intense scrutiny whenever we try to take criminals out of circulation. I often wonder why I do this job: how much more I have to worry about my front-line officers, who get all this abuse and danger too!' (Interviewee BI 35)

The principles by which police officers are held to account are familiar in the long-established democracies of Western Europe, and are increasingly adopted in the emergent democracies as a means of ensuring that the police can be trusted. There are complex and layered systems of accountability, but some strategic police leaders appear to find the proliferation of accountabilities irksome and others (with better justification) have called for the whole criminal justice system to be similarly held to account. The point though is that the public and the establishment alike want their police forces to be accountable for what they do: there are too many examples of what happens when oversight is not rigorous and continuous. For all that, policing is not easily held to simplistic account in the way that some structures and authorities assume, and the police themselves are the first to respond with a pose of injured and defensive innocence when they are challenged too robustly.

The role of politicians: 'magicians in the "art of the possible"'?

Most police forces like to be seen to be above politics and not directly influenced by party political decisions, though in reality of course, strategic police leaders cannot function without their public decisions and opinions having some kind of 'political angle', as this Baltic Region police leader notes:

> 'At this point in my career, nearly every decision I make has political ramifications or a political "angle" of some kind. The politicians generally want reassurance, so that they can go back to their preferred job of stroking their great egos. They don't want to have to think about what I do or how I do it, unless there is a bonus for them in terms of political kudos or votes in praising or condemning me. They'd do either, irrespective of my merits and actual achievements, if it suited them.' (Interviewee Ba13)

These comments by an experienced strategic police leader invite us to consider in more detail the relationship between police and the politicians to whom they are responsible. Interviewees were not generally impressed by the quality of the politicians or what they contributed (see Table 3.1).

Table 3.1: What are your relations with politicians and your views on political governance of the police?

Predominantly positive	Predominantly negative	Predominantly neutral
35 (32%)	**58** (54%)	**15** (14%)

Out of 108 respondents, the 'predominantly negative' response represents over half of the sample, and, judging by the vehemence of the comments made in response to the question, there is widespread distrust of politicians and the ways in which they hold strategic police leaders to account, for example:

> 'You should never think that these people are there for you. They are there for *them*, and "the people" come a long way second, and you are round about the bottom of the heap as far as consistent support and long-term political planning are concerned.' (Interviewee M3; speaker's emphasis)

Another strategic police leader from the same region observed:

> 'Politicians do not hesitate to use you for their own advancement or purpose and I know at least two of my

chief officer colleagues who have been placed on an altar [sacrificed] for political expediency.' (Interviewee M16)

Part of the reason for the mistrust appears to stem from the limited amount of time that politicians spend on policing as a political topic, and the short-term nature of their interest:

'I have never believed that politicians are there to support me and my officers. They can move too easily between portfolios, so one day they are hot on justice, the next they worry about education and a week later they are concerned with the numbers of single mothers.' (Interviewee A12)

An equally sceptical strategic police leader observed that politicians:

'[...] think that they are magicians in the 'art of the possible', but they are just ordinary people who have been given the power for a short time. The trick comes in getting them to work with you, and that's not taught in policing textbooks.' (Interviewee Ba4)

A leader from another region agrees, adding:

'Politicians want what works quickly but most criminal justice solutions need ten years to bed in and ten years to show results – during which time they are modified of course, but not substantially altered. But this is too long a time frame for politicians who want a quick grab of the chances [opportunity]. So you as a chief have to fight expediency and their meretricious solutions and that means in turn that you have to have a really firm idea of what is needed. They don't teach you to be a diplomat at chief school, but this is what you need to be.' (Interviewee M15)

For all the evident need for diplomacy and tact, more experienced (or perhaps wilier?) strategic police leaders have worked out other ways to manage politicians and their expectations:

'Politicians are nervous people: they worry about the media, they worry about the voters and they worry about keeping their jobs. So I reassure them, calm them and help them to have confidence in me, a professional, doing my job properly.' (Interviewee A57)

Another officer showed himself to be an astute politician in his own right, when dealing with a recalcitrant minister who wanted to accept an American initiative on illegal trafficking. It would have entailed US Drug Enforcement Administration personnel being stationed on the country's borders in some strength:

'I knew what that would mean: American interference with, or domination of, our border operations against illegal trafficking, particularly drugs – where our main problem there is not drugs but people trafficking. When I told the Minister that I would resign and go to the media if he insisted on pushing this through, the issue was dropped.' (Interviewee C58)

Threatening resignation is a tactic that can be overdone (and there is always the risk that the resignation will be accepted when all that was intended was a gesture, as here), so the interviewee realised that he needed other tactics too:

'I'm Machiavelli[an] enough to know that [resignation] won't work as a tactic next time: I'll have to think of other, more subtle ways, to put pressure on politicians when they have mad ideas. Inertia might be one answer.' (Interviewee C58)

Some are rueful about the methods they have to resort to in order to get their way, but, as with this Alpine region interviewee, understanding the motivation of a politician enables the officer to manage expectations:

'Politicians run on well-trodden paths and their responses are predictable and pretty easy to manage. If it's bad news, they look for someone or something to blame, and I have become quite skilled at giving them a general target whose competence they can deplore without actually attacking an individual.' (Interviewee A80)

The practical application of this tactic lies in knowing the drivers, political and personal, which motivate the individual politician:

'That's useful, because if you can generalise bad then you can generalise (or more strictly, contextualise) good. When it's good news, they are eager to take the credit for themselves and it is also a skill to suggest that something was achieved *because of* the politician not – as is often the case in reality – in spite of him or her.' (Interviewee A80; our emphasis)

Not everyone is as clever as that strategic police leader, but others combine long experience with a manipulative approach:

'I have been around long enough now to have experienced most initiatives and to know what politicians want (or are satisfied with), and I can use that experience to modify political drivers if I think that they are too short term. Also, I can refer to my US experience which […] politicians generally do not have. A couple of times I was able to say "Oh, the Americans tried this while I was at Quantico, and the result was this", which once stopped a really silly proposal in its tracks. Sometimes I made it up that the idea had been trialled and failed in the US; but I knew that I was right, and the outcome was the same.' (Interviewee M14)

At the back of a lot of the strategic police leaders' distrust of politicians is a searing experience of political interference (in Britain, policing the Miners' Strike in 1984, for example; see Reiner, 2010). Some have noted to us that there is often an extensive history of corruptibility on the part of the politicians who then have political oversight of the police and that, although there are checks and balances to ensure that politicians do not exceed their powers or remit, some still try to do so, as this Alpine region leader observes in relation to a major corruption scandal in his country:

'I think that they start wanting to do a good job but a very small number becomes corrupted by the system. The problem with politicians is that they think they are above the law and the reluctance of the courts to prosecute them only reinforces that. I wish we had a more powerful and independent media to help investigate political abuses. Meanwhile, we watch and wait; one day we will have enough evidence to take some of these peacocks down.' (Interviewee A25)

Others are more sanguine or inclined to think well of those in charge:

> 'I have always advocated a healthy and open relationship with political leads and the police. There is the long-standing debate regarding "operational independence" of policing. It would be naïve to state that these relationships will be without challenges, but the principle that police officers command police operations and police activity, whilst politicians debate with senior police officers the policing priorities through their democratic mandate and the policing budget, are achievable and sensible goals.' (Interviewee BI 32)

A canny Alpine region police leader considered that 'it is better to cooperate [with] than to oppose' politicians and learned to offer them a 'half-success' that would not disrupt policing plans. He offered this instance of how the tactic works:

> 'One small example was a politician who asked me to use his plan to improve the image of tourism by stopping visitors going to an area where prostitutes openly approached people. Now it is silly to stop tourists from going to places, so what I did was get my officers to move the prostitutes to another area or be fined continually, and so the women moved. Not very glorious as an episode in policing, but the politician had his success, I had an ally and the problem seemed to be solved. Of course, there were complaints from the area we had moved the sex traders into, but by then there was another politician asking me to do something else.' (Interviewee A12)

Some police leaders think that positive relationships with those in power are both inherent and required in strategic policing:

> 'My relationship with local [provincial] politicians is important because I will have more chances for success if I am linked in with those who make the strategic decisions. It's important not to get sucked into the politics of decision-making and to keep a clear distinction between the policy side and the active policing side, but that sort of juggling act is what I'm paid for and what I do well.' (Interviewee A26)

Another officer believed that having the skills to work with politicians was fundamental to success at the strategic level; and that such abilities should be looked for when selecting candidates for promotion:

> 'The question is, what skills should a strategic police leader have? S/he should definitely be able to negotiate with the political apparatus. The road to the target is not necessarily a straight line, but often long and winding.' (Interviewee B29)

Another interviewee put the political oversight of the police back into the context of accountability:

> 'Governance and accountability are essential for the police, we are an organisation that has power over citizens; it is absolutely right that we are accountable for that power and have proper governance in place. Police forces are also multimillion Euro businesses, it is right that there is proper, robust governance in place for that amount of public money.' (Interviewee A43)

The police view of politicians

The police, especially at the top strategic end, regard politicians with largely tolerant disfavour. They appear to believe that political expediency is par for the policing course and realise that short-term considerations are likely to be dominant. Some strategic police leaders have learned to offer the politician a 'half-success' that does not compromise policing operations but nonetheless gives the politician some small triumph to brandish. We did not get the impression that such manipulation was widespread. There are others who are as expedient themselves and who do not scruple to gain advantage from a politician's naivety.

In general terms, police leadership sees the political aspect of oversight and accountability as both inevitable and something that they have to learn to work with (or around). Some deplore the lack of training or development at the beginning of their leadership careers in how to handle politicians, but do not offer proposals how 'wily diplomacy' might be taught and who might deliver it as a learning package, or indeed, how it would fit into a suite of leadership skills. Such means of dealing with the often contradictory demands of both local and national politicians are probably the result of experience rather than any formal learning input.

On the media challenge: 'the story is everything'[15]

The media have no qualms whatever about holding to account strategic police leaders (or investigators or district commanders), and it is worth examining the nature of the process, taking as our starting point this comment by a leader from the Alpine region:

> 'I answer directly to the Minister of the Interior as far as political accountability is concerned, but of course I answer to the courts through the criminal justice system and ultimately to the people through community policing and their feelings of safety and security. When I was first a strategic police leader, I thought that these three things were the limit of my accountability and, because I am a professional working in a democracy at a regional level, that is fine with me. But I became aware of the "fourth estate",[16] the media, as another thing to which I was accountable and that is actually the hardest one.' (Interviewee A67)

The role of the media in scrutiny of the police and their actions is of course less formal than those of the IPCBs or any of the accountability mechanisms that we have examined so far, but it is arguable that the ubiquity of media interest in the police – and the responses of the police strategic leaders to such interest – actually is more rigorous and stressful than any other relationship that police leaders experience (Cook and Sturges, 2009). The relationship generally between the police and the media is a mixed one, often because the media believe that the police

---

[15]   The gist of this section was presented as a paper, 'European Strategic Police Leaders and the Media', by Bryn Caless at the Fourth Annual Conference of the Higher Education Forum for Learning and Development in Policing, Canterbury Christ Church University, September 2013.

[16]   The reference is a historical one. In pre-Revolutionary France, the '*états*' (or 'Estates') were: first the Catholic clergy; second the nobility; and third (the '*tiers état*') the remainder of the people. Informally and jocularly, the media is seen as the 'fourth estate', scrutinising those in power. Edmund Burke is believed to have first used the term in a debate in the British Parliament in 1787; see Schultz, J. (1998), *Reviving the fourth estate*, Cambridge: Cambridge University Press, p. 49.

are keeping things back and that they may seek to control what use the media make of 'privileged' information.[17]

During our survey of police leaders' opinions, we heard a lot from our interlocutors about what they thought bedevilled the relationship between the media and the police (mostly media cynicism and intrusiveness; occasionally the corollary police attempts to control and manipulate). This next interviewee had strong views about the challenges posed by the media and the difficulties experienced by strategic police leaders in responding to them:

> 'I worry that the media can be destructive – of names, of operations, of reputations – with no responsibility. I have seen them carelessly endanger the lives of informants, or victims or vulnerable families, and all without any conscience at all – *the story is everything*. This is worst in global media, because you cannot even subject them to European Law, let alone the laws of your country. Let me be clear: I am not against the freedom of the press. What I am worried by, is that the media freedom comes without having to answer for their faults. The media must take responsibility for what they do, just as I have to take responsibility for what I do.' (Interviewee A67; our emphasis)

This viewpoint has had particular resonance in Britain, where the inquiry led by Lord Leveson examined during 2012[18] the illegal 'hacking' of phones by journalists working for the now defunct *News of the World* and other newspapers, and examined the apparently widespread practice of bribing police officers to pass restricted information about 'celebrities' to the media. The final outcome of Lord Leveson's report (Leveson, 2012), recommended firm codes of conduct for the media, but little has been achieved so far (assuming that such stringent regulation was actually in the public or democratic interest, which is a moot point).[19] Indeed, some strategic police leaders

---

[17] A brief furore in England arose in April 2013, when the Association of Chief Police Officers considered a proposal not to release the identities of suspects to the media in the wake of the Leveson Inquiry; see Evans, 2013.

[18] Lord Leveson's report was published in November 2012.

[19] Leveson, Lord Justice (2012), *An Inquiry into the Culture, Practices and Ethics of the Press*, HC779, London: HM Stationery Office. It is worth noting that paragraphs 85 –101 of the Leveson Report deal with the relationship between the British police and the press, and conclude that the relationship was 'too close'.

in the British Isles region noted cogently that there was no need for additional legislation, since eavesdropping on someone else's private communications was already a criminal offence.

More worrying for the police was the revelation (and subsequent investigation) of an unhealthily close relationship between some police officers and the media. The covert and illegal nature of these relationships was investigated and charges have been brought against a number of officers,[20] but they exemplify what Robert Reiner believes to be characteristic of relations between the police and the media since the 1960s:

> In fiction, the police are increasingly celebrated as vigilantes who must break the rules of legality to crack crime. News stories more often report police failure and police deviance. [...] Police officers are no longer portrayed as paragons of virtue but as effective if often venal protectors of the mainstream public – 'us' – against risks posed by a variety of demonised others – 'them'[...] (Reiner, 2003, pp. 275-276)

This dynamic, says Reiner, needs both sets of players: the police need media coverage for practical things like appeals for information or for favourable portrayal, while the media depend on the police for a large proportion of news reporting and dramatic fiction. The relationship is not always as symbiotic and mutually advantageous as Reiner suggests; in the phone hacking scandal, it became evident that the police leaked information (for money) about celebrities and prominent figures in major crime investigations. The motivation, on both sides, was sordidly venal.[21]

Another academic article, looking at police/media relations in the emerging democracies of Eastern Europe, concluded that there is ample scope for misunderstandings on both sides, and that a 'blame game' of the kind played by police officers on occasions can be riskily counterproductive (Kešetović et al, 2006), but that is probably the case whether the relationship is newly emergent or already mature. The European Commission Committee of Ministers considered the potential risks in relations between the police and the media sufficiently important to issue formal guidance as part of its 2010 *European Code*

---

[20] Some have already been convicted and sent to prison, see Couldry et al, 2013.

[21] One of the best referential texts on the phone-hacking scandal and the subsequent inquiry is Couldry et al, 2013. Others are: Keeble and Mair, 2012; Watson and Hickman, 2012.

of Police Ethics. The recommendation in the *Code* is that only 'trained personnel' should speak to the media, and generally interaction should be confined to strategic police leaders themselves, trained to deal with the media's intrusiveness, unless forces employed former professional journalists as spokespeople.

Strategic police leaders would largely agree that this allocation of responsibilities is appropriate, although many of them had anecdotes which suggested that relations between the police and the media were often both fraught and fluid:

> 'I was criticised strongly for my selection of [an officer] to lead a murder enquiry. The media said that he was not up to the job [because he was not "telegenic"]. But he was a very good investigator and he got to the truth of the murder very quickly and his investigation was a model one. Now people are saying what a good choice I made, but it wasn't like that at the beginning.' (Interviewee C50)

The interviewee went on to say that he did not have a crystal ball and could not predict events, but even had he selected an investigator who was more 'media-savvy', the choice may not have been as good as an investigator. His conclusion was weary:

> 'Sometimes you can't win! I shrug off "trial by media" when I can, but it affects my family sometimes and I think it must influence politicians and lawyers who have dealings with me.' (Interviewee C50)

One strategic police leader discussed how a positive media image for the police can directly contribute to public confidence. His own approach was to embrace with enthusiasm the opportunity to influence coverage of the police, in which he seems to have been repeatedly successful:

> 'Newspapers especially have a keen interest in policing and I spend a lot of time giving interviews, responding to questions and fronting up for the journos. They seem to find [in] me the acceptable face of policing ... That's what accountability means to me – it's the responsibility that comes with the job, and I do it as cheerfully now as a strategic police leader as I did it as a sergeant.' (Interviewee BI 73)

Another interviewee agreed with the thrust of his British counterpart's comments above, noting that the realpolitik of handling the media is pivotal:

> 'Handling the public image of the police is the true accountability because on that people's confidence in the police rises or falls.' (Interviewee N83)

An Alpine region strategic police leader commented that the media's self-appointed role as guardian of society sometimes encourages a police 'performance', where one looks 'polished and confident' whatever the reality of the situation. He noted that training in media relations was a necessary corollary:

> 'This [the media] has become an intrusive part of contemporary policing which it was not even ten years ago: we all have to be able to go in front of the cameras and look polished and confident, just as we have to recognise the "trap" question from journalists who know that, if they can get you to say something critical of other cops or stupid from yourself, they will sell more articles or papers or programmes. [...] We all need to be trained very carefully and well in how to handle journalists and interviewing, because this can break you if it goes wrong.' (Interviewee A80)

The need for training for media interviews, responding appropriately to questions and generating an aura of warmth and confidence was mentioned by a number of interviewees, one of whom noted that the media were often satisfied (as were politicians) with the mere surface of things, of how matters appeared rather than what they really were. In a moment of candour, this interviewee commented that:

> 'The Minister has impact of course, but he will be swayed by the media, and if you are a popular police officer in the media, you can go very high. A top chief got there only because [he was media savvy and] the public thought he was nice and [...] you could trust him. Actually, he was a bastard and incompetent as hell.' (Interviewee M3)

The same officer noted how important it is to understand that, in the media's superficial, almost 'virtual' worlds, policing is a 'brand' like any other, and strategic police leaders need to be able to sell the myth as much as, if not more than, the reality:

> 'You need to do as I did and learn to handle the media in marketing a police "brand". Most of my colleagues are way behind in this media savvy: a new age demands new talent, and my future chiefs will be assured handlers of media and journalists.' (Interviewee M3)

Another interviewee wanted to engage the media in positive reporting about community policing, but he had to overcome initial hostility until he was able to convince the media that there was a percentage in such reporting for them:

> '[An example is] our recent experiment in community policing. The people liked it, so the politicians liked it, but the media were [initially] hostile as were some of the courts because they thought that this was elevating petty crime to a higher level or else it was an excuse for vigilantism. [...] Newspapers and TV have [since] come on board though, because it gives them a supply of local news stories which people want to see or read.' (Interviewee C48)

A final comment, also from Central Europe Region, contrasts the role of the politician and the role of the media. The interviewee agreed that politicians can ask him to justify what he is doing, and they 'still direct the police in some ways', but, because the days of communist party domination have passed into history, the 'great control' of politicians has gone. Instead:

> 'I think that the TV and newspapers are more powerful than the politicians and they ask many more questions and don't shut up asking. I think I am governed by them more than the politicians.' (Interviewee C55)

Summary

It is a long-established principle that accountable policing is a safeguard of democracy and part of governance. There is, in the UN's words, 'a conglomerate of processes' (Osse and Dossett, 2011) involved in the general accountability of the police, ranging from internal inspection regimes, through national legislative and judicial processes, to international bodies such as the European Committee for the Prevention of Torture. This is a complex and multilayered business: the police, while largely accepting of the principle, occasionally jib at the practice of explaining themselves in so comprehensive a way to so many, so often.

Accountability is a fact of strategic police leaders' professional lives and most seem to have come to terms with the many layers and forms of accountability to which they are subject. A robust few respond positively to the challenge; a very small number seem disheartened by the ubiquity of having to justify what they do. This proportion of responses is probably the reality across the continent. What has not been systematically addressed in either the literature or the policies, we think, is a requirement for a similar accountability on the part of the wider criminal justice system.

We turn now to relationships and influences among strategic police leaders and look at how they relate to their peer groups, and to other elites in the criminal justice systems of Europe; to examine how 'grounded' they are and whether there are factors in those relationships and influences that need closer analysis.

FOUR

Relationships and influences

'There are a lot of passengers pretending they are driving the bus. Actually, I mostly see my colleagues in action when I turn on the TV – just before I turn it straight off again.' (Interviewee M3)

In this chapter, we examine the nexus of relationships at the strategic level, including the peer groups of strategic police leaders, the wider criminal justice system of which the police are the 'gateway', and roles or contacts at a local level with community leaders. The purpose of this exploration is to ascertain what kind of networks are used by the policing elite to sustain their positions, expand their influence and enhance their working relationships, and whether, because of this exclusivity, they constitute a kind of 'closed shop'.[1] We shall ask some questions of what seems to be a male-dominated workplace, to which members of minority ethnic groups and women are admitted only in small numbers. This helps us to analyse the nature of the closed shop and to ask whether strategic policing in Europe constitutes a self-fulfilling elite.

Most strategic police leaders in Europe have relationships with the wider criminal justice system through formal subordination to their public prosecutor, who normally oversees and often directs police investigations of crime; and through a parallel political subordination to the local or district mayor (the *Bezirksbürgermeister* in Germany, for example), who oversees police responses to public order and to community needs. In some European countries, this constitutes a

---

[1]   Interest in the role and influence of elites is returning to social science research after an absence of some decades (see also the Introduction). A classic study was *Elites and Society* by Tom Bottomore in 1964, but a revised and updated second edition appeared in 1993 and an online version in 2002. One of the most accessible modern treatments of social and occupational elites is *Remembering elites* by Mike Savage and Karel Williams, 2008. One study has examined the 'new' elites emerging in post-communist European countries in the 1990s (Higley and Lengyel, 2000), but there is little contemporary data or analysis on *policing* elites, even in the US, let alone in Europe.

'triangular' balance of power,[2] where the public prosecutor balances the influence of the mayor (whether appointed or elected) and the strategic police leader sometimes holds the ring between these powerful partners. In other countries, particularly in the Netherlands, the police chief occupies a position beneath the other two (Hoogewoning et al, 2015). The dynamics of this 'triangle' change over time, but the universality of top–down pressure for results[3] means that the police leader understands clearly the status of his or her position in the balance of power.

The relationship between strategic police leader and mayor is consequently not always a comfortable one. Our respondents often reported clashes of personality and strong differences about priorities, even of strategic direction. By contrast, there is seldom any clash reported with public prosecutors, and police leaders often speak in warm terms about the lawyers and judges with whom they deal. Importantly though, both mayors and prosecutors can determine what the police responses will be to both volume crime and to more serious crimes, such as homicide or organised crime, within their jurisdiction or the mayor's locality. Beyond them, there is a larger discourse concerning the criminal courts and the judges who preside over them. In much of Europe, this includes the role of the 'investigating' or 'questioning' judge (the adjectives vary, but are usually understood as variants on the French term *juge d'instruction*),[4] and beyond local politicians to national parliamentary representatives and oversight by ministers of departments concerned with internal affairs.

Even here, there are many national variations. In Italy, for example, there are Financial Police (*Policia di Finanza*), who answer to the Treasury Department (*Dipartimento del Tesoro*). In a number of European countries, the gendarmeries – a legacy of the Napoleonic

---

[2]   See Cathy Schneider, 2008, for example.

[3]   Ranging from Home Secretary Theresa May's comment in England that the police have one task and that is 'to cut crime' (2010) to the politico-legal subordination of strategic police leaders, 'we steer and you row', both in the Netherlands and in Nordic countries.

[4]   The term covers the active role of a member of the judiciary in investigation of (usually) serious crime. In France this is the '*juge d'instruction*', in Portugal the '*examinarjuiz*', in the Netherlands the '*onderzoeksrechter*' and in Norway the '*undersøkedommer*'. Despite the inevitable differences in terminology, the function of the *examining judge* is more or less the same across Europe and gives the judiciary a powerful voice in the conduct of an investigation and on the value or relevance of the material evidence that the police obtain (see Harbeck and Glendon, 2013 and Dammer and Albanese, 2013, for detailed academic and legal commentaries).

conquest that we examined in Chapter One – often answer equally to a national Minister of Defence and to a Minister of Internal Affairs. Indeed, gendarmeries, while locally responsible for law and order in rural areas or country towns, nonetheless have a distinct national and international role,[5] which is steadily evolving at the European level as a species of border force or interim power between a national police and the armed forces of the member state (see Chapter Seven).

Relationships with peers

The task we posed to all our 108 respondents was this: **Describe your relationships with your peers in your own force and other forces**. The results are shown in Table 4.1.

Table 4.1: Describe your relationships with your peers in your own force and other forces

Negative	Neutral	Positive
53 (61%)	**17** (10%)	**38** (29%)

The mixed response suggests that, in some forces, rivalry is a real issue, while in others it is not as important as cooperation in the face of common threats. It is perhaps one of the products of the anonymity accorded to interviewees that they are more open about rivalries and competitiveness within policing than they would be if named and on the record. Some were privately antagonistic:

> 'I do not trust a single one of my contemporaries: I know them well and I know how they got to their posts and that means I despise the way some of them came up the tree. I have no respect for them as people as a result.' (Interviewee M3)

All advancement is in some way a compromise between individual ideals and the requirements of the organisation, and the police service is no exception to this generality. Another strategic police leader learned with dismay about some activity by his contemporaries when he was thought to be out of action through sickness:

---

[5]   Gendarmeries often function outside Europe, usually under the auspices of the United Nations but not always; see Lutterbeck, 2004, and Bayley, 2005.

'I was ill [once], and I heard that some chiefs were ringing up the Mayor or the Prosecutor's Office to find out if my job would be vacant. That is like a vulture starting to eat a body before it is dead.' (Interviewee N9)

However, this response also suggests an unusual sensitivity to a situation which many would laugh off robustly as the typical 'shark infested' strategic police officer cadre[6] – again perhaps, might this be a product of the 'confessional' of anonymous interview? Others to whom we spoke were mordant about those massing to replace them, and they accepted replacement (and jockeying to be considered as replacements) as par for the course at this level of policing. Indeed, most strategic police leaders must have experienced such situations on their way up the ladder from the lower ranks.

Some respondents, particularly in those EU member states emerging from former Soviet domination, were frustrated by the sometimes glacial pace of reform, and were not averse to pointing the finger at those whom they thought were deliberately slowing things down and obstructing progress. For example:

'Many of my peers are clever, intelligent, educated people but there are some who are none of these things and I do not like them. I do not like those people who argue for slow change and gradual movement. I believe in seeing what is wrong and fixing it straight away without waiting, but you would expect a former soldier to say this. I am for reform of the police, and that has made me some enemies.' (Interviewee C58)

Another leader was more sanguine, believing that the policing elite in Europe is actually a broad mix of types, much as one would find elsewhere:

'We don't interact much. Looking across the spectrum, there are some very clever but very frustrated chief police officers in the cadre and some threadbare time-servers too. Like most organisations, we are a mix of the good, the bad and the ugly.' (Interviewee N17)

---

[6]   A chief officer quoted in Caless, 2011, p. 68.

One strategic police leader commented that cooperation between colleagues was a necessity forced upon each of them, but he voiced considerable unease at his own country's selection process when he surveyed the range of those who led the police at a strategic level:

> 'I get on with most of my immediate colleagues because I have to. But I would probably not seek them out as companions unless we were thrown together by work. As for those outside my own force, well, the more I see of them, the more I think that there's something fundamentally wrong with the selection process and training to be a chief.' (Interviewee A24)

He did not go on to specify what the shortcomings were and it would be easy to dismiss such comments as part of a nostalgic belief in the 'good old days' of policing – a type of wishful thinking that has been comprehensively demolished by, among others, the redoubtable Gilda O'Neill (2006).[7] However, a number of leaders from very disparate jurisdictions have voiced the same concerns (which we examined briefly in Chapter Two) about selection and promotion processes, and this may indicate a need for the EU carefully to consider a federal system of strategic police leadership selection, thus obviating skew and bias in national systems operated by member states. Hoogewoning and his colleagues noted that the Dutch, for example, had no equivalent of the Strategic Command Course operated by the British College of Policing (although there is a development programme for senior police operated by the Dutch Police Academy), and therefore had no – or little – systematic exposure to high-level strategic leadership thinking and best practice (Hoogewoning et al, 2015).

Not all leaders blame the selection system; some are focused on the characters of the 'ruthless careerists' who make it to the strategic peaks:

> 'My peers are ruthless careerists who would not stop their cars if they could run me over. I am just the same. In fact, there are one or two people who I would reverse over to make sure they were dead.' (Interviewee C81)

Others believe that it is the system itself that produces friction, rather than the people in the senior positions, because there are not enough

---

[7] In her delightful *The Good Old Days; Crime, Murder and Mayhem in Victorian London* (2006, London: Viking).

jobs. As a result, vertical and possibly lateral movements are spasmodic, and genuine vacancies to advance only occur with the departure of someone higher up:

> 'We all get on OK; it's a case of having to because there are not many of us and for most of the police division heads, this is the pinnacle of the career. I guess it probably is for me too, but you never know. If the Chief falls off a cliff tomorrow, I shall move up one place, if he doesn't, I don't. It's dead guys' shoes at this level.' (Interviewee M88)

There are occasions, too, when strategic police leaders realise that what seems normal to them is not necessarily reflected in the wider European policing world:

> 'Unfortunately, [internally] there is a ferocious competition. These command jobs are not very many and therefore when one is coming up, the sharks start to circle in the water from an early stage. Believe me, there have been instances where the fighting for advantage has been sickening. Astonishingly, it doesn't seem to happen in other countries. When I was on my first [foreign] posting, we all compared experiences, as you do, and not one of my new colleagues had the same kind of blood festival that we have.' (Interviewee M82)

For all these prickly, competitive, 'ruthless careerists' at the top of policing, there are many (nearly half) who find their colleagues amenable, their working conditions congenial and their prospects for advancement bright and not dependent on the deaths or retirements of those above them:

> 'I don't see my colleagues as a threat; most of them I see as friends, despite the competition for jobs at this level. I see fellow chiefs as a group of people who have similar worries and problems, and you need to work with them, not against them. When I've had to front public initiatives for example, I've been able to make use of colleagues whom I know and trust to gain support. If I have one skill, it's networking.' (Interviewee N18)

This is a common theme: most strategic police leaders are more concerned to get the job done, they claim, than to fritter their time in endless feuds or scrambles for dominance. In order to get the job done, they have to influence, persuade and negotiate on as wide a basis as possible:

> 'Relationship with peers: very good. I possess a good network, mostly over the younger generation but also with some good contacts all around. My contacts are in all forces, the least in the judiciary police branch[8] because they are so specific and rather isolated, but I have some good contacts there that I try and use as a sounding board from time to time.' (Interviewee M46)

Networking is a key skill in the strategic leader's portfolio of talents, whether inside policing or in any other leadership position. Police officers need such networks; they need ranges of extensive contacts from whom they can seek advice or a favour or an opinion or an introduction to somebody else, simply because their work is less predictable than, say, retail management, and because most of the time they have to be reactive to developing situations rather than pre-emptive (as commodity forecasters in a retail environment need to be).

A British Isles region strategic police leader regarded his peers with a pleasantly ironic detachment:

> 'I like and admire my peers: they're clever buggers and must suffer endless frustrations because the world is not as they want it to be. I'm no threat to any of them and they often come to me to talk things over and to ask my advice. Makes me feel quite fatherly.' (Interviewee BI 35)

It is probably the fact that he is 'no threat to any of them' which enables him to proffer advice when asked, and to act as a sounding board for younger strategic leaders' concerns. Caless (2011) found in his survey of the chief police officers in England and Wales that many of them were emphatically not paternal:

> 'In a service which prides itself on pulling together (where indeed, *team working* is a specific competence) the sometimes raw savagery which chief officers displayed about each other, was a bit unnerving. ... No doubt it is a release from

---

[8]   The reference is to a 'detective' department for criminal investigation.

being publicly benign and collegiate' (Caless, 2011, p. 68; author's emphasis)

The difference between Britain and the rest of Europe in this respect is striking. As we have seen here, while some European strategic police leaders gave vent in our research interviews to their negative feelings about colleagues, rivals and competitors, many (half) did not. Many looked outward to the larger criminal justice system where, inevitably, they had deeper and more continuous relationships with public prosecutors and judges than with their peers. The British experience could be the product of its highly competitive promotion system, particularly to strategic command (Wall, 1998; Savage et al, 2000; Caless, 2011), or it could be the result of a more or less 'closed' system with few external challenges.[9] Either way, it contrasts with the experiences of many of those who police at the top in Europe, where:

> 'to be honest we don't see that much of each other within the day unless there is a special conference or a crisis or something, because we are too focused on our jobs.' (Interviewee N89)

Perhaps the last word for the moment should be with one laconic strategic police leader who, surveying his terrain, observed:

> 'You know, we waste so much time fighting to get here and believing that it is the most important thing in the world to be at or near the top of policing, that we don't stop to think how mundane policing can be at this level and that, even when you have all the silver braid there is, someone will still be saying to you: "do this" or "do that". You don't ever escape a boss of some kind.' (Interviewee A25)

Even a strategic police leader's bed of roses, it seems, contains one or two thorns.

---

[9] This system changed in May 2014 with direct recruitment to strategic police leader, and other ranks, being available in England and Wales for the first time, courtesy of Tom Winsor, HM Chief Inspector of Constabulary. It is too early to say how successful this opening out to competition will be, but in September 2014, the first nine recruits were in training.

Relationships with public prosecutors, judges and community leaders

> '[M]any [lawyers and judges] are very slippery people, cold and slippery like fish' (Interviewee N10)

In this section, we turn our attention to the strategic police leader's relationships with the wider world of national criminal justice, and specifically to relations with the public prosecutors, criminal court judges and, *inter alia*, with mayors and community leaders in their own jurisdictions. These form the general operating world for the European strategic police leader in many instances; only those in specialist 'silos' operate outside the triangle of local jurisdictions.

The relationship with lawyers, judges, courts and mayors formed the second part of our general question: **Describe your relationships within the wider criminal justice system**. The results are shown in Table 4.2.

Table 4.2: Relationships with the rest of criminal justice and the law/politicians

Predominantly negative	Predominantly neutral	Predominantly positive
18 (24%)	9 (7%)	81 (69%)

Results for the wider justice system were more uniform than the rather abrupt divide we saw in Table 4.1 in responses to relationships with other police between those who could not stomach their peers at any price and those who rubbed along as well as they could in an imperfect world, trying to make use of networks and contacts. The responses from the interviews suggest that relationships outside the immediate police hierarchy are more likely to be cooperative rather than competitive. The general outcome is an indication that, overwhelmingly, most interviewed have what they consider to be a positive relationship with public prosecutors, judges and other criminal justice officials. Only a small proportion of respondents – less than a fifth – admit to relationships that are fraught in some way or negatively competitive for prestige or status. It is worth noting, too, that only a few respondents express neutrality or indifference to the criminal justice system of which they are a part.

It is appropriate now to look at some of the 'rich detail' about relationships with the judiciary and the public prosecutors, and the criminal justice systems in Europe more generally.

Warmth does not always characterise the nexus between police and the wider criminal justice system; indeed, one strategic police leader remarked:

> 'I have a necessarily close relationship with lawyers and judges, and it is very important for me to understand them and influence them. Of course, many are very slippery people, cold and slippery like fish. The thing to do is to leave any dislike or caution outside the meeting and focus instead on what needs to be done.' (Interviewee N10)

In most of Europe, the public prosecutor or the criminal justice equivalent of 'lead investigator' oversees and directs the police investigation of any crime. Normally, this entails the investigation of homicide, serious assault or organised crime, but can also relate to volume crime and series crimes,[10] where there is local unease or some community angle that has an impact on the courts.

The chief public prosecutor is a powerful regional figure. A career lawyer, this person instructs the police what to investigate, what evidence to look for and whom to question (Bomberg et al, 2011; Guild and Geyer, 2008). This is more directive and controlling than police in England and Wales are used to; hence the unfamiliarity of this concept in the UK[11] (though Scotland has a similar feature to the wider continent, where the procurator fiscal plays a broadly comparable role in overseeing Scottish Police investigations). It also means that, in European law, the police have a subordinate role to the prosecutor (following his or her instructions) and to the 'examining judge'.[12] The police are therefore 'neutral' gatherers of evidence, pursuing investigative leads and responding to the legal instructions of those overseeing the investigation. The police have autonomy to

---

[10] 'Volume crime' is relatively low-level crime but committed on a scale that affects a community, such as burglary, mugging or vehicle crime. 'Series crime' is a single type of crime repeated over a wide area, such as impersonation fraud or theft by deception from elderly people.

[11] A good account of the role is in Elspeth Guild and Florian Geyer (eds) (2008), *Security versus justice? Police and judicial cooperation in the European Union*.

[12] We commented on this in note 4. One of the best, if now very venerable, analyses of the function of *juge d'instruction* is found in Ploscowe, M. (1935), The Investigating Magistrate (*Juge d'Instruction*) in European Criminal Procedure, *Michigan Law Review*. Morris Ploscowe went on to write a book in 1936 (alas, now out of print) on European criminal justice systems.

decide on the means of investigation, and in practice, of course, bring significant leads or possibilities to the attention of the public prosecutor or examining judge, but the dogged autonomy insisted on by police in Britain is not at all in evidence elsewhere in Europe (Marshall, 1978; G. Smith, 2009).

As might be expected, relationships are often predicated on mutual esteem. The most productive relationships are those where the police respect the prosecutor and/or the investigating judge:

> 'It's not at all unusual for the Chief Prosecutor to ask for me by name to lead an investigation; [the CP will get the Justice] Minister to talk to mine (having tipped me off) and the thing is quickly a done deal. You trust Judges or Prosecutors or are wary of them depending on your experience of how good or how feeble they are.' (Interviewee A12)

The same strategic police leader went on to describe a different relationship, which was very negative and potentially undermining of the criminal justice system:

> 'One judge we always avoided if we could (by delaying the investigation, "mislaying" court papers or having unexpectedly found another witness to interview), because he would always criticise the police, branding us as inefficient or inept when we were nothing of the kind. He kept complaining that he never had "a juicy case" to try and that's because we all hated him and would keep trials away from him if we could. That was where the Prosecutor and the Chief really worked well together.
>
> [**Interviewer:** Is that judge still hearing criminal cases?]
>
> Oh no, no. He was caught by a patrol trying to assault a girl in a park, and the system threw the book at him. He actually went to jail, you know. We were all so pleased because he'll never work again now and probably had a very hard time in the prison. Serves him right for being unnecessarily anti-police.' (Interviewee A12)

Other strategic police leaders cautioned against too much trust or friendship in the criminal justice system, because they believe that the lawyers are there for themselves and not for any higher purpose:

'I have never subscribed to the myth that the interests of the judiciary and the interests of the police are identical. Lawyers and judges are there for themselves as much as we are, and will defend their profession with the same determination. The huge difference between us is that the law, and particularly the judges, are not subject to the same degree of political interference as we are. That gives them the edge every time, and a freedom to act that we can only yearn for.' (Interviewee M28)

It seems a perennial complaint from the police that they are more interfered with than other parts of the criminal justice system, and it is not hard to see why such interference takes place. It is because the police represent, as we noted in Chapter One, the nation state's monopoly of legitimised civil violence, and most parts of society recognise that this means that the police have to be closely watched. That will always and necessarily set the police apart from the other parts of the prosecutorial system and the judiciary (Guild and Geyer, 2008; Dammer and Albanese, 2013).

However, the complaint itself is a partial one: judges and lawyers *are* subject to appeal and review, and the decisions of judges are often overturned or modified by the appeals system. This tends to be conveniently forgotten by the police, perhaps because this 'interference' with the judiciary is not overtly political or the stuff of banner headlines. Yet penalties for professional shortcomings among lawyers and judges are easily as severe as they are for police officers, and it is not unknown – as Interviewee A12 indicated – for judges and lawyers to go to prison if they break the law. Would we as citizens feel reassured if the police had more 'freedom to act'? Not if the numerous examples in the last few years of miscarriages of justice are anything to go by. Besides, the police all over Europe are adept at 'special pleading', sharing with their British counterparts a kind of default mechanism to a posture of injured innocence or aggrieved defensiveness. A kind of professional envy occasionally characterises the strategic police officer's attitude to the judiciary and public prosecutors, and perhaps we should make allowance for that in some of their comments:

'I should like to see people from the Public Prosecutor's Bureau come to work in the police for a time, just so that they can understand our pressures. I think we should do the reverse too and put police inside the justice system to experience it.' (Interviewee N54)

Others think that some combinations are actively dangerous:

> 'The worst combination of all is the lawyer become politician because there you bring together ruthless ambition with great self-conceit, and that can be very dangerous, because such people do not care who they hurt.' (Interviewee N11)

Another strategic police leader had a corrosively negative attitude:

> 'There is always an assumption that we are artisan workers in the police, with muscle but no brains, while they are the mind workers, the miracle men. We think they are often very stupid actually and most of us have no time at all for the lawyers.' (Interviewee A7)

That said, strategic police leaders would do themselves no favours if they needlessly antagonised the criminal justice system, and would soon feel the weight of collective displeasure. The invariable outcome, the interviewee below says, is 'compromise and consensus':

> 'A chief police officer would be a fool to ignore a Mayor's wishes and equally would not oppose a judge appointing someone from the Justice System to oversee an investigation; but the point is that both people know that they have to cooperate with a chief police officer, not tell him or her what to do. So there's lots of compromise and consensus.' (Interviewee M14)

Occasionally, the relationship, predicated on similar education and upbringing, shared interests or shared 'clubbability', can seem almost cosy:

> 'Of course, they still are the government and the authority, but as a rule they are your fellow-students of the university, with whom you associate socially. It is somewhat ambiguous. It might even be very comradely, but the functional authority relationship prevails.' (Interviewee B29)

One leader noted that the routine contact he had with the prosecutor and with his local mayors was regarded as unexceptionable:

'I have monthly contact with the Public Prosecutor. During this contact, we discuss ongoing legal cases and the policy to be followed in judicial matters. With the mayors, I have a meeting every fortnight to discuss policing and public safety issues. I also have contacts with representatives of the religious community and representatives of traders and artisans.' (Interviewee B44)

In countries emerging from the shadow of Soviet occupation and control, there is a refreshing camaraderie between police and the wider criminal justice system, which has nothing to do with envy or resentment, but rather with shared experience and mutual regard:

'I have respect for lawyers and judges, provided they have come up through the new liberal way and are not those appointed by the old regime. You have to understand that under the old Soviet Bloc system, people were made judges and prosecutors because of their loyalty to the regime, not because they were any good. Most of them have gone now, but there are still one or two who I will not work with. Because I have a law degree and have worked in Brussels, I understand how lawyers think and work and I generally like them and they like and respect me.' (Interviewee C6)

However, in parts of central Europe and the Baltic States, the problem is how to gain the trust and respect of the public rather than the respect of lawyers and judges, and some strategic police leaders are thoughtful about how important this trust is and how it might be achieved:

'We have not become a people's police yet and there is still a great amount of suspicion of the police and what they do, which comes from experiences with the old system. Gradually though, as people see me stand up to politicians or take the part of the public against the prosecutors in a crime issue, trust grows. It is still very small and delicate like a plant, and we will need to bring it carefully into growing well. [...] *We need to give [the people] trust* and the right results, so that they can trust us. If they don't trust us, we cannot do the job.' (Interviewee C48; speaker's emphasis)

This meant that the police had to stay out of politics and be seen to be impartial and aloof from the 'system':

'You have to understand that it is only a fairly short time since the police in this country were part of the State apparatus and the public associates us with control and suppressing freedoms. Now we want to defend democracy and protect the public rights but it is slow going to persuade them. Therefore, I believe that the less the police are influenced by politics or the courts the better.' (Interviewee C48)

Another strategic police leader from Central Europe believed that now, lawyers, judges, police leaders and politicians, 'are all Europeans':

'Relations are good. There are not many of us and we all know each other well, because we have gone up the ranks together since the 1990s and we are not of the old regime. It is easy to trust my colleagues now and we do not have to look behind any more. Not just police, but judges and lawyers too – we have all grown in the new system; we are all Europeans.' (Interviewee C70)

By contrast, this next strategic police leader was evidently happier working in the international field than he was within his domestic, competitive policing structure:

'I prefer very much the wider area of international work where I can cooperate with judges and prosecutors and police from other countries. I am not competing with them (except maybe for national pride) and so if I do a good job it does not threaten them and if they do a good job it does not threaten me. This is not a surprise that I am more comfortable representing my country and my police than I am fighting for my place inside.' (Interviewee N53)

Another actually preferred the company of judges and lawyers to that of his police colleagues, because he found the former to be more intellectually stimulating:

'My best relationships, beyond doubt, are with judges and academics: I just love operating at that conceptual level.' (Interviewee C61)

An Alpine region strategic police leader suggests that the police and the wider criminal justice system operate together informally but effectively to create a 'tightly closed' shop:

> 'Of course, we police and lawyers and judges have all known each other a long time and so we are something like a club (which must seem tightly closed to outsiders), but there is much respect and mutual regard with us. We have differences, of course, everyone does, but if we are troubled by someone from outside, we pretty soon gather closely together.' (Interviewee A65)

Others saw the relationship less in absolute terms and more in terms of pragmatism or realpolitik, in which what mattered was the 'art of the possible':

> 'Work is about possibilities and probabilities at this level, and having well-developed political antennae are important to how well I do this job.' (Interviewee M78)

Another thought that contact with the 'judicial system' was enjoyable and profitable precisely because the two (lawyers and police) shared similar outlooks, were not rivals and had no need to engage in professional jealousies:

> 'By contrast [with fellow strategic police leaders], and probably because we are not in competition, I have excellent relations with the judicial system and the public prosecutors. They are intelligent, cultured people, with a deep cynicism about human nature, just as I have. But because they don't want my job, and would not rival me for a job, we get on just fine.' (Interviewee C81)

One officer noted that active and positive relationships within the criminal justice system, and in several countries simultaneously, were vital for him to do his job properly:

> 'The real linkages are with public prosecutors here and in neighbouring countries, and with the respective judicial systems. Relations there are excellent: they *have* to be. I could not do my job properly, nor could I oversee some of these complex operations [...] unless relations are based

on trust and mutual respect, forged in the fires of criminal investigations.' (Interviewee N83; speaker's emphasis)

There are evidently penalties for insufficiently corporate approaches by the police to the criminal justice system generally:

'I am fortunate that I have really excellent relations with the Chief Public Prosecutor; we are not friends exactly but we respect each other, I think. Some of my colleagues in other States do not have such good fortune. Some argue, some speak to the media about the other one and there was one chief who did not speak to the Prosecutors for months. He was dismissed in the end of it, because that was a kind of madness to do.' (Interviewee A90)

Another saw his role simply as a broker of deals and facilitator to make things work at a strategic level:

'Most of my time is taken up stroking the Mayor's ego and working really hard at the job of strategic policing (don't let anyone tell you it's easy) and of course in making networking and relationships within the criminal justice system. I see my police colleagues perhaps three times in a year, but I will see the Public Prosecutors and judges that many times in a month. Contact in the justice business is frequent and professional.' (Interviewee N95)

Another officer, who commands a gendarmerie, noted that the dynamic of the relationship between him and the judicial or political powers locally was of a different order to those experienced by his equivalents in the National Police:

'I am sympathetic to my colleagues in the National Police because they have been castrated by the political process; I mean to say that the police chiefs have no power and very little influence. The real power is in the Mayors and in the Public Prosecutors, and the police do what they are told. Now the Gendarmerie is different. We always say "we are nationally organised but locally responsive". My officers listen to the rural Mayors and work confidently with the Public Prosecutors, but those do not command the gendarmerie, I do.' (Interviewee B104)

To sum up, there is a spectrum of responses on the part of strategic police leaders to their oversight and direction by public prosecutors, examining judges and the wider criminal justice system, ranging from a minority expressing rather bitter envy through a residue of indifference to a considerable majority who experience camaraderie, shared values and mutual respect.

There is a range, too, of emotions – from the grudging to the wholehearted – which yet contrasts with their attitudes to their own peers, where there is a mixture of negative and positive preponderances, depending on whether or not the individual sees other strategic police leaders as direct rivals.

It is perhaps a greater sense of pragmatism, of knowing that they have to get on with prosecutors and judges in order to complete an investigation and bring a case to conclusion, that contrasts with the often dismissive attitude to community leaders and mayors – whose influence is less direct and perhaps more diffuse.

On minority ethnicities, gender prejudice and women in the police

It would be appropriate now to examine why there are relatively so few members of minority ethnic communities and women police officers in strategic leadership posts, and to ask ourselves if this is the result of a failure of EU political will to follow through on its declarations about ethnic and gender equality.

Minority ethnic leaders

The European Union does not collect or assess information about minority ethnic representation in policing, let alone at the level of the strategic police leader.[13] Accordingly, we have been constrained throughout this project by a lack of reliable official data. We did not set out initially to ascertain the ethnic identity of our interviewees,

---

[13]   We have accessed the Eurostat *Regional Yearbooks* for 2012, 2013 and 2014, which mostly record demographics (age profiles of populations) by region and country, but there are no data on police officers by ethnicity or gender. Data storage goes back to 1985. The comprehensive annual *Regional Yearbook* includes 15 chapters but nothing of merit on the police, except crime statistics. See Eurostat (2014), *Regional Yearbook*, October, published by Eurostat, EU, http://tinyurl.com/mocuxwm. Anne van Ewijk, in her survey of diversity in Europe, bemoans the same paucity of data (van Ewijk, 2011, p. 3).

any more than making a gender analysis was an original aim. These elements emerged as we conducted our research. In all, five of those we spoke to identified themselves as coming from minority ethnic communities and had substantive commentary on how that may have affected their strategic police leadership role. It will be evident then, that we make no claims for comprehensiveness in our comments about minority ethnic 'top cops'; rather that we seek simply to convey an impression of what such origins mean to those concerned.[14]

The position for those police officers with a minority ethnic background is difficult, since there are so few of them entering policing in the first place:

> 'Ethnic minority people are another matter: there are not enough of these in the police to begin with so it is extra hard to choose any for command jobs.' (Interviewee B103 [the speaker is a woman])

It follows that proportionally, we would expect to see fewer members of a minority reaching strategic levels in a police culture that appears 'institutionally prejudiced'[15] in favour of white, indigenous, middle-class males. The struggle for those of a different origin to rise to command in such circumstances can be both tough and painful:

> 'I suffered prejudice on the way up to this strategic rank. I see it all the time, and I am sure that such considerations are still playing in the background. I know that I will never make top rank because of this. No-one has said anything; they are polite and smiling in public, but I know that many are uncomfortable with my being here in this role with my background as a foreigner in their [midst].' (Interviewee X (anonymised))

This could be an exaggerated suspicion founded on past experiences of prejudice – especially since the speaker admits that he cannot point to anything concrete in the attitudes of those around him, but his feelings seem supported by such facts as we can glean.

---

[14] However, to protect the speakers' identities, we have completely anonymised them, not giving region or interview number (since we quote them on other matters elsewhere in the book). We use XYZ instead.

[15] To borrow and adapt a phrase from Sir William Macpherson at the Stephen Lawrence Inquiry, 1999.

In a ground-breaking piece of research in 2011, Anne van Ewijk noted that across Europe the percentage of police recruits from minority ethnic backgrounds has never exceeded 10%. Indeed, the best to date is in the Netherlands, where 6% of all police officers 'had a migration background' (van Ewijk, 2011, p. 4).[16] She goes on to note that recruitment of members from minority ethnic communities to the police service as a whole is low to begin with, and it is clearly the case that this number 'diminishes as police officers' rank increases' (van Ewijk, 2011, p. 2). Not only that, but 'the level of diversity within police organisations in practice is low compared to societal average' (van Ewijk, 2011, p. 2). In other words, something seems to inhibit people from joining the police in the first place, so that a low entry number can only decrease as one goes up the ranks. In Germany, for example, ethnic minorities make up only 1% of the total, while in Denmark, there are none at all, let alone in the higher ranks. Anne van Ewijk's tables for 2011 show that just over 4% of officers from minority ethnic groups make it to strategic leadership positions in the Netherlands, but barely 3% make it in the UK (van Ewijk, 2011, p. 6, Table 2).

It comes as no surprise, in light of these data, that:

> '[...] facts never destroy prejudice entirely, because what people feel is usually stronger than what they think. They do not want to confront their fears and so the prejudice lives on.' (Interviewee X anonymised)

Another strategic police leader with 'a migration background' noted that his struggle began before he even joined the police, but intensified when he did join:

> 'I know that when I said I wanted to join the police my parents went into a huge rage and told me that I was

---

[16]   Compared, for example, with 4.8% across all ranks in the UK and 3% in Spain; but data are sparse and erratic: few EU countries publish figures for either minority ethnic or female police officers. The proportion of female police officers has never reached 50% across Europe. We might note additionally that in some countries the high entry requirements and long periods of training (two years in Sweden), do not always suit women or members of minority ethnic groups; thus there are *systemic barriers* which need dismantling. The success in the UK of the PCSO concept both among women and among minority ethnic communities, may have much to do with short training periods, less responsibility and fewer instances of confrontation than in the police (see Caless, 2014).

betraying my whole family. But they were judging the
police as they were in the old country, not as they were
here in our new country. So I went ahead and joined. Sure
there was prejudice: you get used to it but it still hurts.
To me, judging me by my skin is so stupid: it's like saying
"You can't do a good job because you have blond hair",
or "because you have a large nose". I think the police are
still pretty prejudiced against people of different race and
against women.' (Interviewee Y anonymised)

Academic commentators have found this culture of prejudice in the
police quite baffling. On the face of it, since the police deal with all
parts of society and are familiar to everyone as a part of the 'normal
fabric' of life, and since policing is one of the few public service
occupations where anyone can, theoretically at least, rise to the top,[17]
discovering latent prejudice against people because of their ethnicity
or gender seems inexplicable. Abby Peterson and Sara Uhnoo argue
that barriers to diversity in the police are the products of a 'loyalty
culture', which demands inclusion of some to the exclusion of others,
and this inevitably rejects those who are different. This demand for
loyal adherence to a particular set of values may inhibit many from
joining the police (Peterson and Uhnoo, 2012). van Ewijk (2011,
pp. 4–5) argues as well that some may be put off joining the police
because they see few who 'share their diverse characteristics', their
experiences of the police may be largely negative ('stop and search',
'stop and account', 'heavy' policing of urban areas where there are large
ethnic communities and so on), while there could also be 'a hostile
reaction of friends and family' (van Ewijk, 2011, p. 5) to the notion
of becoming a police officer.

Interviewee Y confirmed this last point as a typical reaction, when
he observed that his family judged the police 'as they were in the
old country'. This may account in part for widespread antipathy to
policing as a career choice for ethnic minorities and may explain why
women from minority ethnic communities are least likely of all to
become police officers: an overlay or patina of cultural inhibitions and
taboos acts as a formidable obstacle to recruitment. Yet in the UK it
has been notable, particularly in London, that recruiting both men
and women from minority ethnic backgrounds to become police
community support officers (PCSOs) has been much more successful

---

[17] Unlike health, for example, where nurses seldom make the bridge to becoming
doctors.

than recruitment to the regular police. According to published data in July 2013, a total of 5% of police officers (including Specials[18]) came from a minority ethnic background,[19] but nearly 10% of PCSOs came from ethnic minorities – twice that of the whole police service (HO, 2013, Table 7). Additionally, 47% of all PCSOs are women; a proportion far higher than the 27% in policing as a whole in the UK (HO, 2013, Table 7, para. 5.1 and Table 2).

The attractiveness of the largely non-confrontational role of the PCSO probably helps to balance the poor percentages of recruitment into the regular police (though minority ethnic representation of 5% in 2013 represents an increase over 3.3% in 2004). It is still a long way from the 25% in London alone that was called for by Sir William Macpherson in 1999,[20] but, discouraging though it is, at least the recruitment data for England and Wales are transparent and openly available.

Very few other European police organisations publish such data at all. France, for example, has no official data, because French policy rejects registration on the basis of race, ethnicity or religion (van Ewijk, 2011, p. 3). This is despite a 1993 report from the Council of Europe, which recommended that 'the composition of police forces should normally be representative of the communities [they] serve' (Council of Europe, 1993).

The fact remains that there are complex barriers in European policing to a truly proportionate representation of the minority ethnic composition of the population as a whole and there seems to be little political will to do anything about it. As Justin Greenwood notes, 'interest representation' in Europe, where special interest groups lobby for attention, is a product of a political structure that is not actually representative of the citizens of Europe (Greenwood and Turner, 2011). This is because the EU, unlike its constituent members, is not subject to robust parliamentary scrutiny and accountability through election.[21] It is no surprise that the political will to change the police culture is as dormant in the EU as the urge for rigorous parliamentary democracy.

---

[18] Special Constables, volunteer and unpaid, but fully warranted police officers who work a minimum of 16 hours a month.

[19] See Home Office (2013), *Police Workforce England and Wales, March 2013* (http://tinyurl.com/kx87hpy). The broad numbers were 6,537, the same as in 2012. Women made up 47% of all PCSOs.

[20] See Llewellyn, J. (2012), Life as an ethnic minority police officer, *Daily Telegraph*, 24 January, http://tinyurl.com/lmcxyac

[21] This is often called the 'democratic deficit' in the EU.

Nonetheless, the police 'culture' of prejudice is not uniform. The same interviewee who noted how he had been subjected to prejudicial treatment within his own police force found a very different experience when he served in an EU institution and met police officers from other member states:

> '[...] colleagues in the EU have no notion of my ethnic minority background and they treat me entirely as a colleague with no carefulness and no roughness either. Just as a colleague. So I am teased and welcomed for myself. It's very refreshing.' (Interviewee X anonymised)

This officer's ethnicity is not designated by appearance, so his European police colleagues may have treated him as one of themselves without actually knowing his origin. Had they known more, their attitudes towards him might have been different.

Gender

We have published elsewhere our research data and analysis of women who reach strategic police leadership rank and will simply record the salient points here.

Studies of women strategic leaders in European policing are few and far between. A recurrent problem in this specific field, just as for minority ethnic representation, is a lack of data. In fact, very few data generally on European policing are gathered, and there seems to be a lack of interest in any purpose to be served by such collection.[22] We did not set out to ascertain what the experiences were of women aspiring to become strategic police leaders, but the responses we had from women interviewees suggested that this was something that we should look at critically, because many of them across the whole EU suffered gender discrimination, obstruction and prejudice at the hands of their male colleagues.

---

[22] We enquired of Eurostat (the European Union office for statistics and analysis) what data they held on women strategic police leaders and were told that these are not data that are routinely collected. We then submitted, in June 2013 and again in March 2014, formal requests to the European Commission through Eurostat, for this kind of data to be gathered, including gender representation and the proportion of ethnic minority community members in strategic policing. We have yet to receive any response.

Some 71% of the female officers interviewed indicated that at some point in their police careers they were the target of discrimination and prejudice. One noted that it was not until she reached strategic leadership rank that discrimination began, while others commented that their attempts to move into specialist areas such as detection and investigation were obstructed by senior males in the police force. Many men regard policing as 'an unsuitable job for a woman' (Heidensohn, 1992, p. 199).

The bare numbers alone tell a story: we interviewed 108 strategic police leaders, of whom 24 are female (23%) but 84 are male (77%); the male police officer predominates at the strategic level and women are outnumbered here by at least 4:1. Aigi Resetnikova, in a 2006 study of women in the police in Estonia, noted that women made up a third of the entire police force (33%), but only 12% make it to the senior ranks (Resetnikova, 2006, para. 16). Her findings may be indicative of a larger state of affairs in Europe or even further afield, but we need to be cautious. Such studies are isolated research projects and there is no larger picture within which specific research can be contextualised, since the study of women strategic police leaders is still in its infancy, even in Europe, let alone in China, India or South America. What we can say with confidence is that it is not easy for women to break through 'the blue glass ceiling' in Europe and they do so in disproportionately small numbers, largely because male officers dominate and it is the latter who formulate the 'rules' of membership of the policing elite.

One area in which this male thinking is dominant may be seen in the remarkably persistent idea that women are best at dealing with sexual offences, domestic violence, prostitution and crimes against children and that they are less good at matters such as public order and the investigation of serial murderers (Brown, 1995, p. 62). One interviewee (C6) noted a kind of embedded cultural hostility when she applied to join the detective branch and was told that she would be better at 'women's policing' tasks. This is an experience that Frances Heidensohn also came across in her pioneering 1992 study of women in American and British policing, where she identified themes deriving from women's experiences in policing that were variants on the notion that policing was unsuitable as a female career. It may be this entrenched and stereotypical view that militates against women applying for strategic leadership jobs in the first place. Cressida Dick, an Assistant Commissioner in the Metropolitan Police Service in London, noted in an interview in 2014 that many police women look at their female role models in senior ranks and decide that childlessness in pursuit of a career is not for them.[23]

Research by Anne van Ewijk in 2011 noted that diversity levels in policing are low to begin with, and that the proportion diminished as people are promoted (van Ewijk, 2011, p. 3). The range of intake for female officers across Europe varies from 38% in Estonia to 4% in the Spanish *Guardia Civil*, but then there is a marked decrease as one reaches strategic policing rank, from a little under 14% in Sweden to a fraction over 2% in Austria (van Ewijk, 2011, Table 2, p. 6), for example. In other words, there is an erosion of female presence as one goes up the rank structure.

Some countries have tried to remedy this by the introduction of quotas at the higher ranks. The practice in France, for example, leads to an inversion of the proportion of female officers; 18% of high-ranking *Commissaires* are women, while only 14% of women are patrol officers (Pruvost, 2009). According to Geneviève Pruvost, this is the French government's policy, which focuses only on the higher ranks where intellect and strategic thinking are needed rather than the sheer physical strength required on the front line. Some of our interviewees told us that they did not agree with such quotas, because the act of imposing female presence on male strategic leaders merely reinforced the latter's prejudice, and meant that the women officers had to be even more resilient and determined to succeed. It rather mutes European Commissioner Viviane Reding's claim that 'gender equality is a European achievement' (European Commission Memo 14/156 of 7 March 2014), where even in business and commerce the number of women in strategic leadership positions has failed to reach the EU target of 40% (in fact reaching only 17.8% in 2014). It may be an improvement on an already feeble proportion, but it is still nothing to crow about, and no mention is made in Reding's memo of the representation of women in strategic police leadership roles.

In many other professions and in most large businesses, there is systematic 'barrier analysis', where hierarchical organisations can check where there are obstacles to women performing on an equal basis with men and do something about removing them.[24] Such points at which

---

[23] Interview in *The Times*, 11 March 2014; it may be of interest that AC Dick was interviewed because, for the first time, she headed 'an all-female leadership team in counter-terrorism' in the Metropolitan Police – something apparently she herself had not registered until it was pointed out to her by the (male) interviewer. She has since moved to another post.

[24] A good study is Matthies et al, 2012.

'barrier analysis' can be carried out include vacancy advertisement, interview, recruitment, reward/bonus, selection for promotion or (for high-profile jobs) assessment methods for identifying potential, and development programmes. Already in place in human resources departments in the UK and US (though not, to our knowledge, in policing in either), there is no reason why the EU could not adopt 'barrier analysis' to detect cultural or gender bias in policing as well as elsewhere.

Summary

It matters significantly to policing that leadership selection systems in the EU may be disadvantaging women and members of minority ethnic communities. Gender and racial equality *should* be observed in practice at all levels of the police yet currently, even in the most apparently socially enlightened of countries, fewer than half the available senior women police officers make the advance to strategic leadership posts and a very small number of those from minority ethnic communities achieve command rank in the police.

As one of our interviewees remarked, when men set the rules, men will prosper within the system, while women will continue to be disadvantaged until those rules are amended. The implications of this for diversity within policing, for the representation of women and members of minority ethnic communities in the top strategic posts, and for the message that this sends to society as a whole, needs extensive debate and further research and analysis. Having access to reliable data would be a start.

One of our interviewees said:

> 'My mother told me I was a fool to enter policing and she may have been right. It has been the hell of a struggle to succeed and climb up.' (Interviewee C94)

If this is a typical experience for a woman or for a member of a minority ethnic community, then European strategic policing is indeed a closed shop, staffed by a smug elite of pale males, much in need of extensive and immediate reform.

FIVE

The preference for cooperative bilateralism among European strategic police leaders

'I get frustrated by all this talk about multilateral cooperation in Europe: much of it comes from bureaucrats with vested interests in keeping their jobs. My own experience, and that of many of my colleagues, is that the organisations which are supposed to encourage police cooperation do nothing of the kind, and take weeks about it. The simplest way is to pick up the bloody phone, call your opposite number in the other country and take it from there!' (Interviewee B103)

Beyond the national: policing across borders

Increasing mass population movement and advancements in information technology have contributed to globalisation and substantial challenges in both the management and security of the nation state (Block, 2011; Yar, 2013). These developing pressures, over the last twenty-five years or so, have resulted in the emerging requirements to: police beyond national borders; develop political and police cooperation to make use of technology; create treaties, partnerships and protocols to counteract dangers and risks related to global crime threats (Bowling and Sheptycki, 2012); and devise ways in which, somewhat paradoxically, police forces can cooperate simultaneously at strategic, tactical and operational levels without compromising national integrity.[1]

---

[1] It is worth noting here that what is perceived as a dilemma in policing is reflected elsewhere in the politics, economics (including the currency zones) and legislative activities of the EU. Noises in Britain in recent years about withdrawal or renegotiation are probably as much political party positioning as they are symptoms of unease about the 'surrender' of national sovereignty to 'supra-national', that is, EU, control. This unease is evidently wider than just the UK: the elections to the European Parliament in May 2014 saw a tangible increase in the right-wing anti-federalist vote, and the number of nationalistic right-wing seats more than doubled: the UK and France with 24 apiece, followed by Denmark, Greece, Italy and Germany.

Adaptations to an evolving global and European policing context are undertaken through a range of policing models (as we saw in Chapter One), themselves made more complex because of national histories, political administration, channels of legitimacy, governance, roles and a state's functions, responsibilities, resources and capabilities. These complexities are not static: they evolve alongside changing political ideologies and swift but profound developments in technology and social media, all set against a background of uncertain economics and financial constraint. The pressures that result encourage a slow convergence of police practices, exacerbated by inevitable tensions between those that favour development towards a federal European police service and those committed to the protection of the Weberian 'nation state' (Biersteker and Weber, 1996; Frank et al, 2000).[2] One example of this from Britain may make the point. A suggestion was floated in early 2013 that the next commissioner of the Metropolitan Police might be the former chief of the New York Police Department, William ('Bill') Bratton. The notion of a foreigner occupying the most senior English operational police officer's post provoked, predictably, furious responses, particularly from retired police officers, exemplified by this comment by a former chief constable in *The Times* letters page:

> Policing here [in Britain] is a complex amalgam of political, economic, sociological and demographic factors which impinge upon local, national and international issues. Management of a [...] police service requires a blend of experience, practical application and operational skills which are not readily gained in the boardroom, on the battlefield or even in foreign [police] forces. (Former Chief Constable Ben Gunn, QPM, *The Times*, 26 January 2013[3])

Gunn is too parochial: these are factors which 'impinge upon' policing in Europe as a whole and upon strategic policing in particular; they are not peculiar to Britain. The larger point is that there is widespread resistance to the notion that one strategic police leader can work in the jurisdiction of another with equal effectiveness, even when the

---

[2]   See our discussion in Chapter One. 'Europe' as a quasi-state entity has no monopoly of force, and cannot compel other than by law; see Gustafsson (1998, pp. 189-213).

[3]   To be fair to Mr Gunn, the context of his letter was about external appointments to top command of police forces, not specifically about a species of national protectionism, but his views are commonly held and, as we shall see, not solely in Britain.

problems faced are identical, such as in transnational organised crime. Eduardo Ferreira put the point with admirable forensic detail (if little in the way of evidence):

> Transnational organised criminal groups will certainly keep profiting from [...] all sorts of trafficking – from human beings, industrial goods and waste, arms, drugs, to rare raw materials [...] Global inequities will also remain for many years, continuously feeding all kinds of extremism and terrorist activities aimed at the healthy and secular EU Member States. (Ferreira, 2011, p. 22)

The problems facing the police forces of European states in dealing with these threats and risks are very similar. In difficult circumstances, European strategic police leaders are expected to combat transnational organised crime (of which terrorism is a part), modulated through a functional partnership of member states, to create a trouble-free, non-parochial, fully cooperative, wholly selfless, pan-European and multilateral investigation (Verhage et al, 2010). We need to explore in more detail the nature of this idealised police world and we must also try to explain why, on an operational level, it does not seem to work. At the same time, we need to understand why those strategic police leaders who spoke in confidence to us seem to be more comfortable with bilateral operations. Ferreira comments that:

> Different and/or conflicting national legislations are frequently reported as a major obstacle to international cooperation because they also affect the gathering, storage and exchange of information, the sharing of police intelligence and joint investigations or operations. (Ferreira, 2011, p. 25)

But he also observed that:

> There are, however, several legally binding instruments supporting, at least theoretically, international and European police cooperation [...] These cover, for example: jurisdiction, confiscation and seizure, controlled deliveries, witness protection, surveillance, undercover operations, extradition, mutual legal assistance, transference of criminal proceedings or freezing illegally obtained assets. (Ferreira, 2011, p. 24)

Ferreira implies that these 'legally binding instruments' have not entirely succeeded in persuading strategic police leaders to conceive of their work in pan-European or overarching terms. Put bluntly, multilateral police cooperation, despite the creation of organisations like Europol and Eurojust, does not seem to have taken root effectively in Europe, and some European strategic police leaders, when we asked them about the quality and nature of such cooperation within the EU, expressed impatience with the bureaucracy of consulting any of the 'supra-national' organisations which were set up within Europe to facilitate precisely that kind of cooperation. It seems to them that pan-European policing cooperation is monolithic: processes have overtaken, or have formalised, opportunistic joint operations (predicated on local networking and bilateral contacts), resulting in slowing matters down and becoming ponderous or self-serving.

The problem is exacerbated perhaps by 'top-down' initiatives that, while they have created the machinery for action, have not given EU-wide organisations any power to command or override national concerns. One strategic police leader observed:

> 'Cops are pragmatic; they have to be. They know that the best thing to do is to go with what will produce quick-time positive results. That invariably means going with an informal, bilateral, "seat-of-your-pants" arrangement which focuses on the crime and nails the bad guys rather than trying to catalyse the inertia that attends institutions like Europol. You simply can't wait until these organisations get themselves in gear.' (Interviewee M38)

These do not seem to be just the irritations of the moment: a number of strategic police leaders have voiced these criticisms and they are reflected too in work by academic commentators. Our research suggests that a significant proportion of strategic police leaders in Europe share the views of the officer quoted above. We asked strategic police leaders directly about their views on cooperation in policing and how this related to the pan-European organisations that are intended to facilitate such cooperation.[4] Table 5.1 shows the data that resulted (from 108 respondents).

---

[4] **Question No. 8:** *What cooperation exists between you and your equivalent in other countries? What is your experience/what are your views of multilateral organisations such as Interpol, Europol, CEPOL and so on?*

Table 5.1: Bilateral and multilateral cooperation: extent of cooperation with other EU countries

Predominantly positive	Predominantly negative	Predominantly neutral
75 (69%)	**8** (7%)	**25** (23%)

Most strategic police leaders are very positive about the need for mutual cooperation in the face of criminality and crimes that cross borders, and they evidently believe that, in most cases, fostering pragmatically good relations between forces is a worthwhile and desirable end. However, when it comes to multiplying this cooperative impetus across the entire EU, and embracing 'supranational' organisations like Europol, the preponderant responses (from 108 respondents) are nearly inverted (see Table 5.2).

Table 5.2: Bilateral and multilateral cooperation: extent of cooperation with multilateral organisations (such as Europol, CEPOL, Eurojust)

Predominantly positive	Predominantly negative	Predominantly neutral
64 (59%)	**39** (36%)	**5** (5%)

These data suggest that more than a third of strategic police leaders harbour some reservations about the complexities involved (and the surrender of national sovereignty entailed) in the pursuit of multilateral police initiatives. All the same, they view this mostly positively, because of outcomes or personal experience. But this is not a simple matter of either/or, even of contrasted choices. It is much more complex than that. Strategic police leaders, when questioned privately, admit to considerable frustration with formalised and 'top-down' multilateral cooperative ventures in policing. A strategic police leader put the frustration like this:

> 'Now, that doesn't mean that we're not all trying [to be multilateral]; we are. It's just that the difficulties to overcome are almost insuperable: there is no shared criminal law, no shared jurisdiction, [...] and there is no collective political will for such a system. And that's where it has to start – in the Council of Europe. Until there is a political imperative [...], we'll be stuck with creaking systems, well-intentioned bureaucracies and police forces

which rely on informal connections to get things done.'[5] (Interviewee B75)

Pan-European mutualism

Monica den Boer argues that overregulation and 'initiative fatigue' may have alienated the police from the policy makers, arguing that the 'most visible aspect' of this is the 'vast number of initiatives' and a 'proliferation' of laws and statutory instruments which have come from the European Union (den Boer, 2010, p. 42). This amplifies the observation made by the strategic police leader quoted at the head of this chapter, that there is a deal of bureaucracy in police cooperation but little in the way of tangible evidence that pan-European mutualism works, particularly at the police operational level. Indeed, den Boer goes on to describe police cooperation as having a distinctly two-tier character, with 'ample progress' in strategic policy making but a tangible lag in multilateral 'operational or executive cross-border cooperation' (den Boer, 2010, p. 43). There is nothing new in legislators and protocol-framers being ahead of, or divorced from, realities (for example, the Labour Government in the UK from 1997 to 2010 passed laws to make people behave better, with a conspicuous lack of success[6]),

---

[5] A nationalistic journal in the UK averred that the enactment of coherent pan-European criminal law is 'imminent' and (February 2011) describes it apocalyptically in these terms: 'The EU project to build a "single country called Europe" includes the establishment of a single criminal law for all. A blueprint for a pan-European criminal code, called "Corpus Juris", was unveiled at a seminar hosted by the EU Commission in Spain in 1997. It is based on the Napoleonic-inquisitorial system of law used on the continent, and will explicitly do away with our British safeguards of Habeas Corpus, Trial by Independent Jury, protection against double jeopardy, etc.' (www.tfa.net/2011/02/04/the-pan-european-criminal-code/). 'Imminent' is clearly a relative term, as there are as yet no definitive proposals before the Council of Europe, though the concept is debated in a fairly desultory way from time to time. See also Browne (2005), in which Browne observed: 'The European Commission listed seven offences that it insisted should become European crimes immediately, including computer hacking, corporate fraud, people-trafficking and marine pollution.' Other, more temperate, views on *corpus juris criminalis* may be found in Klip (2002) and Archick (2013). We debate this further in Chapter Seven.

[6] As evidenced in research by the Centre for Crime and Justice Studies at King's College London, which in 2007 showed that successive Labour Governments had introduced more than 3,000 pieces of criminal legislation between 1997 and 2007; see CCJS (2007).

but in terms of police cooperation within Europe, the practicalities of multilateral cooperative ventures at the operational level do not appear convincing. One strategic police leader commented:

> 'I do not have a good opinion of multilateral organisations of any kind – they are slow, cautious, inward-looking and resistant to real change. Europol might be an exception, but I doubt it because it has to please too many masters and cannot direct police forces to do something. It can only request. It calls itself the "hub" but it isn't really. It is more like a gearing mechanism which helps a machine go smoother, but it doesn't have control of the motor.'
> (Interviewee M82)

It is easy enough to understand that the motivation for mutual cooperation arises from the internationalisation of criminal enterprise and the frustrations of police forces in trying to coordinate, investigate and disrupt illegal entrepreneurialism. Dean et al have identified the contemporary distance between the effectiveness of organised criminals and the relative ineffectiveness of police practitioners, and they comment that there is a need for 'smarter, better educated and better trained' law enforcement agents to counter the criminal entrepreneurs (Dean et al, 2010, p. xxi).

Our empirical research data suggest that the modern strategic police leader is actually far better educated than his or her predecessors: 88 of the 108 interviewed have Bachelor ('first') degrees, 54 have postgraduate qualifications, 26 strategic police leaders possess two or more degrees, while fewer than 10% of our sample had no formal higher education qualifications at all. We do not claim that these data are actually any more than indicative of the character and profile of the modern strategic police leader, especially as the issue is peripheral to the thrust of our own enquiry.[7] The point is rather that there are plenty of very bright strategic police leaders, so the apparent 'distance' between criminal and law enforcer, claimed by Dean et al, may not be the product of relative intellection, so much as systemic inertia or bureaucratic stasis on the part of the police, and pragmatic opportunism (of a kind normally denied to state organisations) on the

---

[7] However, this might well form part of the remit for subsequent longitudinal researches into strategic police leadership in Europe suggested by CEPOL, and noted earlier in the comments about our Methodology in the Introduction, page 18.

part of the criminal. Most of the contemporary literature and analysis of modern transnational organised crime has rejected the notion of masterminds, whether the fictional 'Moriarty' or the 'Mr Big' beloved of the sensationalist media. This contemporaneous viewpoint may be summed up in the words of Peter Klerks:

> Many law enforcement practitioners [...] hold rather simplistic views [...] they often think in rigid terms of leaders, chains of command, bag carriers and stable criminal infrastructures, where I observe mostly improvisation, fluid networks and ad hoc coalitions, opportunistic and very flexible individual entrepreneurs, criminal omnivores and organisational chaos.[8] (Klerks, 2003, p. 99)

Klerks suggests that such police and other law enforcement agency conceptions about organised crime may be vested in the need to attract funding and structure. Expanding the policing 'empire' may be the only activity respected by bureaucrats or espoused by strategic police leaders, intent on explaining to politicians why they need more resources to counter organised crime. In other words, Klerks says, law enforcement agencies try to mirror what they claim is the organised crime structure, while intensifying the 'fear of crime' among those in authority. Yet, such contradictions can be beside the point. It is not altogether a simple matter of pitting brains against brains. Investigating and disrupting international criminals requires flexibility, clarity of aims, fierce purpose and a ruthless concentration on the 'endgame'. These are also characteristics of the successful organised international criminal, of course (Mallory, 2012). However, if you multiply those requirements by the number of police forces engaged in the operation, with their different priorities, jurisdictions, practices, shibboleths and political

---

[8]   See also the pioneering 1995 work by Cyrille Fijnaut and a group of researchers in the Netherlands [Fijnaut, C. and Ouwerkerk, J. (eds) (2010), *The Future of Police and Judicial Cooperation in the European Union*, Leiden and Boston: Martinus Nijhoff Publishers], who comprehensively disposed of the notion of the untouchable mastermind pulling the strings at the back of international criminal enterprise. This is not to say that there are not clever criminals in organisational positions; rather it is to argue that flexibility and opportunism rule. The international criminal enterprise is just that: a profit-making supply of illegal goods and services. Dean et al (2010) and Mallory (2012) are good contemporary commentators on these aspects of transnational crime, which we look at from a strategic policing point of view in Chapter Seven.

drivers, what you get may be progressive diminution or dilution, not increasing strength and solidity.

Commenting on a European Police College (CEPOL) TOPSPOC seminar (see Chapter Two) in 2010, Eduardo Ferriera notes that one of the conclusions reached after extensive debate among strategic police leaders was that 'no one is one hundred per cent sure [...] how European police cooperation can or will develop in order to respond to [...] risks or threats' (Ferreira, 2011, p. 22). This suggests strongly that there is no homogenously cooperative thinking at the top of policing. So, although European strategic police leaders are bright enough intellectually to combat transnational criminality, and although there is recognition at the strategic policing level that forces face similar challenges, there is no apparent appetite for concerted mutual action. Trailing behind the entrepreneurial acuity of transnational criminals is one thing; it is something else again that the police may also be at a further disadvantage because of the inherently monolithic structure of pan-European cooperative organisation. Ironically, it may be that part of the problem for police forces and their strategic leaders is located within the very architecture that has been provided to help them deal with transnational and cross-border crime. One strategic police leader was enthusiastic about the bilateral levels of cooperation but sceptical of the 'value added' of EU institutions:

> '[There is] lots of cooperation at all levels, because partnership across borders and frontiers is the future – at least in Europe under Schengen. I'm not impressed with EU institutions, though the European Arrest Warrant (EAW) is good and very valuable to us. Other organisations just talk but do nothing. [...] Bilateral relations with police partners is the only way to get things done well.' (Interviewee A24)

Craig Paterson and Ed Pollock have noted that the creation of Europol in 1999 was a top-down political decision, not 'formed from the bottom up by police professionals', and they come to the perhaps inevitable conclusion that 'Europol is not an executive police force' (Paterson and Pollock, 2011, p. 137). It is relevant to observe that Europol was an EU creation, deriving from political will to coordinate policing responses. In that sense, it was not a 'bottom-up' initiative, but it is surely misleading to suggest that its creation took place in some kind of law enforcement vacuum? It seems at variance with the facts to suggest that Europol was conceived on paper in a strategic boardroom and that was that. In reality, the initiative for Europol was developed in close and comprehensive consultation with police forces, in the same way that the EU's 'Judicial Cooperation Unit' (Eurojust, created in 2002)[9] was developed in consultation with prosecuting lawyers and judges, or as the Joint Investigations Teams (formally created in 2000)[10] were developed in consultation with public prosecutors and investigative practitioners in European police forces.

Bilateral and cooperative structures

Ferreira (2011) points to many cooperative law enforcement structures in which the police played a pioneering role, ranging from protocols to interdict human trafficking through to 'legal instruments concerning asset confiscation or recovery' and cooperation to investigate and prosecute terrorism, drugs smuggling and cybercrime,[11] and concludes that 'the existing judicial cooperation instruments provide, at least, an important platform on which to build such cooperation' (Ferreira, 2011, pp. 23-25).

What happened subsequently to each of these initiatives might have been predicted, as inevitable in any 'top-down' process: formality, procedure and caution held sway over informal operational effectiveness. This was succinctly summarised as "simply noise" in a comment by a strategic police leader:

> 'I have real problems with [formal] international cooperation in Europe because I think much of what passes for multilateral cooperation is simply noise and doesn't mean much out there on the ground. [By contrast] there are plenty of *bilateral* successes, including joint drugs operations between the Dutch, Germans and Belgians and there was a good case a year ago between the French and the Italians over stolen luxury cars, but I can't think of a genuine pan-European prosecution in the last twenty years, I really can't.'
> (Interviewee B23; interviewee's emphasis)

---

[9] See www.eurojust.europa.eu

[10] See http://tinyurl.com/pwa6n95

[11] Ferreira also instances the many and various protocols and agreements (such as Schengen (1995), FRONTEX (2005), Prüm (2008), the Standing Committee on Operational Cooperation on Internal Security (COSI) (2009) and others) in a clear and intelligent statement of the evolution of 'legal instruments' to assist cross-border cooperation. See pp. 23-28 of his excellent 2011 article.

Europol and Eurojust are all very well, argue their critics,[12] but these 'supra-national' organisations have no teeth: they cannot insist on coordinated action or override an individual country's refusal to cooperate in any larger scheme or design. It is this dichotomy that appears to concern European strategic police leaders, operating as they do at the practical/utility end of policing, because they see what the European institutions are capable of doing, which is often sharply differentiated from what they actually achieve:

> 'I can do more with two emails in five minutes than Interpol could do with a 300 page dossier in a week. I wish though that the people who do Interpol's publicity worked for me; I'd be President in a month! Europol tries hard and is getting better at being relevant but it can't escape the fact that it is a political creation, not a police force.' (Interviewee M37)

The essential dichotomy in all of this, for police leaders, is that Europol has to persuade because it cannot direct; it relies on other law enforcement and security agencies, because it cannot investigate autonomously.[13] Ultimately, it is operationally impotent, because it cannot override national jurisdictions. This is where the 'hub and spokes' metaphor, which Europol itself supports in its literature,[14] gains resonance, and possibly, some credibility. Europol centralises intelligence searches and, uniquely, can access all European states for traces, links and data, which it can analyse. It can be the 'umbrella' that it seeks to be, when other nation states freely cooperate in, but are not necessarily subordinate to, its 'bigger picture' role. How do we know that this sometimes works and that Europol's claims to be the 'hub' are not merely hubris? The example instanced by the interviewees concerned a 'lone wolf' terrorist attack in Norway in 2011.

On 22 July 2011, Anders Breivik, a right-wing Norwegian extremist, exploded a bomb in Oslo, killing eight people, and then carried out a mass shooting of a further 69, mostly teenagers, in an island 'camp' (Utøya) near the capital. He subsequently claimed kinship with a number of right-wing groups elsewhere in Europe, and a

---

[12] Such as France; see Nadia Gerspacher's essay (2010); and van den Wyngaert's thoughtful article from 2004.

[13] Routine transnational crimes anyway; it has carved for itself a role in investigating international football match 'fixing'.

[14] See, for example, http://europoljsb.consilium.europa.eu/about.aspx and www. europol.europa.eu;

computer statement recovered from his hard drive suggested that he had formal membership of some as well.[15] A number of strategic police leaders remarked to us that Europol had moved quickly to coordinate information on right-wing movements across Europe, and was particularly alert to trace any supporters of Breivik and what he stood for and to ascertain whether such people posed a copycat or other political violence threat in their own country or elsewhere.[16] A comment from a Nordic region police leader may serve as an exemplar, though even here an innate scepticism is pervasive:

> 'Europol did a good job in coordinating responses and intelligence leads on right-wing groups in Europe in the wake of the bombing and shootings in Oslo by Breivik in July 2011 – but that's its strength, it isn't a 'super-cop' or a force above the state and it's silly to pretend that it is.' (Interviewee N98)

Another strategic police officer observed drily that while Europol was opening its operational centre, individual security services across Europe had already briefed their ministers (see also Interviewee BI 73 below). All the same, it was Europol's swift exchange of data, pursuit of intelligence leads and rapid compilation of threat assessments that earned it grudging accolades from normally sceptical strategic police leaders. Some police forces in Western Europe responded directly to Europol's requests, such as investigating Breivik's (exaggerated) claims that he had links with far-right organisations.[17] For all that, and no matter how effective Europol proved to be in the wake of this attack, it

---

[15] Good general summaries and analyses of Breivik's statements, before and during his trial, include Rosenberg (2011) and Cave (2012).

[16] As explained by Europol's Director, Rob Wainwright, in an interview: 'As soon as it happened, we opened our operational centre to connect the investigation with an international platform of counter terrorism analysts. It has taken a lot of people by surprise. We've been monitoring the right wing extremists in Europe for many years' (reported in the Brussels-based *Euobserver* and quoted in SETimes, 25 July 2011, www.setimes.com/cocoon/setimes/xhtml/en_GB/features/setimes/features/2011/07/25/feature-01

[17] See, for example, an article by Vikram Todd and Matthew Taylor entitled 'Scotland Yard called in over Breivik's claims he met "mentor" in UK', subtitled 'Europol ask for information because gunman wrote of visiting London for secret far-right gathering in 2002', *The Guardian*, 25 July 2011, www.guardian.co.uk/world/2011/jul/25/scotland-yard-gunman-mentor-uk

is an organisation that has an 'imposed' structure rather than an 'organic' one, and it was suggested by a number of the strategic police leaders that the 'organic' relationships are the ones that work first and fastest. One British Isles region strategic police leader, currently working in Europe, commented:

> 'I am sure Europol did an excellent job of coordinating intelligence on Breivik's network, but I can guarantee this work had already been done via the PWGT[18] and the Club of Berne before Europol had even called together its first meeting. Europol may well present information as fact, but I know that the Ministers of the Interior across Europe rely more on their own security services and their national coordinators for counter-terrorism investigations than they would on Europol.' (Interviewee BI 73)

The simple fact persists that an organisation that was the creation of the Council of Europe can coordinate intelligence products and act effectively in information-gathering, but because it has no jurisdictional command, it cannot lead a police investigation or mount an arrest operation. Inevitably then, it is always going to be, in BI 73's words, 'playing catch-up'. Back in 2002, Monica den Boer argued that organised crime itself was the catalyst that brought European police agencies together, and that crime successes induced cooperation between the agencies (den Boer, 2002a). This argument suggests pragmatism at the heart of law enforcement cooperation and that the joint working that followed was a result of the criminal threat. Yet while pragmatism explains bilateral cooperation in operational terms, it does not justify an assumption by the European Commission (EC) that the strategic solution to countering transnational organised crime would be multilateralism on the part of police and law enforcement agencies. Perhaps, as den Boer seems to argue, the siren call to multilateralism is one heard by politicians rather than by police officers?

Many of the strategic police leaders we spoke to were agreed that it was the political will to create 'pan-European' organisations that overtook their informal bilateral relationships, themselves predicated on simple but flexible operational necessity. This flexibility, argue strategic police leaders, which was the key to bilateral success, has not been a feature of the new organisations intended to make cooperation

---

[18]   Police Working Group on Terrorism.

coherent and systematic; instead there was more bureaucracy and greater delay. A Mediterranean strategic police leader remarked that:

> 'These bodies [Europol and others] have no direct contact with the ground and have difficulty in understanding cross-border crime as we know it.' (Interviewee M28)

The penalty for a more coherent, more inclusive but formalised structure seems to be a drop in the speed of response and this, in turn, suggests that in police operational situations, the organisations that are designed to coordinate are often unwieldy and slow to respond.[19] The EU itself has produced a number of protocols that encourage lateral cooperation, some of which have been effective (at least initially) and some of which have been allowed to lie and remain dormant. Examples include: the Data Retention Directive; the Prüm Treaty of 2008 (facilitating access to DNA records, fingerprints, and so on); the Visa Information System; and SIRENE (Supplementary Information Request at the National Entry). Member states do use many of these systems and processes, and others such as COSI (the Standing Committee on Operational Cooperation on Internal Security) and OLAF (the European Anti-Fraud Office) are developing well, because police officers can see an advantage in utilising them.[20] That is not the same as achieving multilateral cooperation across the EU, since police forces will only access such systems on an 'as need arises' basis. To be fair, that is what the systems themselves were designed for, not to promote geopolitically strategic integration between disparate police forces. A Mediterranean region police leader rather mischievously suggested that, in his experience, international cooperation is of three kinds:

> '1) Bland, superficial, ceremonial and vapid
>
> 2) Strong, strategic, with a community of interests
>
> 3) Political, necessary, beleaguered' (Interviewee M15)

---

[19] In Europol's case, it may be of point that 'The Europol Management Board is staffed with Interior Ministry officials with one representative from every participating member state' (http://tinyurl.com/l5jk4w9), which may not be conducive to a police-focused responsiveness nor to an understanding of the imperative of speed in police operations.

[20] See, for example, entries for the Directorate-General, http://tinyurl.com/kyf46n9

He went on to observe that:

> 'I of course prefer 2), but all cooperation is probably a blend of all three and it is really a question of which one dominates. Interpol perfectly fulfils the first kind, Europol falls between 1) and 2) and bilateral relations between forces are a blend of 2) and 3). You seldom get 2) alone, but when you do it is professionally highly satisfying. Of my "collegiate nations", I think Germany and the UK are often 3), France and Greece almost always 1) and The Netherlands, Norway and Poland often in or predominantly 2).' (Interviewee M15)

However, there appears to be a reluctance among strategic police leaders themselves to promote international cooperation at the strategic level. Andreas and Nadelmann thought that policing practices are normally so much a part of a nation's sense of sovereign independence, that they can seem in need of protection more than other parts of a state's international relations (Andreas and Nadelmann, 2006, pp. 10-11). There can be an element of inherent confusion in some of the European initiatives on international organised crime, some of which is traceable to different jurisdictions or different legislative emphases (Caparini and Marenin, 2004), even to different priorities for framing criminal law. A persistent inhibitor appears to be a form of nationalism, or, more precisely, a protective self-interest that is most often expressed in nationalistic terms. In some countries, the powerful police unions pose obstacles to reform. Understanding this parochialism, den Boer observed that police organisations were 'reluctant players' in international cooperative ventures, constrained by national politics and conscious of their amateur status in any field but policing (den Boer, 2010, p. 48).

Putting your country first: the police and 'national protectionism'

It should not surprise us that police forces entering the international cooperative arena take considerable direction from their political leaders; to do otherwise would risk running contrary to a country's 'on-message' position on a given issue. However, den Boer goes on to suggest that the reluctance of European strategic police leaders to play in the international arena is more often the product of a defensive mindset than of a political 'line-to-take'. To some extent, this mindset is confirmed in research undertaken by Laure Guille, who identifies a 'vicious circle' that can only be changed if member states focus on the 'crime issue' rather than on 'a strong nationalist vision' (Guille, 2010a, p. 36). A Nordic strategic police leader substantially agrees, noting that:

> 'Liaison is time consuming of course and because direct experience of international cooperation is so scarce, it creates unease among police officers when crimes occur that are not "local".' (Interviewee N40)

Ferreira, observing the responses of strategic police leaders at CEPOL's TOPSPOC seminars, commented:

> European police cooperation will remain limited to what is best for national interests – even when a national interest is the worst outcome for other States or to the European Union as a whole. Senior police officers are and will remain key players, but until tackling transnational risks or threats becomes essential for winning *national* favourable appraisal and recognition, it is difficult to blame them for not doing this more often. (Ferreira, 2011, p. 29; our emphasis)

Another British Isles region police leader, based in Europe, argued thoughtfully that political science does not recognise the concept of the 'supra-state' and that, in fact, the EU itself is in transition to become a kind of 'mega nation-state' but that, until it could demonstrate that it controlled 'unified force' to impose its will, the EU could not be regarded as such an entity, no matter what the trappings that surround it:

> 'Now the EU has many of the characteristics of a nation-state – defined territory, legislative body, currency etc, but it lacks the Weberian embodiment of "force", as represented by the police and army, and therefore is not yet a nation-state. And until it is, member states will defend their territory through bilateral agreements, especially in the field of terrorism.' (Interviewee BI 73)

This suggests that, along with other strategic police leaders, BI 73 believes that any sense of the EU as an operative body in law enforcement will not become fact until its agencies (Europol, Eurojust) have independent power and can subordinate individual member states to their overarching policing, political and jurisprudential wills.

James Sheptycki argued 20 years ago that 'Europe urgently requires a security blanket. What appears to be emerging is a patchwork quilt of agencies' (Sheptycki, 1995, p. 613). He went on to cite Lode van Outrive as telling the European Parliament in 1994 that 'we do not have the political, legal and procedural structures we would need for an operational European federal police force' (Sheptycki, 1995, p. 614).

Not much development has occurred in this respect; so little in fact that in 2010, Verhage et al could argue that 'supranational police cooperation continues to be highly dependent on national circumstances and cultures', ironically citing Sheptycki's 1995 argument that there is 'diversity and fragmentation' as a result (Verhage et al, 2010, p. 7). What seems to be happening as a result of Europe's inability to create a 'supranational police force' is that strategic police leaders have become very cautious about grand schemes of international cooperation. A strategic police leader commented on this caution, arguing that:

> 'The problem with international cooperation is that often the most stereotyped national characteristics emerge and you have to aim off for a kind of "national protectionism" where simple self-interest rules. The Dutch have been burned this way in the EU a time or two, especially when they gallantly subordinated their own national interest to the greater EU good and got pissed on. They don't do it now and that's why.' (Interviewee B75)

An Alpine region strategic police leader recognised the way in which past history can sometimes modulate current approaches, but asserted that there is no alternative to trying to make international cooperation work:

> 'I find international cooperation urgently necessary. It is almost a platitude that transnational crime entails properly organised police cooperation. However, internal security is still one of the bastions of the nation state in Europe, and we have to be alert to implicit messages that we may send without meaning to. But there is no alternative to international cooperation against international crime, and it is necessary that I find ways to work with my counterparts in other countries, whatever the resonances.' (Interviewee A57)

There are many examples where bilateral and trilateral investigations are effective and well conducted (Spain and France on dismantling drugs networks; the UK and the Netherlands on people-trafficking from Bulgaria; trilateral cooperation between Belgium, the Netherlands and Germany in the Meuse/Rhine Region; and Operation 'Java' in 2010 that coordinated police forces from France, Italy, Germany, Austria, Switzerland and Spain against Georgian organised crime groups).[21] What seems evident, though, is that police forces prefer to evolve their own ways of working, rather than have protocols imposed on them (this was certainly the case in the joint UK/Netherlands investigation team; see Schalken and Pronk, 2002; and Kapplinghaus, 2006, p. 32). What is more, forces do it on a smallish scale, regionally or geographically focused; involving, at most, four or five national jurisdictions, rather than the huge 'cross-Europe twenty-eight member-state mutualism', which is dreamed of in the political stratosphere of the EU (Santiago, 2000).

A larger and more intractable problem can often be found in one country's reluctance to accept another state's priorities as its own. The UK found 'common ground' with Europe quite difficult during the late 1980s and early 1990s, when a terrorist group, the Provisional Irish Republican Army (PIRA) was particularly active on the UK mainland and also operating against British armed forces personnel in Europe (NATO HQ in Brussels; British Army of the Rhine and Royal Air Force bases in Germany; British military garrison in Gibraltar). It proved a challenge for the British to interest European countries in joint interdiction or joint surveillance. This may have been simply because other countries did not share the UK's sense of urgency about PIRA's threat (see, for example, Jongman, 1992; Chaliand, 2007, p. 251), or they thought it a specifically British problem rather than a European one. It is perhaps a noteworthy irony that a debate in Britain in 2013 about withdrawal from the EU police mechanisms provoked an impassioned plea to remain from Europol's (British) director.[22] However, there is no tangible evidence that the chimera of 'mutualism' has become any more real: few nation states did more than register the facts of Brevik's attacks in Norway in 2011, and assure themselves that the likelihood of copybook attacks in their own

---

[21] See Soeters et al (1995) and Lemieux (2010); see also http://tinyurl.com/mrgoqut for an account of joint interdiction operations.

[22] See O'Neill, S. (2013), Director warns of 'unmitigated disaster' if Britain quits Europol, *The Times*, 2 October, p. 2. Rob Wainwright's comments were cited in note 16 above.

jurisdictions were low, before going back to their everyday business. Economic migrants heading for Britain in 2014 have soured some cross-border policing arrangements between England and France at Calais, and politically between France and Italy/Greece (where the migrants are 'landed' in Europe). This example of a 'spat' suggests that national interests continue to override the larger European notion of being open to refugees.

Perhaps the most that can be hoped for when there is such a conflict of priorities is that some space is found to accommodate each nation's requirements (Guille, 2010a), but that is going to be infinitely easier and simpler between two or three cooperating countries than between many. A strategic police leader was sceptical that multilateral cooperation across Europe was feasible at all:

> 'Getting 27 countries to sing in tune is hopeless. They are in 27 different keys and have 27 different conductors – and they are all performing different songs.' (Interviewee A7)[23]

Bilateralism rules OK?

Nadia Gerspacher, researching 'shifts in cooperative behaviour' between France and Europol, suggests that a 'coalition of interests' might be more effective than legalistic protocols, and that a 'pooling of resources across borders' might start to match the 'deep pockets' of criminals operating transnationally (Gerspacher, 2010, p. 159). In a perceptive article, Vito Breda argued that two prior conditions are required for a shared criminal law on this scale: the first is that there is some sort of mandate arising from public consultation for the subordination of its national law to international law; and the second is that any constitution embracing '*corpus juris criminalis*' takes account of divergence and difference between member states (see Breda's 'theory of constitutional multinationalism', 2006). Eduardo Ferreira notes judiciously that:

> 'It is obvious that international conventions or protocols, and EU directives or decisions, are not immediately and automatically included in the national legal frameworks and that they certainly do not enhance good police and judicial international cooperation practices.' (Ferreira, 2011, p. 25)

---

[23] The interview took place before Croatia joined the EU in July 2013.

If such structures do not enter national law in member states – as is *de rigueur* with the European Convention on Human Rights – then it should not surprise us that such 'conventions or protocols' remain aspirational or in the realms of the merely theoretical. This notion of sharing criminal laws, though self-evidently a precursor to the EU's becoming a Weberian 'nation-state' with its own federal police force (Aden, 2001; Schalken and Pronk, 2002), may remain continually elusive, because drawing up a constitution (embodying Europe-wide criminal law) on such broad grounds, however closely public and legal opinion is sampled, may end up pleasing no one and prove unworkable. It also begs the question how the popular will can be convincingly expressed when there is no current machinery for pan-European plebiscites and, indeed, when there is neither political will nor money to pay for them (Walsh et al, 2002). In other words, it seems clear that there is a requirement for some kind of embracing cooperative framework, allied to pan-European law and mechanisms for coordination, but as yet there is no agreed means to make it happen.

It is, however, untenable for European member states to ignore the increasingly international dimensions of crime and criminality, nor is it now acceptable for one of them to act unilaterally and without regard to impact elsewhere. Two observers of European policing, Cyrille Fijnaut and Toine Spapens, are uncompromising in their declaration that it is now 'impossible' for one European country to act against transnational criminality without impacting on another state, adding that the EU is determined to strengthen 'operational police and judicial cooperation between member states' to prioritise actions against 'terrorism, human trafficking, the drugs trade, the arms trade and fraud' (Fijnaut and Spapens, 2010, p. 121). This view was echoed by a strategic police leader, who remarked:

> 'I think it's important to say that at the strategic level in policing, and certainly in Europe itself, there is no chance of getting the job done without international cooperation. From drugs to human trafficking, and from terrorism to internet fraud, most organised crime is international and so the police have to be as outward-looking [as the criminal].' (Interviewee B103)

Another strategic police leader commented wryly that it was not so much the need to investigate and disrupt international criminals that was the problem, but more the very human possibility of lacking common interest or understanding:

'The usual problems are in shared understandings: cultures differ and attitudes can do so too, such as in the understanding of restorative justice: what I think of as "restorative" could be interpreted by another in a different culture as either very weak or very tough, depending on the shared understanding of the concept.' (Interviewee M39)

However, the realpolitik of this is that the EU at the very top can be as politically resolute as it likes; if strategic police leaders do not see that multilateral cooperation will impact on their bottom line of crimes investigated and deliver outcomes of 'brought to justice', *and* that there is a national willingness to make this happen and pay for it, then the corollary will be that they won't bother. As a strategic police leader observed, the highly strategic, pan-European multilateral element has yet to be achieved, while at ground level, pragmatic bilateral relationships are alive and well:

'International criminal law, allowing a common investigation and prosecution route across Europe, is still a chimera – especially as this needs political will rather than a police initiative to set up. But we are well down the road in terms of protocols for "hot pursuit" and there are some instances already of jointly-staffed desks which facilitate cross border liaison.' (Interviewee M16)

It does not take a crystal ball to see that police forces will continue to default to pragmatic, cost-effective, bilateral cooperation for specific operational purposes (picking up 'the bloody phone'), while the multilateral, strategic, cooperative but insubstantial ideal lingers uneasily and ghost-like somewhere in the background, creating what Ferret calls a 'problematic tension' (Ferret, 2004). The reluctance of the police to engage with EU multilateralism seems only partially a product of their reluctance to surrender control operationally and strategically. Much more, it is unease about large concepts and apparent threats to autonomy, compounded to a degree by nationalism and defensiveness, as well as an acute sense that surrendering local police control for pan-European gestures will ultimately be futile if there is no federal police force to run with the problem. We might conclude that only when the external criminal threat is so persistent, overwhelming and impactive as to presage imminent disaster, will the police cede their default parochialism. As van Buuren comments in his analysis of bureaucracy in the European Police Chiefs' Task Force: 'it appears that national structures always prevail' (van Buuren, 2012).

SIX

The challenges facing European policing today

'The problems here are what they've always been: dodgy businesses cutting corners, criminal entrepreneurs making use of our liberal laws on trade, global companies thinking we'll do anything for a few Euros, and being a transit point for international trafficking of all kinds. That's reflected globally and internationally, which is where I come in because my job is to plan the criminal interdiction upstream of the country and that means thinking ahead and beyond the purely nationalistic. Sometimes it's hard, and people get quite scared at going out on a limb, but policing properly is about assessing risk properly and that's what our work is in the international sphere: it's a form of risk management. I have to say that not many of us are any good at it because we keep thinking too much inside our own narrow national concerns. The time will have to come when we think together rather than just cooperatively.' (Interviewee BI 69)

Introduction

Understanding the challenges facing policing is usually hedged about with caution, given the potential for unforeseen developments to change the basis of any analysis. This chapter is no exception to this general observation. Some expectations about challenges to policing may not materialise at all (Crawford, 2002), some may mutate into something altogether more sinister (Europol, 2011),[1] and a few may make the impact predicted for them (Edwards and Gill, 2003).

The states that make up the regions of Europe interpret such 'hard' policing challenges differently, depending on what social, economic, political, historical or national compound lens they look through: what is a jurisdictional problem in Latvia may not be in Greece. Aspects of illegal trafficking that impact heavily on the Slovenian

---

[1] See, for example: Europol (2011), *The Future of Organised Crime; Challenges and Recommended Actions*, http://tinyurl.com/lp9yh4y

police (smuggling routes through the high mountain passes) may barely register with Portugal's gendarmerie. Stolen vehicles may be a problem for the Belgians, but the Slovak police are more preoccupied with drug smuggling. To try to bring coherence to this very disparate, and often fragmented, picture of the challenges facing Europe's police forces, sometimes complicated by the remits and approaches of the law enforcement agencies involved, we group the views of strategic police leaders thematically, we analyse their proposed solutions and we identify some of the likely barriers to potential success.

Again, we must warn that none of this is definitive: we are dealing with the mutable perceptions of strategic police leaders, set against political, economic and social flux in their own countries and regions, and modulated through their individual experiences and prejudices. 'Rich detail' doesn't often give neat criminological solutions to challenges: rather it gives one a sense of how bewildering, frustrating or exhilarating it feels to be the strategic police leader tasked to try to meet those challenges.

Contemporary European police cooperation

Peter Andreas and Ethan Nadelmann (2006) argue that the 'convergence of crime control' in Europe is nothing short of 'remarkable', given the large number of states and the intense and complex 'transnational interactions' within Europe. Despite the distance already travelled in convergence, police cooperation is persistently seen as a problem by nearly all the leaders who were questioned. Chapter Five addressed this in relation to supranational institutions and Europe's bilateral and multilateral structures, but it is important to acknowledge here that the perceptions of poor cooperation can also be directly related to lack of success against criminal groups. If criminals get away from the operation designed to catch them, it is very human for the agencies to start blaming each other; goodwill between allies can be a fragile thing.[2] Respondents were very clear that less bureaucracy and more harmonised principles are keys to achieving greater success at a federal level. Some officers pointed to politicians as barriers to improvement and others cited the implementation of human rights in member states' law as precedent for a similar, federally applied criminal law. A Nordic strategic police leader noted that:

---

[2]   As evidenced between, say, France and Britain in the Second World War, or between the US and Germany over the interception of Angela Merkel's private phone calls in 2014.

'The real challenge is going to be getting all the EU countries to sign up to an overarching criminal legislation that we can all follow – a criminal law equivalent of Human Rights – but that is still some years away, I think. Meanwhile, many criminals are not investigated or tracked because my law doesn't work in this other country and this other country's law doesn't work in mine.' (Interviewee N9)

A Benelux region police leader thought that too often the temptation was to 'displace' a crime problem to an adjacent country:

'Disruption is often as effective as prosecution, though I know from colleagues in other countries that one merely displaces the problem (like drug smuggling). We also need to get organised on a federal basis for the pursuit and investigation of the bigger criminals and crimes.' (Interviewee B103)

This view is echoed by a Mediterranean strategic leader, who agreed that the problem was a lack of 'pan-European' jurisdiction:

'Drugs, organised crime and cybercrime – but more important even than these serious manifestations of crime – is the absence of international jurisdiction to deal with crime on a pan-European level. We urgently need an international criminal law applied to all member states so that we can take coordinated action against criminals. Drugs smuggling routes are a case in point, especially Heroin routes from Turkey to the rest of Europe. We could deal these a fatal blow if we had a) the political will and b) a common criminal law.' (Interviewee M15)

Although pessimistic about the likelihood of implementing 'a common criminal law' in the near future, many officers saw legal reform as fundamental in developing effective responses against cross-border and organised crime, a form of criminality that was most regularly quoted as the most significant challenge to the police. A strategic police leader from the Mediterranean region, acknowledging the temptation for the police to seek what works rather than what is permitted by law, expressed it like this:

'The philosophical difficulty is that of keeping the balance between individual liberty and society's security and safety. In any attempt to engage with organised crime or with terrorism, it is tempting to do what is expedient rather than what is lawful, and public support for what you do is vital.' (Interviewee M12)

An Alpine region officer (Interviewee A7) refers below to the absence of a 'world policeman' and the need for flexibility among national police services. The vested interest of the US as a 'global policeman' was mentioned by a minority of respondents questioned; the inconsistency of interests and priorities between the US and Europe was further seen as an underlying problem (Smith, 2013). Interestingly, the national interests of countries within Europe are also cited as a barrier to success, as problems can be displaced to the benefit of one nation over another or priorities between countries can be very different:

'The centre to all this is that there is no "world policeman" and I don't think there is likely to be. The UN tries to be, and so do the Americans, but I don't think that they succeed. Criminals are clever, they know what they have to do, they are loose groups which are hard to enter and hard to detect. The international problem is that the police are slow in getting clever like the criminals, slow at knowing what to do to fight crime, and we are all stopped from changing by two things: we are too nationalist and we are too bureaucratic to be able to respond with flexibility to threats.' (Interviewee A7)

In the absence of a strong but flexible law enforcement structure that can match the 'loose' criminal groups, there are examples of good local partnerships between neighbouring countries, but even this has limitations depending on national interests:

'International crime is rising in importance because of the weakness in our police investigation and because we do not have coordination of operations. It takes much effort and really hard negotiation – I can say 'strenuous' – to persuade states to cooperate over a long geography. Our multiple cooperation along the coastline is very good, but that is because we all buy into it. Relations with countries which do not have such a sharing coast is hard: how do you persuade countries like Latvia or Italy to cooperate against people trafficking, if the routes only just touch them and the crime itself is not a difficult end problem?' (Interviewee M92)

National priorities and cooperation between bordering nations can be fluid and subject to change, requiring a similar response by police services (see Chapter Five). Although politicians are often blamed in responses from interviewees for not providing resources, infrastructure or legal frameworks for the police, these themes are very much aligned to issues relating to sovereignty – national or international perspectives that are sensitive issues for populations and therefore for politicians seeking election. While from a police officer's perspective 'what needs to be done' might seem straightforward in terms of developing a generic criminal law across Europe, in practice it is a highly complex challenge. The police may cite human rights principles as an example that any federal criminal law could follow, but counterarguments would cite pan-Europeanism itself as a debilitating or inhibiting factor.

A Balkans strategic police leader believed that with some effort, such a '*corpus juris*' that enables international police cooperation within Europe, was at least possible:

> 'Our laws are not like your laws, and both of us have laws that are not the same as those in the USA, so it will be very hard to make one law for everyone. But we did it with human rights, so we might do it for drugs, or paedophiles and I hope for that day. A single law which is the same everywhere and applied everywhere will be bad for the criminal because nowhere he will be safe, and this is not too hard to do, is it? We must try.' (Interviewee Ba2)

Ben Bowling and James Sheptycki (2012) critique the 'European transnational state-system' in the context of police operations and evolving powers. They argue that the European Arrest Warrant (EAW) has provided a streamlined approach to extradition of criminals, while acknowledging the need for recognition of 'dual criminality'[3] in the states involved in the EAW request. However, citing 'Fair Trials International', Bowling and Sheptycki also argue that the EAW has been used disproportionately for minor offences, 'dated' crimes and

---

[3]   That is, the crime must be considered a crime in both the requesting and receiving jurisdictions.

evidence obtained by brutality. They summarise their argument like this:

> 'In Europe we see [a] police subculture adapting legal rules and shaping enforcement jurisdiction to suit operational requirements. In rather undemocratic ways police have decisively shaped EU regional state systems.' (Bowling and Sheptycki, 2012, p. 46)

Therefore, while some politicians might be reluctant to give up the autonomous and considerable powers of the nation state in favour of a European-wide federal system, police discretion and the adaptation of rules are also important considerations in any reforms to legislation and police powers in a European context. Bureaucracy, legislation and police services predominantly set up to reflect fairly narrow national interests are the principal strategic barriers identified by police leaders in our research. Although solutions in the form of harmonisation of laws and procedures were almost routinely suggested by them, strategic police leaders' concerns about how policing frameworks have evolved and become operationalised have been raised with us. It is dealing with this impasse that appears (from the respondents' perspective) to be key to the success of various forms of organised crimes and to the ability of the police across Europe to deal more effectively with such threats.

One Alpine region strategic police leader identified the drawbacks to a slicker criminal justice system, or at least to 'integrated police services', as residing within police procedures, those time-hallowed formal activities that *have* to be followed, sometimes at the expense of common sense. The interviewee uses the standard police response to domestic violence as an example of the often costive effect of procedural rote on police thinking:

> 'The police across Europe really have a most inefficient way of dealing with criminal evidence – a legacy of the ink-and-paper 1950s which does not sit at all well in the digital age. The demand for integrated police services responding to a first incident is high, but the response is piecemeal and fragmented – not joined-up at all. Domestic violence is a good example of this fragmentation, where successive processes take too long, are lugubrious and outmoded, and desperately inefficient. The victim is visited by different specialists and interviewers, has to tell the same story over and over and the processes to stop repetition of the violence

are ineffectual. This too often leads to the victim or injured party refusing to continue with the case, and withdrawing evidence.' (Interviewee A17)

The perspective of interviewees in a majority of cases (across all regions) was that the police were losing the war against crime and that the gap between criminality and police interdiction was widening. The dominant view was that officers did not have the legal tools or resources to tackle organised crime effectively. Les Johnston (2000: 180) described 'optimal policing' as: '... neither quantitatively excessive[4] nor qualitatively invasive[5] [but] which satisfies the conditions of public accountability, effectiveness and justice for all'. If these ideals are to be satisfied, it is not only important to provide an effective framework for law enforcement, but also to ensure that legitimacy is maintained through appropriate accountability, proportionality and transparency of the police and their operations.

What are the major challenges facing policing?

We asked our respondents: What do you think are the major challenges facing policing?

While inevitably this involved some future forecasting (which we deal with in more detail in Chapter Seven), the majority cited what an Alpine Region strategic leader characterised as 'the usual core of problems' (Interviewee A61) to do with international organised crime: *terrorism*, *drugs* importation and use, *trafficking* for sex and other forms of trafficking, and *money laundering*.

Interestingly, most made little distinction between the challenges they faced in their own countries and those they faced internationally, with the exception of a parochial focus on *police reform*. A large number suggested the widespread need for such reform, which had to include the resolution of questions about police legitimacy and accountability, and ways in which to restore trust in the police.

---

[4]   To the detriment of alternative social values and objectives.
[5]   To the detriment of public freedoms.

A separate concern was *cybercrime* and a number of respondents indicated *budget constraints* and funding cuts as significant.

The major category, though, concerned *social issues* and what many saw as social breakdown; 'a feral world' (Interviewee C68) 'of social upheaval' (Interviewee BI 97), which includes public order issues and crimes of violence.

Finally, there were a number of calls for a pan-European criminal jurisdiction (the '*corpus juris criminalis*') to tackle transnational organised crime within the EU.

The statistics[6] are shown in Table 6.1.

We propose now to discuss some of these issues in more detail (others are considered in Chapter Seven).

Table 6.1: Themes identified as challenges to policing now

Topic	Numbers
The 'usual core of problems' of which:	**68**
terrorism	11
drugs	14
sex and other trafficking	20
transnational organised crime	23
Cybercrime	**48**
Police reform	**78**
dominant among which were:	
legitimacy	12
trust	15
budget constraints	19
Calls for 'corpus juris'	**23**
Social tensions	**83**
dominant among which were:	
public order issues	17
violent crime	20

NB: The numbers represent proportional values, since respondents included several categories in their replies

---

[6] Note that respondents considered a number of options in response to this question, so there are no percentages, only 'absolute' numbers.

Police structures and legitimacy

In the previous section, the challenges of global enforcement were discussed in the context of respondents' views focusing on reduced bureaucracy and federal legal reform to improve the effectiveness of policing transnational crime. The challenge of maintaining legitimacy while at the same time changing police structures remains an important but fraught challenge to Europe's young democracies. One Central Europe region police leader noted that the challenge is one of credibility:

> 'The biggest problem for us is to show that we respect human rights. Crime is inherent here (it was almost the only thing we exported under the communists) and we were heavily criticised last fall for being a "police state". We're not – that was what it was like twenty or thirty years ago – but we do have a long way to go to prove that we are as good as any other EU country.' (Interviewee C58)

Substantial police reform does not only reflect changes in political systems, but attempts to modernise and improve police services have to be integral to such effort. Structural reforms of the police include the gradual nationalisation of police responses to organised crime (examples include the creation of the National Crime Agency in the United Kingdom and, in 2012-13, the wholesale reorganisation of the Police Service in the Netherlands), and these changes reflect governments' views about police reform in an increasingly globalised and economic context. These changes occur in the context of budget cuts and increasing competition from multinational 'private security' companies winning increasing numbers of government contracts.

Achieving legitimacy on a pan-European basis is therefore likely to be difficult in the context of what some have called the 'hollowing out' of the state and 'pluralisation' of policing (Crawford, 2002). However, interviewees like this strategic police leader from Central Europe also pointed to the importance of legitimacy within their own national boundaries:

> 'Inside my country it is the challenge to be a democratic police. We must change the belief that we are repressive and we must do this by reaching out to the people and trying to gain their trust. I find it hard to convince my policemen, and even harder to convince the people, but

> this is the main mission for us now and for at least another five years I think.' (Interviewee C69)

This comment reflects change to a more democratised policing system, predicated on legitimacy of function and responsiveness to the rule of law, emphasising the importance of public trust in an organisation in transition from a previously authoritarian and unaccountable policing model. While respondents from Central European countries were positive about democratic reform and appeared to value the importance of public legitimacy, there was greater emphasis on the challenge of convincing populations (and some police colleagues) that the police were no longer repressive but were now entirely citizen-focused. This anxiety was particularly prominent among officers in Central Europe, more so than any other geographical region. Some respondents in other regions included public legitimacy as an important challenge or priority for the police, but these were only in a minority of cases.

The Baltic region also contains countries that have changed to a more democratic mode of governance. Interestingly, police officers here focused more on how to tackle crime effectively within a democratic framework, rather than discussing public legitimacy. (The number of respondents in this group, for obvious reasons, was significantly lower.)

> 'Policing is really very simple; it's the law and powers to apply the law that are fraught and complex. The major challenge is to find ways through in a democratic and accountable way to effective policing, and that begins (and ends) with effective police leadership.' (Interviewee Ba5)

Interviewee Ba 5 concurs with the views of other interviewees on the obstacles created by different jurisdictions between countries, but this strategic police leader also emphasises the importance of accountability. Accountability is important for the public police because, as we noted earlier, the 'hollowing out' of the state and increasing pluralisation of policing provision present a serious challenge to reformers who want to establish a viable system of accountability across a wide range of different 'police' providers (Johnston and Stenning, 2010). Although respondents from the British Isles and the Alpine regions mentioned privatisation as a concerning factor in terms of accountability, other regions did not raise this issue as a challenge for the future. Most regions mentioned the importance of the legitimacy of the public police.

The privatisation of security and 'policing'

Police legitimacy is important for public confidence, but questions persist around how sustainable legitimacy can be achieved in the face of continued change and pluralisation. The 'privatisation of policing', as governments tender for services with multinational companies, and as the latter progressively take over roles previously delivered by the public police, is progressive and seemingly implacable in some jurisdictions. Concern has surfaced about large companies becoming monopolies, not subjected to the rigorous frameworks of accountability common to public policing. Equal concern has been expressed about governments becoming overreliant on commercial monopolies in key areas of security (van Steden and Sarre, 2007). This reliance goes further than policing, because contracts have been awarded to run probation services, prisons and child protection services. This 'creeping privatisation'[7] of security and 'policing' occurs in spite of recurrent scandals relating to Secro, Securitas and G4S[8] and questions about whether such organisations have appropriate governance. The evidence for ineptitude and poor standards is growing, with examples ranging from charging the UK government for 3,000 tags on 'phantom' offenders, to the non-renewal of a contract with the European Parliament because the security company concerned had been 'deeply complicit with Israeli violations of international law' (European Coordination of Committees and Associations for Palestine [ECCP] chairperson Pierre Galand, 2012).

Nonetheless, government contracts across Europe continue to be awarded.[9] Growing concern in some public policing circles is reflected in comments by our interviewees, one of whom noted the ubiquity of the challenges of privatisation to conventional policing:

---

[7] First used in 1994 in comments in the UK about outsourcing in the Health Service, but rapidly adopted by commentators and journalists across Europe to describe the exponential growth in 'private' policing provision; see http://tinyurl.com/l2bd9qs; and also Button, 2012.

[8] Such as those for the Olympics in London in 2012, when G4S admitted that it had not recruited enough people to handle security at the Games and the government had to call in the military to assist.

[9] Not only Europe, of course. A number of 'private security' scandals are global, including one in South Africa, where a contract to run a prison had to be revoked because of the company's failure to sustain security, and another which provided a security fence along the US/Mexican border that continually malfunctioned (see Busch and Givens, 2012).

'If we don't do it, the private sector will and we all know how unaccountable [private security] organisations are (and how incompetent and venal). Do we really want our security provided by them? I hope not.' (Interviewee BI 85)

Another British Isles region police leader suggested that the bifurcation between public and private policing went even deeper than 'creeping privatisation', and that:

'[...] as a society – even as a European society – we need to decide what we want policing to be and what it should consist of. Security is increasingly provided on a private basis, surveillance is as much commercial as public, the police are expected to do more and more with smaller budgets and the natural default for people is to augment shortfalls by buying in things like a uniformed presence or patrols in neighbourhoods. If we don't supply a perceived deficit, rich people will buy it and the poor will continue to be victims as a result of our inadequacy.' (Interviewee BI 100)

Strategic police leaders from the British Isles were particularly vocal about the increasing privatisation of policing. The regular failures of some private sector organisations in the region reflect concerns about which areas of public service should be subject to bids from commercial interests and which areas are too important to be left to the market economy (Brodeur, 1998).[10] Globalisation lends itself to mass privatisation of public services, but national (and international) security is important for stability, reassurance and the demonstration of public legitimacy in the police. The problem with increasing pluralisation is that citizens are becoming confused about which services are responsible for which key areas and how those responsible for the provision of such services are to be held to account if things go wrong (Holmqvist, 2005). Despite some fundamental failings on the part of commercial security providers – ranging from insufficient presence at the London Olympics through to evidence of substantially overcharging the state for work not completed – threats of a ban on awarding further contracts to individual private providers do not appear to have materialised.

---

[10] The US has consigned 85% of its security to the private supplier (Busch and Givens, 2012).

While national public police structures across Europe are changing (and causing concern to some of our respondents), the pluralisation of policing services is set to continue. The strategic leaders in this research have emphasised the importance of police legitimacy as a challenge, but the ability of public police services to maintain and increase public confidence in them is likely to be much more challenging (Kääriäinen, 2007). Few police forces can aspire to the 97% public satisfaction enjoyed by the Finnish Police; even though Finland has a relatively low crime rate.[11] How much more important it is, then, to ensure the legitimacy/accountability of commercial providers of 'security' and 'private policing'.

There is little doubt that the role of private policing providers vis-à-vis the public police will continue to be discussed, at least by the police and by academic commentators, if not by commercial 'security' companies themselves and the national governments that use them (Brodeur, 1998; Johnston, 2005; Button, 2012). At the same time, policing models across Europe that explicitly accommodate private policing delivered by multinational companies will probably develop further. And you can see why: restricted by budget, coping with cuts, 'firefighting' a number of criminal issues, the public police appear to be stretched very thinly on the ground. The private security companies offer (gated) community safety, patrol, visibility and reassurance – all at a price, of course. The boom in the provision of private policing has at least as much to do with people's preparedness to pay for a 'perpetual' security presence as it has to do with governmental-level contracts.[12]

Criminal threats and challenges

Responses from strategic police leaders described organised crime as a serious problem and a priority for them when considering challenges within policing. Almost all respondents referred to 'organised' crime followed by more detail in relation to the *type* of organised crime (and

---

[11] These are the annual findings of the *European Social Survey* (ESS), in which 'data were compiled from a total of 39,000 face-to-face interviews across 20 countries'; see a February 2012 article by the Economic and Social Research Council entitled 'How Europeans trust courts and the police'(http://tinyurl.com/ms7t9hu). See also Kääriäinen (2007).

[12] The European Parliament noted in 2011 that 'the European Union (EU) and its member states are increasingly relying on private contractors in multilateral operations' (see http://tinyurl.com/mmmsdel), while evidence of community and individual use of 'private policing' similarly shows an increase (Tsifakis, 2012).

we look at some of these types in more detail Chapter Seven). Within these views, respondents denote organised crime activity as human trafficking, illegal drugs distribution, terrorism and, to a lesser extent, illegal arms trafficking and the sex trade. Beyond the organised crime emphasis, cybercrime and fraud were also considered significant threats.

Maggy Lee (2011, p. 88) observes that transnational organised crime networks exploit gaps in countries with 'weak-states', 'states in transition' or 'capacity gaps'; thereby 'neutralising the state through corruption'. Although those approached in our research identified problems in dealing with trafficking of various sorts, the role of 'public service corruption' was raised on only a few occasions. We acknowledge that persuading respondents through an interview or a questionnaire to discuss police or political corruption in any significant detail is unrealistic, and the topic was not part of our prepreared questions. We cannot therefore quantify how wide-ranging such problems are; nonetheless, the accounts given below illustrate that some problems do exist and we should mention them.

First, this police leader from the Mediterranean region, when asked what challenges faced the police, seemed to think that corruption of public service by crime is endemic:

> 'Corruption in public service and politics, drugs and internet crime, I think. These are common to all countries. Perhaps "trafficking in illicit goods and services" is the better way to describe the problem we all face?' (Interviewee M56)

A similar observation of the concatenation of crime with corruption was made by a strategic police leader from the Central Europe region, who noted that corruption 'of state officials' and 'trust [in] the police' were possibly two sides of the same coin:

> 'We face the same threats internally as externally from organised crime and corruption of the state officials, the smuggling of drugs happens inside and outside my country. That means that we should be aware of how drugs come in and if they transit our territory, as well as looking at disruptive migration, movements of terrorists and the trafficking routes.' (Interviewee C105)

Another officer echoed concern at the corrupting power of transnational organised crime:

'[...] organised crime in all its manifestations is our major current and future worry. Organised criminals make colossal profits, they can suborn governments and bribe officials, they can buy silence and procure the services of just about anyone from accountants to judges, and they have their hands in many activities.' (Interviewee Ba 13)

Selectivity in crime priorities

Tackling crime operationally is challenging in itself, but the strategic selection of priorities is inherently politically charged. In 2006, King's College London hosted a conference entitled Policing Transnational Crime. The conference involved academics and practitioners discussing the problems of tackling effectively organised crime across borders, boundaries and frontiers. The summary of the conference included criticism of the lack of transparency in how crime priorities across Europe were identified and that there seemed to be a disproportionate focus on crimes relating to commercial interests. A focus on human trafficking, in particular, increased its profile among both practitioners and politicians, but there are competing high-profile criminal activities (such as the illegal trade in animal horn and ivory from Africa to China) that do not attract the same intensity of police or political interest.

In light of this, it may be useful to assess the context in which most strategic police leaders view the transnational challenges as 'traditional' or 'typical' crime. One from the Central Europe region was among very few in our survey who questioned the sense in which 'crime' was being considered. The officer not only makes reference to offending by 'legitimate' business organisations, but also to the scale of criminal profit making; it no longer makes sense to see crime parochially, when it is simultaneously global and local:

'Some of these drugs cartels make more illegal money than small nations do, and they can hide it successfully inside legitimate moneymaking. It has been argued that if we really did work to get the profit out of crime, the entire world economy would collapse. I don't buy that, but it does indicate to you the enormous amounts of money that criminals can make for relatively little risk.

'I would also pursue criminal companies too, like Enron and some of the banks, who engage in outright criminality (like the Libor scandal in the UK for example[13]). You can't separate any more what happens globally from what happens on your doorstep: the drugs that were grown in Afghanistan are being sold on your street corner right now, and you can't hope to break, or even reduce, such crime simply by acting locally.' (Interviewee C50)

While concerns over the distribution and equity of surveillance and police operations among different sections of society are often raised, this debate comes under more intensive scrutiny in the context of developing technologies, national and supra-intelligence orientated institutions (such as Europol), and the movement of populations; while at the same time there are arguments for streamlining legislation and criminal justice processes across borders within Europe. The recent exposure by Edward Snowden of the US National Security Agency's surveillance activities (apparently shared with Britain's GCHQ) calls further into question the selection of national security priorities and the impact – or abuse – of state powers.[14]

Changing police structures, increased pluralisation, cuts in budgets, tensions between a federal approach to policing and national sovereignty are difficult to balance in the context of investigating flexible, skilled criminal groups.

Regional differences in perceptions of policing challenges

Although, as one might expect, there is a degree of consistency between different countries and regions and their strategic police leaders in what they understand as the most serious challenges to policing, there are

---

[13] 'Libor' is the rate that banks charge to lend to each other. It was a scandal in mid-2012, when British banks, including Barclays, were implicated in manipulating the Libor rate to their own advantage. In October 2014, the first (unnamed) individuals were given prison sentences and banks involved were heavily fined (see Bowers, 2014).

[14] George Lucas observes 'programs [sic] that are implemented in secret, out of public oversight, lack [...] legitimacy, and that's a problem', in his analysis of the effect of Snowden's whistle-blowing. See Lucas, G. (2014), pp. 29-38. An alternative, highly critical view of Snowden's activities was provided by *The Economist* senior editor Edward Lucas, published rather gleefully in *The Times* on 24 May 2014 as *Lobbing a leaky bucket of bile: the case for Edward Snowden is naïve, cartoonish and flimsy* (*Saturday Review*, p. 13).

also subtle differences. In this section, we compare those differences regionally.

Alpine region

Officers in the Alpine region had a strong identity with particular crime types. As we shall see Chapter Seven, there is a clear recognition that cybercrime, organised crime and drug trafficking are key current and future challenges.

Prominent concerns in the responses for the Alpine region also included terrorism, the procurement and sale of illegal weapons, human trafficking and the tensions arising from immigration and a multicultural society.

Bureaucratic challenges are also widely cited; from slow administrative processes through to a lack of willingness to cooperate, as made clear by this Alpine region police leader, who believes that policing should be more focused and surgically precise:

> 'There is a core of problems that we all have: drugs, international crime, trafficking routes, terrorism and cybercrime. We all have shrinking budgets too. So we need to apply police pressures more exactly, like a doctor treating a disease. We should not aim to police everything, though many of my colleagues do. What I mean is that we should focus policing where we are needed most, in the criminal world and perhaps leave little crimes and little problems to the private section of policing. My staff should not be wasting their expertises [sic] on anti-social behaviour, but instead investigating what they are best at: on homicides, people trafficking, drugs and illegal weapons for example.' (Interviewee A65)

Benelux region

Officers from the Benelux region seem to have a particular focus on police structures, population demographic changes, and identification of tensions associated with multicultural communities. The challenges here are not necessarily primarily with crime types (although they are well represented in responses), but are focused more on police organisation and internal tranquillity, and on police cooperation between countries.

Overall, responses from officers in the Benelux region reflected a broader range of issues and concerns than the officers from the Alpine region. This is a typical example:

> 'Obviously, a major challenge for us is to prevent being bothered as little as possible by internal reorganisation and we must ensure that we push back the bureaucratic burden as much as possible and that we release ourselves from the system-driven work. In my opinion, that's really an enormous challenge here.
>
> 'Another challenge is to keep in touch with society. The legitimacy issue will really become a challenge for us. You see that differences are growing, that people are pitted against each other. In my view it is an important remit for the police to ensure that inequality is counter-acted as much as possible. The improvement of our information position is vital, certainly in relation to Intelligence. And Intelligence in relation to information which is being generated from neighbourhood policing.' (Interviewee B29)

Another Benelux strategic police leader was a firm convert to organising police services 'on a federal basis':

> 'I shall be biased of course because I work [exclusively] in serious crime and my view is [determined] by my professional interest. So, all kinds of cross-border entrepreneurial crime, frauds, money-laundering and trafficking in people and services are going on all the time and we need to be able to disrupt such criminality collectively and individually. [...] We also need to get organised on a federal basis for the pursuit and investigation of the bigger criminals and crimes.' (Interviewee B103)

Mediterranean region

The Mediterranean region includes 22 respondents from seven countries. The characteristic responses of these countries include challenges to the region's police forces in getting a grip on illegal immigration in one of the busiest trading waterways in the world

(REMPEC, 2008).[15] Despite the geographical commonalities between countries in this group, respondents shared concerns with other regions in terms of police cooperation, expressing a clear view that the police are lagging behind criminals in terms of their effectiveness and efficiency in responding to cross-border crime. Opinions about police responses ranged from Europol 'not being strong enough' to 'over-slow' responses from some countries in relation to the issue of European Arrest Warrants. For a minority of respondents, the question of expectations from policing with a much-restricted budget was coupled with a concern that community policing was being pursued at the expense of adequately investigating serious crime. Human trafficking, organised crime, cybercrime, terrorism, drug-related crime and immigration issues are regarded as among the most important challenges. A large number of respondents in the Mediterranean region raised concerns about how tardy the police (and their governments) are in recognising the threats posed by the entrepreneurial criminal:

> 'The big ones [threats] are drugs and internet crime and the smuggling crimes like slavery and sex. To beat these we will need better cooperating, closer working and joint police operations. Some of this is there, but we don't have a good appreciation of criminal markets and criminals who are good businessmen. They are just like other entrepreneurs – they chase the profits and will not go after ventures which have no big gains. So we [police] need to be business-like too and as clever as them in finance and exploiting opportunities to make money. Where money is, will be criminals. We don't just need to work together as police, but cleverly as [in] taking profits out of the crime.' (Interviewee M14)

Another Mediterranean police leader considered that more attention needs to be paid to the machinery of justice itself and how it can be accelerated in outcomes:

---

[15] The Mediterranean Sea is among the world's busiest waterways, accounting for 15% of global shipping activity by number of calls and 10% by vessel deadweight tonnes (DWT). In 2006, some 13,000 merchant ships made 252,000 port calls totalling 3.8bn DWT at Mediterranean ports. See the *Lloyd's Marine Intelligence Unit report* for the Regional Marine Pollution Emergency Response Centre for the Mediterranean Sea (REMPEC), July 2008, p. 4, http://tinyurl.com/l5aqoae

'If I commit a crime in England and then run back to my home here, it will take a very long time for the machinery to bring me back to face what I have done, or what you allege that I have done. [...] So let me say that integrating the EU's justice systems through Eurojust should be a priority call for all of us. Otherwise extradition will stay complicated and prolonged.' (Interviewee M46)

Baltic region

Officers from the Baltic region identified their main concerns with regard to crime as terrorism, drugs importation and human trafficking. Frustrations with international policing and cooperation revolved around the lack of effectiveness, in part due to a perceived ineffectiveness of Europol (again with the corollary suggestion that 'it needs more power'), and the problems related to working with different laws and jurisdictions.

Internally there appeared to be concerns about social cohesion and the threat of public disorder. One strategic police leader noted that his worries included 'the exponential growth of organised crime':

'At the moment, the ease with which terrorist attacks of all varieties can be mounted, and the exponential growth of organised crime [concern us]. Since one is a facet of the other, I suppose I'm saying that organised crime in all its manifestations is our major current and future worry. [...] Look at money-laundering, drugs, people trafficking, smuggling, internet scams, banking fraud, third-world exploitation and identity theft as examples. It costs us billions of euros and we, the police, are limping along well behind them and hopeful only that, in their greed, they will make mistakes. Otherwise, I tell you, we don't have much chance of catching up.' (Interviewee Ba13)

Central Europe

The responses from officers in Central Europe reflected the political changes in the countries making up the region and the police reform generally moving from an authoritarian policing approach that sustained the governing one-party state and suppressed dissent, to one that aspires to embrace human rights, establish legitimacy for the police and re-engage trust with the people. Interestingly, many of the senior officers who spoke to us seemed as interested in how to gain public trust as in combating crime, and rather earnestly desired the police to be identified by the population as entirely distinct from politicians or the state. They also raised issues regarding illegal arms smuggling from the Russian Federation and indicated a widespread belief that police cooperation across Europe was poor. Their proposed improvements range from harmonising criminal laws to providing a European-wide enforcement capacity. Drugs and human trafficking appeared to be the most prevalent crimes, with internet crimes also high in the list of respondents:

> 'Oh hard questions! I do not think we know what our police should be. We have been a free country only a short time so there is no tradition for the good relations with the people. But we have to learn to do this, because the people must support the police – not be fearful of police. Criminals make the great profits because there is no top jurisdiction. I mean that there is not a Euro or global law that says we can get the criminal in any country. [...] The UN is not a good model, but who else can make China and Russia and India work with Europe against drugs and the trafficking?' (Interviewee C6)

The responses from Central Europe region's strategic police leaders were perhaps less representative of Europe as a whole, but were focused more on crime-related issues than on police organisational issues. Like interviewees from the Alpine region, Central European strategic police leaders raised the importance of improvements to international police cooperation.

Nordic region

The strategic police leaders from the Nordic region identified challenges around crimes involving sex, the internet, organised crime and fraud. Concern around social divisions, violence and social unrest because of immigrants were also voiced (and are explored in more detail in Chapter Seven).

Strong themes coming out of this group of officers include the need to improve cooperation across countries in the EU and the need for consistent priorities and laws or principles, within which the paradigm of the EU-wide application of human rights legislation was seen as paramount. The role of technology and the challenges of internet crime feature in the majority of responses, of which the following is expressive of the range of crime that Europe faces:

> 'I think that many threats, aside from public order or neighbourhood policing, are simultaneously national and international. The challenges to policing in these categories are cybercrime, the criminal use of the internet for financial crime and fraud, terrorism of course and the exploitation of "diaspora communities" by criminal groups (like Vietnamese families in growing cannabis or Albanians in gun smuggling) and these are often crime types that are not too obvious to the police.'[16] (Interviewee N9)

Another strategic police leader from the Nordic region was sceptical of some of the received opinion about criminality in Europe:

> 'It depends who you believe, and I am sceptical of those who, not experts themselves, tell me how to do my job. The media will tell you that terrorism is everywhere. It is not. It is actually diminishing, but that doesn't sell news stories. The courts will tell you that violent crime is on the increase because of the number of criminal cases reaching the court. Actually, I don't think violent crime is rising (except perhaps in domestic violence) but I think we are bringing more cases to the Public Prosecutors and they are taking more of them to court, so that explains the increase I think. If you speak to politicians, they will say that international crime is on the increase, and I think that there is some truth in this, but not for the reasons that the politicians give. This crime

---

[16] One could argue that they should be *more* 'obvious to the police'. A recent study of 'mobile banditry' in the Netherlands noted that organised criminals from four newly emergent democratic countries (Poland, Romania, Bulgaria and Lithuania) sought to steal methodically from Dutch communities (Siegel, 2014). Such studies can run the risk of racial or national stereotyping, but Professor Dina Siegel's research is cool and objective; it is a model of its kind and shows the long Dutch lead over the rest of Europe in empirical investigations of transnational criminality that began in 1995 with Cyrille Fijnaut. There is also growing evidence that Albanian criminals are being displaced by organised criminals from Georgia, leading European police forces in 2013 to combine in Operation Java to disrupt Georgian crime groups; see Odintsov, V. (2013) The Scope of Activities of Georgian Organised Crime Groups, NEO, 12 September, http://tinyurl.com/kvaujbl

across borders is rising because we in the police are slow to coordinate and respond to what they are doing with people, sex, drugs, goods and illicit services.' (Interviewee N68)

British Isles region

The overwhelming response from officers in the British Isles region focused on resources and the need 'to do more with less'. This is clearly a product of the recession and economic downturn that began in 2008 for all the countries in the region. For a minority of respondents, the cutbacks led to concerns about privatisation and the implications for this on public policing. This group also focused on internal challenges around civil disorder, again probably as a result of geopolitical events, including the widespread inner-city riots in the summer of 2011. Technology also featured heavily in officers' comments, but mainly because of a concern that the police were well 'behind the curve':

'Resources: doing more or as much as before with 20%–25% less is a real challenge and it's not one that will go away. If we struggle with that we only have ourselves to blame because we grew fat on the Labour government's fear of crime. Now the Coalition is saying "Crime's going down, so can police numbers and budgets" and it's a cold welcome to the real world. [...] We're individually aware, but not collectively geared to deal with it. I mean that Europe is a bit like Britain's independent police forces: we all retain our independence but moan that we're not effective against transnational crime. You can't have it both ways: we have to drop the nationalism bit if we are to succeed internationally. Europe has to act collectively, not in penny packets, against the transnational criminal' (Interviewee BI 85)

Summary

Our respondents' perspectives have offered an insight into the minds of officers engaged in international policing. However, we must acknowledge that analysis of this kind is still fraught with substantial difficulties, sometimes because of inaccuracies between member states in their interpretation of official data on organised crime, including human trafficking. The challenges identified by the strategic police leaders in this study represent interrelated issues in immigration, cybercrime, organised crime, terrorism, police legitimacy and legal frameworks relating to enforcement. All this is linked together and modified by economic fluctuations, globalisation and the mobilisation of populations.

While there is widespread and vocal concern about declining budgets, interviewees put greater emphasis on the problems of judicial bureaucracy and different criminal laws providing slow responses to crime, in contrast to flexible and adaptable organised criminals. In key areas of organised crime and cybercrime, respondents were very concerned about police responses and worried that the police were not effective in tackling these problems. Officers regularly advocated overarching laws (the *'corpus juris criminalis'*) and a pragmatically federalised approach to policing, neither of which appears likely in the short term if the European Parliament elections of 2014[17] are any indication. There is simply no political appetite for pan-European jurisdiction or for a *'corpus juris'*; in fact, all the indications now are that a greater parochialism or national self-interest is more strongly to the fore among the nation states in Europe. The corollary to this includes reduced cooperation and less interest in federalism.

---

[17] A largely anti-federalist vote, in which right-wing parties across Europe gained votes and seats, especially in France and the UK, but also in Greece, Germany and Denmark.

SEVEN

The future of policing

'Politics is the ability to foretell what is going to happen tomorrow, next week, next month and next year. And to have the ability afterwards to explain why it didn't happen.' (Winston Churchill, speech in 1922)

It is always something of a risk to write about the future, especially when it is as diffuse as the future of policing, which is subject to change, vagary and political initiative to a greater extent than many public service activities, with the exception perhaps of medicine or of politics itself.[1] Nonetheless, we felt that we should give our respondents a chance to comment on the future of policing, both in Europe and further afield, trusting that their experience and wisdom would inform the debate.

That debate has been rumbling quietly for many years, and seems to consist – with Churchillian consistency – of explanations why something did not happen. The hubris of William Bratton's 'crime in New York is down; blame the police'[2] is perhaps the nadir of such explanations, especially as it was shown that Bratton's much-vaunted 'Compstat' process actually did little to address the underlying causes

---

[1]   Nils Bohr, the Danish Nobel Prize winner for Physics, said "Prediction is very difficult, especially if it's about the future," quoted in Hughes, S.A. (2014), Coastal engineering challenges in a changing world, *Journal of Applied Water Engineering and Research*, Vol. 2, No. 2, 72-80.

[2]   William (Bill) Bratton and Mayor Rudy Giuliani jointly claimed credit for the sudden fall in crime rates in New York in 1997, claiming that new 'zero-tolerance' policing and the introduction of Compstat (see next note) were responsible. Bratton later asserted that falling crime rates had nothing to do with demography, economics or social issues, in: Kelling, G. and Bratton, W. (1998), Declining crime rates: Insiders' views of the New York City story, *The Journal of Criminal Law and Criminology*, Vol. 88, No. 4, pp. 1217-1232.

of crime.[3] Crime analysis has since revealed that crime and criminality were declining anyway across the Western developed nations, and the police were often tangential to this process.[4] But one cannot blame them for trying to take some of the credit, since, when crime goes up, they get the blame, irrespective of other social factors.

At the same time, discussions have been taking place at European police conferences, seminars and on academic courses (including those run by the European Police College), in which topics have been aired such as the future control of civic unrest, the nature and character of policing to come (especially in the opposing 'civil police versus gendarme' schools of thought), the positioning of the police with regard to the expansion of cybercrime, and to what degree policing itself needed to change to reflect profound and sometimes seismic shifts in society (Ekblom, 2005), such as in employment, diversity, gender, education, ethnic proportions and the stratification of society. All this shows variation across Europe as well as within the forces themselves: a number of EU states in central Europe are still in the process of

---

[3]   'In 1994, New York City instituted CompStat, an initiative to hold local commanders accountable for achieving crime reduction goals in their areas, which Police Commissioner William Bratton and others credited for the decrease in crime in the city. The problem-oriented component of this era emphasized analysis as a crucial ingredient in framing effective policing strategies.' (Greg Treverton et al's (2011) research paper *Moving Toward the Future of Policing*, published by the Rand Corporation, p. xv). Compstat never 'took' in the UK or Europe, possibly because it seemed to be merely a public pillory and it has subsequently fallen away in the US, but that has not inhibited Bratton from claiming it as 'his' success and himself being viewed by non-practitioners (including the British Government) as some sort of moral crusader for police reform. As commentators dryly pointed out, crime was going down anyway, and it is not easy to attribute directly to Compstat any of the benefits of this phenomenon. Compstat served a purpose in revitalising local police accountability to communities, but larger claims about it being a potent law enforcement weapon seem exaggerated. It may be another example of American practice being imported to Europe without analysis and careful evaluation, like 'zero tolerance'. Bratton became chief of the Los Angeles Police Department, where, in 2008, he co-wrote a defence of Compstat, some time after it had ceased to be significant, before returning to NYPD in 2014 as chief once again. See Bratton, W. and Malinowski, S. (2008), Police performance management in practice: taking COMPSTAT to the next level, *Policing, a Journal*, Vol. 2, No. 3, pp. 259-265.

[4]   See the arguments summarised in an excellent piece by Ben Bowling in 1999: The rise and fall of New York murder: zero tolerance or crack's decline?, *British Journal of Criminology*, Vol. 39, No. 4, pp. 531-554.

formulating the detail of the democratic/accountable police model they have adopted from practice in western European countries (as we noted in Chapters One and Six), and at the same time, the Germans are considering to what degree they need nationally based policing functions in the name of economic efficiency, rather than their familiar 'dispersed' model of lots of separate hubs in their autonomous *Länder*.

What follows in this chapter is a snapshot of opinions about what lies ahead for European policing and police leadership: policing is itself in perpetual flux and may look very different in a few years.

What will policing look like in 5 or 10 years' time?

We asked European strategic police leaders: *What do you think policing will look like in 5 or 10 years' time?*

We chose these two time periods carefully, because they represent together a decade of public finance strategies, and separately at least two general elections in European countries in which police policies might be changed (witness the introduction of police and crime commissioners to England and Wales in 2012 or the structural reorganisation in the Netherlands in 2013 and the 'rightward shift' in the 2014 European Parliamentary elections) and the nature of contemporary criminality reassessed.

Reponses to the question, as might be expected, were varied and occasionally idiosyncratic, but out of 108 replies, the summary data are shown in Table 7.1.

We shall examine four of the larger themes in more detail later, but it is worth first noting the spectrum of other suggestions on offer.

The range of opinions

Rather specialised comments suggested that environmental crime should be more rigorously policed (5)[5] and that drugs should be decriminalised (10). Thirteen thought that public policing was in decline (12 did not) and 5 thought that there would be an increase in police accountability. Five others thought that languages would become an issue and that European forces should now be recruiting Arabic, Chinese and Russian speakers to deal with future criminality, while a lone voice thought that 'hacktivism' would become an issue

---

[5]   The numbers in brackets represent the number of responses out of a sample of 108.

Table 7.1: What do you think policing will look like in 5 or 10 years' time?

Theme	Number[*]
Concerns about cybercrime and policing the net	49
Worries about international crime	31 (see Chapter Six)
Concerns about social unrest	33
Economic problems	27
Better coordination needed between police forces	31 (see Chapter Five)
The development of a pan-European police force	23
The creation of a comprehensive *corpus juris*	24 (see Chapter Six)
A decline in terrorism	21[**]
A decline in nationalism (subordination of interests to a greater European ideal of federalism)	18

Notes: * These are not percentages but total numbers, since interviewees usually selected several issues to consider for future development. ** With four believing it would rise.

needing police intervention if European information systems, banks or governments were targeted by, among others, 'Anonymous'.[6]

The numbers involved in the responses are merely relative (because most officers indicated a variety of criminal, social or policing activities that they believed would dominate the future), but even the single mention here of 'hacktivism' suggests that some strategic police leaders are alive to potential problems in the future and are concerned to position themselves and their forces to take account of possible

---

[6] "Anonymous" is a loose affiliation of 'hackers' and computer experts who have attacked systems that they believe to be ill-intentioned or big Brother-ish. Famously, they disrupted the Church of Scientology in the US and have claimed success in an attack on Home Office data in the UK. In public, their supporters wear white 'Guy Fawkes'-style masks. Some members have been caught and imprisoned, others have become disillusioned with Anonymous's focus on the US rather than other places where 'service denial' would be effective, such as Russia and China. Others have supported Julian Assange and the Wikileaks phenomenon. See for example: Hampson, N. (2012), Hacktivism: A New Breed of Protest in a Networked World, *Boston College International and Comparative Law Review*, No. 35, pp. 511-603; or Walker, J. (2012), Unmasking Anonymous , *ITNow*, Vol. 54, No. 2, pp. 28-29. A short analysis of the politics of 'hactivism' and Anonymous can be found in Gabriella Coleman's 2011 paper: Hacker Politics and Publics, *Public Culture*, Vol. 23, No. 3/65, pp. 511-516.

trends.[7] Some concerns are undoubtedly the product of professional preoccupations, such as those who drew attention to the perturbing rise in 'private' policing at the expense of public policing[8] (8), or those who argued for more and higher educational qualifications for entrance to strategic policing (7), or the 4 who believed that police forces had wilfully held back or concealed useful information from others because of 'power-broking' and parochialism (one citing 'the British' as particular offenders). A few idealists argued for a pan-European police strategic leadership qualification (4); a number saw social urban breakdown as inevitable and "a brutalistic response to anarchy may be the only available response" (Interviewee N18), while some believed that in the longer term "we will all end up working for the Americans" (Interviewee M77).

Dystopian views, other than concerns about social unrest (discussed later), were actually fairly rare. Most strategic police leaders gave optimistic or positive comments on the future of policing in Europe, though one opined that "who thinks to be able to know [what will happen] in 2020 is mad or a fool" (Interviewee C105), while another refused to provide any comment about the future except "I don't know. Ask me then" (Interviewee A1), which might have been the product of interview fatigue as much as disenchantment with the act of prediction itself. Another strategic police leader, describing himself as "only a gypsy telling fortunes", believed that ideas about federalism in European policing could be translated into reality if the political will existed (as we explored in Chapter Five). He continued:

> 'Importantly, we must have an idea, a plan, of where we want to go and how we might get there. To start with, we could begin to abandon small nationalist positions and become truly a "greater Europe".' (Interviewee A24)

This had resonance with other leaders, who argued that "What solves international crime is international police and judicial cooperation" (Interviewee M28) and looked to Brussels not only to encourage such

---

[7]   "Hactivism" receives academic attention too (see note above), with authorities as eminent as Majid Yar devoting an entire section of his book on *Cybercrime and Society* (2013) to 'Hacktivism and the politics of resistance in a globalized world' (3.2, pp. 46-50), and good accounts too in Jordan and Taylor (2004), and Vegh (2002).

[8]   We looked at this in some detail in Chapter Six.

cooperation but also to describe what is entailed by strategic police leadership:

> 'Leadership will be "joined-up" or properly networked as the criminal justice system will be more and more complex to sort out.' (Interviewee N41)

But when pressed, police leaders acknowledged that, in many respects, these were idealised positions and the realpolitik in Europe in 10 years' time would probably be muddle and inertia:

> 'the politicians will still be arguing, the EU will still be passing grand resolutions, the media will still be criticising us, the criminals will be laughing at us and we'll all still be saying that we need an international law enforcement agency to handle international crime.' (Interviewee C81)

All the same, the lure of integration, the notion of effective policing utilising "public support and engagement", can seem very appealing to a strategic police leader attempting to evaluate what leading the police will mean in years to come:

> 'I hope in ten years' time, when finally I might be leaving strategic policing, we have a better sense of who we are and what we are doing, from Cardiff to Krakow, and that we are doing it together, with public support and engagement.
> 'When international criminals start looking over their shoulders and when trafficking is too risky to do without being caught, then I'll know that policing is on the up.' (Interviewee BI 100)

A police leader from Central Europe, noting that "it is not easy to see so far" into the future, gave a deeply sceptical response to the mythology that crime does not pay, when he described criminality's "new clothes":

> 'Crime will be big, still, and we will be struggling to contain it. Why? Because people will find soon, if not today then tomorrow, that crime pays better than most kinds of work. Why work hard in the fields or factories when you can make ten times your money by dealing drugs or selling sex? It is an old problem and although it has new clothes

in Europe now, it needs police and courts together to make deterrence.' (Interviewee C108)

Bearing in mind the distinct probability that "crime will be big, still" in the future of policing in Europe, let us turn now to look in greater detail at the four main themes that emerged from the answers to our question.

Policing cyberspace and cybercrime

Nearly half of all our respondents drew specific attention to the problems they saw in trying to police a 'virtual world' that crosses borders with ease and which enables criminality to flourish.[9] A strategic police leader from Central Europe commented:

> 'I do not have a crystal ball to predict the future, but it must be obvious that *technology in the service of crime* must be our main focus. Young people now spend so much time in cyberspace and have so many tools for communication that they hardly at all interact outside those social media. When did your children last read a book or sit in a concert? Some don't even physically go to university today. The crime will also become hidden on the net rather than in the streets and on the borders. Why risk being stopped at a checkpoint when you can cross whole worlds inside the computer?' (Interviewee C71; his emphasis)

This is very characteristic of the responses from other strategic leaders. They acknowledge that crime is shifting tangibly to the internet, but some feel helpless when it comes to policing within the virtual world – a place where criminal laws and police jurisdiction appear meaningless:

> 'Now the most of the police are being left a long way back in line because we cannot police the cyberspace. The move outside our own jurisdiction is an urgent one that society and the police must address. At the moment it is anarchy with very little in the way of "policing" the net in any real way. The police, the governments and the ISPs [internet

---

[9]   This is the focus of Majid Yar's *Cybercrime and Society* (2nd edn, 2013), in which, among many good things, he argues that the internet should be seen as 'a set of *social practices*' (p. 6, his italics) rather than as 'simply a piece of technology'.

service providers] must reach an agreement for the way forward, or we will be helpless, I think.' (Interviewee M82)

This sense of impotence, sometimes even a kind of baffled rage, may be the product of the thinking of a generation that has not grown up with social media, smart-phones, pads/tablets, text messaging, internet communication and 'anywhere' computing to the same immersive degree as the generations aged under 40. Yet some respondents noted that since criminals themselves are proving very adaptive to the 'bot generation' and are exploiting new opportunities to commit crime, the police would do well to emulate that flexibility with their countermeasures. One Alpine strategic police leader put it like this:

'There is one place where the police are not well equipped to go and patrol or make investigations and arrests and that is the world of the internet. In this world, all our young people live – some of them only have "virtual lives" (their real lives must be "half-lives", like decaying uranium) but all rely on the net in some way – for social contact, for information, for student research, for films and entertaining, for communication and for images. The criminals very well know this and so the future of crime may be in the virtual world, where there are no police. This is what we have discussed in Pearls and other forums for chiefs for three years now, and although we have informal agreements, there is no EU strategy or action plan to work together. A community of many millions would surely have influence with service providers? If we acted together on this, we might start policing the net, and that would be good for democracy but also good for the individual security.' (Interviewee A90)

Coordinated action with internet service providers (ISPs) is one way forward, but the ISPs themselves have often proved to be most reluctant partners. Indeed, in one case in the UK where a woman was maliciously made the target for trolls,[10] she herself had to seek judicial action against the ISP responsible for a messaging site, because the police claimed

[10] A 'troll', derived from the name of a brutalist monster in Scandinavian folklore, is commonly regarded as someone spreading discord and mischief on messaging sites. At its most extreme, trolls hound people with criminally malicious intent, but usually hide behind anonymity and thus cannot be 'outed' by the victim(s) unless the ISP cooperates in releasing the name(s).

that they could not help her. Only the prospect of losing an expensive legal judgment forced the particular ISP into releasing details of the troll, who was eventually charged with a criminal offence.[11] But it was really vigilante action by a determined individual, rather than deliberate investigation by the police, that brought about this result. The Alpine police leader above who calls for coordinated action between police, governments and ISPs, acknowledges that no such cooperation is yet in place in Europe and that calls for it to happen may remain wishful thinking instead of hard-edged strategic police planning, unless Europe can persuade other countries or international groups to join. Essentially, the jurisdictional dilemma persists – just on a larger scale. Yet there is no denying the essential truth that, once coordinated, a "community of many millions" will of course influence ISPs, which exist to make money, not morality.

The inability, or reluctance, of the police to become involved in investigation of cybercrime may partly be the result of insufficient understanding of the threat at the strategic level in policing, or a lack of skill sets among police investigators, too many calls on police time elsewhere, and often vague or imprecise targets for their attention. This is of a piece with the views of academic commentators, some of whom have noted that, while private companies have embraced 'new technology' with enthusiasm and flair, the police have been traditionally reluctant to adapt (Hughes and Love, 2004). A thoughtful essay by Peter Sommer on policing cybercrime wondered whether the public and the police expect too much of each other when it comes to controlling what goes on in cyberspace (Sommer, 2004). Jessica Lichy, making a comparison between policing the internet in France and Britain, noted that regulatory structures – including relevant criminal law – tended to evolve in the face of specific crime examples; there did not seem to be a deliberate attempt to impose strategic controls (Lichy, 2012). Greg Treverton et al (2011) observed that there is a functional mismatch between the ways that criminals swiftly exploit advances in electronic technology, and the police's organisational slowness to adopt changes. In fact, they argued '[t]he key to the future of policing [...] is not technology [itself], but the ways in which police forces adapt it to

---

[11] See http://tinyurl.com/mwu27mr. The ISP was Facebook against whom in 2012, Nicola Brookes won her case in the English High Court; four trolls were eventually charged under the Malicious Communications Act 1988, which makes it illegal to send grossly offensive messages. Prosecutions under the Act have more than tripled since 2004. In 2014, the maximum penalty for conviction under the Act was increased to two years' imprisonment.

their purposes (Treverton et al, 2011, p. xvi). They added that: '[T]he environment in which criminals operate will morph as technology, law and law-enforcement change. None of these dimensions operates independently of the others: they are all interconnected in complex ways' (Treverton et al, 2011, p. xvii).

None of these observers of the 'interconnected' crime-and-policing scene has noted in any detail the exponential rate at which cyberspace, and crime in cyberspace, is developing. It seems unfair to single out the police alone for criticism when entire criminal justice systems across Europe seem equally reluctant to adopt fully the techniques and capabilities of operating in cyberspace (Yar, 2013, pp. 15-17). It is perhaps more often the case that the police have to juggle competing priorities within the broad task of 'policing' rather than any stubborn Luddism about new technology and 'e-crime' (Pease, 2001). On the contrary, one strategic police leader believes that "crime on the internet is growing very fast", and the police themselves need to be thinking about recruiting a different kind of police officer to deal with the phenomenon (though she does not specify how or where this might be done):

> '[...] crime on the internet is growing very fast and we need cops who can patrol cyberspace and act [in] a coordinated way across the whole EU. We must keep recruiting those kinds of police, so that in five years they can be running small or medium units of cyber cops.' (Interviewee C91)

She goes on to note the deterrent effect that "a few cases" brought to successful prosecution might have on potential offenders:

> 'On the cyberspace, the problems will be stopping illicit goods and services and the difficulties of policing across the Net because it is simultaneously personal and global. But a few cases of paedophiles and traffickers caught on the Net by police and service providers working together, and then punished by the EU, will warn others that we are not an easy conquest.' (Interviewee C91)[12]

---

[12] A total of 660 arrests for downloading indecent images of children was an 'internet bust' across Britain by the National Crime Agency in July 2014, led by 'cybercops', so perhaps there is more development in this area than Interviewee C91 knows about; see Symonds, 2014.

A Mediterranean region strategic police leader attempted to describe the inability, or incapability, of the police to cope with these new threats as a product of the inherent police focus, which is, he says, "parochial, local". Only when the police can coordinate action globally (in other words, on the same basis that the criminal can), and operate equally effectively in both the real world and the virtual world, might policing on such a scale "work ... everywhere":

> 'The criminal is increasingly international, global maybe, while police are still parochial, local, community-aimed. The world criminal is becoming slowly a real factor, and that can be in cybercrime as much as real crime in the physical world. We do not grasp the importance of fighting both: it goes in the "too difficult" box for most of us. We need strong protocols internationally, a better understanding of the strategic importance of cooperating en masse, and something like a world criminal law which will work for all jurisdictions everywhere.' (Interviewee M92)

Such a utopian vision of 'world policing' has been a dream since the Victorian heyday of the British Empire and has been central to US foreign policy since 1945, and even underpinned some of the hopes for the United Nations after the Second World War, but it is no nearer reality now than it was then. The speaker above (Interviewee M92) went on to note that it was almost the case that respect for human rights had become global except in rogue or oppressive states,[13] and that if respect for human rights can be codified, then so can global policing. He is realistic though about any timetable for such massive coordination:

> 'We almost have it in civilised countries for human rights, so it cannot be beyond belief that we can do it for criminal investigations. But it needs the will of many to make it

---

[13] But if we pause a moment and consider this claim, it hardly stands up. Only in the developed Western hemisphere broadly, in most Commonwealth countries and a few in Africa or South America, are such freedoms permanent and guaranteed. The number of autocratic and 'oppressive' states easily outnumbers those with liberal constitutions. The UN states that there are 192 distinct countries in the world, but at best only 50 or so of those could claim to be liberal democracies; the remainder are autocracies, "illiberal democracies" or absolutist states (see Farid Azaria, 1997, http://tinyurl.com/l62mca5)

occur. Do I think it will happen in ten years? No, we will still be talking about it. But I hope very much that I am wrong and we start to act like a UN or at least at EU level, against this threat to society everywhere.' (Interviewee M92)

A Nordic region police leader agreed, but thought that recruitment of police officers who would be at ease in the internet should begin now:

'[...] there should be more internet police officers, more police software engineers, more police fraud experts to follow money-laundering and more experts who know how to harness science in the service of policing. If we can do all that, and cooperate internationally, we may make a difference.' (Interviewee N96)

A Benelux strategic police leader noted that all this discussion and speculation was fruitless unless the emergent generations of social media and messaging were themselves alerted to how crime and criminality stalk the virtual world:

'Things are changing very fast: the use of technology in crime is going forward all the time and the police are in the back of this a little bit. So the communications of the young are leaving the older people behind: my children live all their lives in social media and the internet, Wii and Wi-Fi and all the rest. They share so much more than we ever did and so things like identity theft and personation is so much easier than in our "buttoned-up" generation. But that also makes crime easier and some of the present generation learns the hard lessons of cruelty and violence for they are not as prepared for it as we had [been], coming in the post-war generation.' (Interviewee B104)

Nearly every interviewee who mentioned the problems of policing cyberspace noted the parallel inadequacy of the police to deal effectively with such problems, a comment reflected in the academic literature (Ekblom, 2005; Carson, 2007). Naivety among the young might be one factor – even though their communications techniques are effortlessly superior to those of the police leadership generation – but another is the reluctance fully to embrace the new 'paperless' world, and consequently a clog on developing a criminal justice system that could respond to cybercrime (Wall, 2001). ENISA, the European Union Agency for Network and Information Security founded in 2009, is intended to coordinate investigations into, and prevention of, cybercrime, but actually had its budget reduced in 2012 (Yar, 2013, p. 16). ENISA continues to work at coordination, common protocols and joint action, but its effectiveness does not yet appear to be objectively measured.[14] Such innovative mechanisms may also come up against time-honoured police practice and procedure, which in turn may hobble the flexible responses necessary to tackle cybercrime. A Baltic region strategic leader, himself still in his forties, told us that:

> 'Policing should adapt to the modern communications and make more use of social media; criminals do, and so do citizens. We are too paper-bound still and we need to empower cops at the front-end to use the new social media and messaging trends to communicate with youth. As you know, very few strategic police leaders systematically use Twitter or Facebook. There are very few "police" apps and we don't exploit YouTube for example, to post details of people we'd like to interview.[15] But those places are where all the kids are and we're not there yet. Mind, we are really progressive compared with the courts: I hear the Brits are experimenting with virtual courts but I don't know of many in Europe and certainly not in my country. It's all still based on paper.' (Interviewee Ba106)

'Virtual courts', where defendants (and some, mostly young, witnesses) appear by video link or some other Skype-type means, have been used rather piecemeal in the UK since 2009, and are in use in some other European countries, but the practice is still not widespread. A UK

---

[14] See www.enisa.europa.eu/; the home page claims that ENISA's 'objective is to make ENISA's web site the European 'hub' for exchange of information, best practice and knowledge in the field of Information Security. This web site is an access point to the EU Member States and other actors in this field.' It goes on to note that it 'is helping the European Commission, the Member States and the business community to address, respond and especially to prevent Network and Information Security problems.' All this may be true, but the claims are not validated with evidence.

[15] Not entirely true; many police forces use YouTube to spread messages, particularly those aimed at the young, but it is not a medium amenable to 'Wanted' posters anyway.

Law Society advice note of December 2012 notes that a 'virtual first hearing', linking magistrates' court to police station by video link, is in common usage now.[16] But the production of a physical body to answer criminal charges (*habeas corpus*) is still a powerful freedom; subsequent hearings at Crown Courts or their equivalents to answer serious charges still require the corporeal presence of the accused. It remains demonstrably the case that the virtual world of the internet, social messaging and communications are "places […] where all the kids are and we're not there yet". We have to compensate for strategic police leaders perhaps being out of touch with the latest developments in cyberspace, but they do have plenty of colleagues who are fully attuned and many academic contacts for whom research in these fields is a commonplace.[17]

Summary of views on policing cyberspace and cybercrime

The generality of the message from the 49 strategic police leaders who mentioned cybercrime and cyberspace as places where police strategic concerns should exist, is that whether the police catch up or not, this is an area of exponential growth. In 5 or 10 years' time, they say, the 'Net' will be unrecognisable and what concerns us at the moment will be long consigned to history. Speed in the virtual world is much greater than that in the real world, but the essential fact on which many of our interviewees dwelled was that recruitment of 'cyber-savvy' police officers should be a priority now, and not in 5 years' time, simply because the criminals who exploit cyberspace are already operating in large numbers there.

Social unrest

Another powerful concern expressed by strategic police leaders, this time completely located in the physical world, indicated a belief in the probability of widespread social unrest in Europe in the 5 to 10

---

[16] See www.lawsociety.org.uk/advice/practice-notes/virtual-courts/; advice for 19 December 2012. A long (and frankly tedious) trawl through the deliberations of the European Court system online (http://tinyurl.com/o2573v6) yielded almost no information on virtual appearances, though much was made of 'virtual documentation'.

[17] One of the authors was for some years a 'vetted' External Examiner for Master's level research in Cyber Crime at a UK university, dealing almost exclusively with confidential research by police officer students.

years that they looked ahead (a concern somewhat paralleled in the academic literature; see, for example, Reiter and Fillieule, 2013). A Nordic region strategic police leader explained why this was such a prevalent concern:

'In five years not very changed [...] but by ten years, there could be real social disorder. It will start in the minority communities where there will be too many unskilled people looking for basic provisions. Then the population may resent all the hand-outs to the immigrants and tensions will grow. Then the ultra right will come along and say "Solution! We will send them all home" and we could be plunged back into a Nazi type era of intolerance and prejudice. I studied Gordon Allport's model for genocide[18] and this can be adapted to present conditions, where immigrants are "bad-mouthed" by the media, by commentators and by the populace.' (Interviewee N45)

One demonstration of "intolerance and prejudice" was the July 2011 attack in Oslo by Anders Behring Breivik, bombing and shooting members of the Norwegian Labour Party (the *Arbeiderpartiet*) – including a large number of young students – whom he held responsible for policies of toleration and mass immigration of 'Islamists' into

---

[18] Gordon Allport, an American academic, investigated Nazi activities against minority groups (particularly, of course, the Jews, but also against gypsy travellers, people with physical or mental handicaps, gays and other powerless minorities) and extrapolated from his research general principles that could be applied to all forms of prejudice. His original 1954 book is out of print now, but *The Nature of Prejudice* (Gordon W. Allport, Cambridge, MA, and Oxford, England: Addison-Wesley) is a potent demonstration of how prejudicial actions begin with minor demonisation ('bad-mouthing') but lead eventually, if the demonisation is sufficiently organised and widespread, to genocide. Allport devised a five-step model (known as 'Allport's Scale'), which depicts this progression. For more modern interpretations, see, for example, Ekehammar, B. and Akrami, N. (2003), The relation between personality and prejudice: a variable- and a person-centred approach, *European Journal of Personality*, Vol. 17, No. 6, pp. 449-464. Allport's Scale is widely used in police forces in diversity training.

Norway.[19] Confused and mad though Breivik's reasoning is, police strategic leaders across Europe see his violent racist response as likely to be symptomatic of tensions to come. More generally, one police strategic leader looked ahead to the "real challenges" of "social anarchy in the cities" from immigrant populations:

> 'The real challenges are [...] social anarchy in the cities, especially in deprived areas and where there are large immigrant settlements, unless they can be more rapidly assimilated into the prevailing culture.' (Interviewee Ba76)

It is a general observation that assimilation of immigrant populations into the host country takes at least two generations, and that the migration westwards of Muslims from the Near and Middle East is a relatively new phenomenon (Castles et al, 2005), occasioned currently at least in part by the displacement that followed conflicts in, variously, Iraq, Afghanistan, Libya, the Yemen, Somalia and Syria. According to the EU's official data:

> On 1st January 2011, the EU's total population was 502.5 million, with an increase of 1.4 million from 2010 which is equivalent to an annual rate of +2.7 per 1000 inhabitants made up of a natural increase of 0.5 million (+1.0‰) and net migration of 0.9 million (+1.7‰). The 20.2 million third-country nationals in the EU amounts to some 4% of the total EU population. (European Commission, 2012)[20]

The proportions in Europe are not high relative to total population, but it is the speed of the increase – nearly a million and a half in the years since 2010, including half a million in 2012-13 alone, at nearly

---

[19] See, for example, Adam Bergström's unpublished Master's dissertation in 2012, *Anders Behring Breivik*, Lund University, Sweden (available in Swedish at: http://lup.lub.lu.se/luur/download?func=downloadFileandrecordOId=3052001andfileOId=3052074), and Moustafa Bayoum's 2012 article: Breivik's Monstrous Dream, *Nation*, Vol. 294, No. 21, pp. 17-22. There is also a useful 2012 BBC report post-sentencing on Breivik ('Anders Behring Breivik: Norway court finds him sane', *BBC*, 24 August 2012), which summarises his background and what he did (www.bbc.co.uk/news/world-europe-19365616). Breivik was sentenced in August 2012 to 21 years' imprisonment for his mass murder the year before.

[20] Immigration in 2013 reached nearly half a million: see Eurostat 14/46, March 2014, http://europa.eu/rapid/press-release_STAT-14-46_en.pdf

3 per thousand of the population – which will be at the centre of social unrest, say strategic police leaders. This prompts questions about assimilation into some European cultures, because it is unlikely that immigrant populations, especially from Syria and Russia, will already know minority languages like Swedish, Polish or Greek, even though they may know some English or French. The current major immigrant groups are identified by the Commission research as:

> *Syria* (50,000 asylum applicants, or 12% of the total number of applicants) became in 2013 the first main country of citizenship of these applicants, ahead of *Russia* (41,000 or 10%), *Afghanistan* (26,000 or 6%), *Serbia* (22,000 or 5%), *Pakistan* (21,000 or 5%) and *Kosovo* (20,000 or 5%). (European Commission data for 2013, see previous note; our emphasis)

But other refugee groups from the Middle East and from Southern Asia have also moved into Europe during 2012-14, following conflict and disturbances in their home states and regions, including outfall from the 'Arab Spring'. Relatively small numbers are dispersed in each member state, even with accumulated totals, but the impact of immigration (when it is a net increase over emigration) is felt in numerous ways, such as in social housing, schools, hospitals, health/welfare schemes, local amenities and policing. This impact leads to almost apocalyptic visions on the part of some strategic police leaders:

> 'The real internal problem is immigration and the inability of societies to integrate their new groups into the whole. There will be inner city disturbances for years to come and that will be across Europe, not just here. There will be a backlash against the immigrants too, and more people like Breivik, taking the law into their own hands and carrying out massacres.' (Interviewee N83)

Tackling organised crime is also challenged by perceptions that organised crime is associated with particular ethnic groups, leading inexorably to tension between 'established' populations and immigrants. The 'rightward shift' in politics in some areas of Europe increases this tension:

> SOCTA [Serious and Organised Crime Threat Assessment] makes notable findings about the continuing evolution of

a new breed of 'network-style' organised crime groups, defined much less by their ethnicity or nationality than has been the case hitherto, and much more by their capacity to operate on an international basis, with multiple partners and in multiple crime areas and countries. This calls for a shift in our strategic response in the EU, away from one centred on individual ethnic types.... (Rob Wainwright, Director of Europol in 2013, p. 5)

The Director of Europol's cool judgement here is not reflected in the anxieties of some of our respondents. This, from a Benelux region strategic police leader, may be regarded as typical:

'There are worrying signs of a kind of social polarisation happening now, where people take extreme positions about things like immigration, military involvement in Islamic countries and the growth in ethnic communities in EU countries. [...] I believe it is a shared problem across the whole EU whether it is migration from Asian countries, from North Africa or from Islamic communities. It is often the trend of migration from economic poverty to economic plenty (though with the Eurozone crisis that is not so great a contrast as before). The existing citizen seems ready to resent this flood wave of new people coming in and wants to force them out of any jobs, so the tensions are very strong already.' (Interviewee B103)

Developments in 'ultra-right' politics (ranging from UKiP in Britain, Marine le Pen's *Front Nationale* in France, *Vlaams Belang* in Belgium and Gert Wilders' *Partijvoor de Vrijheid* in the Netherlands to the 'Golden Dawn' (Λαϊκός Σύνδεσμος) in Greece and the *Lega Nord* in Italy),[21] foreign policy and population movement all act as drivers for tension within European societies, particularly in relation to jobs and a perception of uncontrolled growth in ethnic communities. The view of the Benelux police leader quoted above relates directly to what Jo Goodey (2002) describes as 'demonization of the "other"'. However, this is not reserved for countries outside the EU but is applied also to

---

[21] There are good studies of the politically ultra-right in Europe and the threats posed by them; among the best is Paul Hainsworth's comprehensive *The extreme right in Western Europe*, 2008 and a short study by LubomirKopeček (2007), *The Far Right in Europe*, available as an e-text on www.ceeol.com

new and 'candidate' members of the Union. The political debate in the United Kingdom about the 'fears' of a huge influx of Romanian and Bulgarian immigrants[22] fed into criticisms of EU membership and concerns for the employment of British workers:

> Links between long-established demonization of the 'other', in the form of the criminal threat posed to the EU by undesirable 'outsiders', and increasing pressures for migration into the EU from outside, have allowed for an easy marriage between crime concerns and migration concerns as focused on certain non-EU citizens. (Goodey, 2002, p. 137)

While concerns over immigrants from within the EU or beyond have fed an intense debate, particularly among right-wing political groups, Pascouau (2014) argues that the combination of economic recovery and an ageing EU population requires migrant workers to satisfy both skills and labour shortages:

> ...EU Member States are exposed to a key challenge which will impact on their needs regarding migrant workers: Europe's demographic trends, which will result in a shrinking workforce and the ageing of Europe's societies. While the shrinking of the work force will impact on labour and skills shortages, taking care of an ever increasing number of 'elderlies' will also create additional labour demand. In addition, if a sustained economic recovery can be achieved it will intensify the need for a bigger part of the workforce coming from outside the Union. (Pascouau, 2014, p. 24)[23]

---

[22] Stoked by Nigel Farage, the UKiP leader in May 2014, when he remarked that he did not want Romanian families living next door to him (and his German wife); see a BBC report at http://tinyurl.com/ojavb5u; the 2014 EU elections showed a general increase in right-wing representation.

[23] Pascouau's conclusions are matched by the EU's own research data. In a paper published in 2013, the EU noted that: 'It will not be long until Europe starts to feel the impact of its ageing population and shrinking workforce. Even today, despite high levels of unemployment, there are around 2 million job vacancies across the EU, such as in the fields of health, information communication technologies, engineering, sales and finance. While immigration is not the only answer to fill skills gaps where they exist, it is certainly part of a common solution supportive of EU's economic growth strategy' (see European Commission (2013) *Commission report calls for forward-looking policies on migration*, IP/13/552 17/06/2013).

So crime threats and tension over population movements are heightened, particularly in tough economic times.

An instance in England paralleled that of Breivik, in intent, not in scale, when in 2013 a Ukrainian student, Pavlo Lapshyn, murdered an 82-year-old Muslim and carried out the bombings of three mosques in Birmingham and nearby towns. He was preparing to bomb further targets when he was arrested. The police found a file on his computer called 'You Must Murder', which 'contained a racist rant by East European extremists calling for a violent race war', much as Breivik had had on his computer.[24]

Police reported that it was only because Lapshyn mistimed his bomb explosions at sites where Muslims foregathered for Friday prayers, that there was not greater loss of life. So perhaps the police strategic leaders like Interviewee N83 are correct in identifying *potential* for attacks on immigrant populations settling in countries where there are ultra-right-wing political extremists, either resident as with Breivik or temporary like Lapshyn. One Alpine region police leader noted that suspicion of strangers is a characteristic response of communities across Europe, and considered that the generation of violence might be from the native population against the immigrant:

> 'Communities are often suspicious of strangers and we can be very cold against people who migrate into our country, and that may be where the first future tensions grow. We are seeing more and more migrations from poor countries to rich ones and you know, if one EU country lets someone in, they can then go to any EU member state for work or welfare. So in 5 or 10 years' time we will all of us in Europe have very large communities of non-Europeans living among us. There will be violence and crime from them and from our citizens to them.' (Interviewee A90)

Perhaps we might cavil at the supposition that there will be "very large communities of non-Europeans", and we might suppose that the

---

[24] Report in *The Independent* newspaper, 25 October 2013, http://tinyurl.com/ m5tdvxa. Passing a sentence of 40 years' imprisonment on Lapshyn, the trial judge described him in these terms: 'You clearly hold extremist right-wing, white supremacist views and you were motivated to commit the offences by religious and racial hatred in the hope that you would ignite racial conflict and cause Muslims to leave the area where you were living.' (*BBC News*, 25 October 2013; www. bbc.co.uk/news/uk-england-birmingham-24675040).

speaker exaggerates the doom-laden future, but another police leader, from the Mediterranean region, agreed that "tensions will grow in the cities because of increased migration of people from poor to rich countries" (Interviewee M93), but went on to explain that he had taken part in a discussion forum that had highlighted the difficulties of integration without fluency in languages. Facilitators had encouraged the participants to experience typical dissociation:

> 'I went a seminar last month where we imagined the reverse, where our people were moving from Europe to China, Brazil, India and what the reception we would get. I guess it would be very brutal and it would take years to learn the languages and become part of their society. Why should we expect anything different here? The new comers will not know our languages except maybe some English, they will not know our ways and our customs and they will not be welcomed by our people, so of course they will go into places where they are all together for protection. These city "ghettoes" will be the centre of crime and unrest, which we will need to police and control with carefulness and understanding. We should be preparing now for that.' (Interviewee M93)

There is no suggestion currently that there is anything like a pan-European policing approach to potential or actual immigration tensions, and police forces appear to be making contingency plans only within their own force areas and in response to their own immigrant populations (della Porta et al, 2013). The corollary to this, argued Interviewee M93, is that we must extend our command of languages in the police – at least to cover Arabic – and recruit police officers directly who can command "hard" or minority languages:

> 'I have only two officers in my staff who speak Arabic and none who speaks Chinese or Indian languages. We should be thinking ahead, Europe-wide and spending money to make police linguists, or recruiting from language programmes at universities to get police speakers in these hard languages.' (Interviewee M93)

A British Isles region strategic leader considered that social unrest was only partly the product of racial tensions caused or catalysed by immigration. Drawing on the lessons learned from the widespread rioting and looting in cities, particularly London, in the summer of 2011, he commented:

> 'I think policing is going to be more about civil unrest, anger at governments, anger about unemployment, anger about the waste of resources and conspicuous consumption, and competition for scarce things like fuel.' (Interviewee BI 73)

This scenario suggests a much broader breakdown of law and order in a dystopian future than that caused only in relatively restricted geographical areas because of a community's suspicions of 'outsiders'.

Social commentators have noted that civic disturbance can have complex causes and motivations. Leonard Berkowitz, one of the first to comment on modern urban social unrest as a phenomenon, believed that a number of factors were in play, ranging from aggressive acts as responses to hostility or authority, through to 'appropriate situational cues' (Berkowitz, 1972), which means that some people riot because they can. This combination of opportunity and anarchy was certainly evident in London in 2011[25] and earlier in the French *banlieues* of 2005.[26] Analysis of social unrest in the US in the mid to late 1960s talked of 'rage' against liberal education (Edy, 2006), but it is certain that any unrest in the EU would be more complex than that rather self-indulgent emotion. Jacopo Ponticelli and Hans-Joachim Voth propose instead that societies can become unstable after severe budget cuts in public services, but they went on to observe that severe economic downturns did not, of themselves, provoke the same response (Ponticelli and Voth, 2011). Donald and Phyllis Tilly ascribe social unrest to a lack or absence of control over one's life (Tiffany and Tiffany, 1973); powerlessness is felt by members of immigrant communities trying to adjust to often bewildering new lives. We may observe that same sense of powerlessness among the disaffected and underskilled young in any European population, which led one police leader to observe:

> 'If the Eurozone breaks down, and the recovery is not global (say China and Brazil doesn't rack up more real growth until 2020, and the recovery in the US is temporary), then we'll face a real life breakdown of the law here in Europe. [...]

---

[25] See, for example, Murji and Neal, 2011, p. 24.

[26] See Flint and Powell, 2012, p. 20.

There are plenty who would profit from such a situation and it doesn't take much for this nightmare to happen. Look at New Orleans when the levées broke[27] – look at Cyprus with the banking crisis in 2012. We are a whisper from violence and crime on a massive scale.' (Interviewee M88)

Jens Hainmueller and Michael Hiscox, in their 2007 study of the assimilation of immigrants in Europe, noted a contemporary explanation for ethnic tensions and unrest because 'incomers' were resented as competition for work at the unskilled or semi-skilled level. This in fact had little or nothing to do with the relative education levels of those coming into a country against those already there. Indeed, Hainmueller and Hiscox showed that educated 'natives' welcome immigrants, irrespective of the immigrants' educational achievements. It was the cultural clash at the lower skills end of society, partly predicated on fear and partly on racial prejudice, that forms the real focus of tension. Educated people were likely to have less prejudiced views than those with little formal education. Tomas Weiss by contrast argues that in the rush to obtain integration, the EU has inadvertently blurred the borders between internal and external security and has created a concept of 'inside and outside' that was not there before (Weiss, 2012). However it was created, the police now have to deal with the outfall of a federal geography that is under a prolonged external assault by those who want a piece of the better life.

Summary of views on social unrest

The police anticipate that future tensions will arise between working class indigenous populations and poorly educated immigrants, because 'foreign' cultures are viewed with suspicion and there is a widespread belief that those coming in will take away the jobs of those already here. If that happens in general terms across Europe, there may be some foundation for the rather doom-laden pronouncements by strategic police leaders about the consequent breakdown of social order. Certainly the prospect of 'backlash' preoccupies them as far as law and order are concerned. Some of this is merely contingency planning, which any competent strategic police leader should be doing as a matter of routine. But there also seems, on the one hand, to be a genuine and consistent theme emerging from the interviewees' comments

---

[27] Following Hurricane Katrina in August 2005, social order broke down within three days.

that ethnic tensions leading to widespread social unrest, compounded by budget restraints and cuts in public services, allied to growing unemployment and an ageing demographic, may combine at some unspecified point to make a potent threat to stability in Europe. On the other hand, since Europe has a history of absorbing migrants over time (Leigh-Fermor, 2013), police fears may not be realised after all.

'New' policing

> '[...] we may find two different cops: clever ones who do their hunting in the virtual world, and tough cops who walk the streets. So we may recruit different kinds of people to do these things.' (Interviewee C66)

This comment by a Central European region police leader is echoed by a number of others in response to our question about police futures. There seems to be some agreement that future police will be recruited at two levels, one for 'clever' policing and one for a tougher, more 'physical', level to sustain law and order on the streets. A strategic police leader from the Alpine region suggested that:

> '[...] policing will become more about holding law and order together than about investigating crimes. I believe that we are entering a period of civil unrest which will boil up swiftly and die down again, before coming somewhere else. It will cross borders and focus itself in conurbations.' (Interviewee A80)

In order to cope with the likelihood of extensive urban unrest, he thinks that:

> 'What we need is a mobile European detachment of say 4,000 police officers directed to swamp the trouble spots. That will seem to the member states like a step too far even though the Gendarmerie is thinking exactly in that way. It may come because circumstances change and that is the way forward. It would be hard to go back to national police once we let the genie out of the bottle.' (Interviewee A80)

This would be pan-European policing on a large scale, and would require a considerable shift in current policing politics to make it a reality. Currently, very few European member states, if any, would permit foreign police officers to control their urban unrest (Reiter and Fillieule, 2013), but it is entirely possible to imagine a situation where the scale of unrest, and the fact that it may cross national borders, would stimulate governments into cooperative riot control.[28] As Interviewee A80 comments, this may "let the genie out of the bottle" so that:

'In ten or fifteen years, we will probably have a permanent cadre of riot police drawn from all member states, ready for deployment anywhere in the EU. That really would be a Federal solution, wouldn't it?' (Interviewee A80)

Such an elite force already exists, in name if not in function.[29] The European Gendarmerie Force (EGF, often referred to by gendarmerie officers as 'EuroGendFor'[30]) was formed some time ago under the auspices of the Dutch *Maréchaussée* and consists of protocols for mutual support and cooperation between the various gendarmerie forces of Europe. Hans Hovens noted the membership of this formidable police grouping:

On 18 October 2007 France, Italy, Spain, Portugal, and the Netherlands signed the treaty for the European Gendarmerie Force. The treaty meant a new step in the cooperation between the French *Gendarmerie*, the Italian *Carabinieri*, the Spanish *Guardia Civil*, the Portuguese *Guarda Nacional* and the Dutch *Koninklijke Maréchaussée*. In the following years the membership increased. The Polish *Żandarmeria*, the Lithuanian *Viešojo Saugumo Tarnyba* and the Romanian *Jandarmeria* joined the EGF in [respectively] 2007, 2008 and 2009. The Turkish *Jandarma* was granted the observer status in 2009. (Hovens in Hovens and van Elk, 2011, p. 139)

Eight gendarmeries, with possibly a ninth in due course, would easily contribute the "mobile European detachment of [...] 4,000 officers"

---

[28] And not that fanciful either. An article by Alice Hills in 1998 noted that the Secretary-General of NATO had called for a 'global gendarmerie' to pacify the world's trouble spots, but she argued that a permanent cadre of mobile gendarmes was no answer to an absence of policy (Hills, 1998).

[29] It was Napoleon who first referred to the gendarmerie as an elite: "'*C'est un corps d'élite*", disait Napoléon de la gendarmerie'; see Luc, 2002.

[30] See www.eurogendfor.org/. The site has pages in a variety of European languages.

envisaged by Interviewee A80, though whether they would be able to form, deploy and carry out tasks on European streets with the ease that is suggested on paper is another issue entirely (Reiter and Fillieule, 2013). It is probable that the *lingua franca* for the EGF will be English, which in turn may presuppose a higher level of linguistic capability across Europe, particularly among the newly joined gendarmeries, than may actually be the case. Nonetheless, this is a considerable shift by the gendarmeries in the mass and may indicate a greater strategic awareness of future police roles than was previously apparent (Arcudi and Smith, 2013).

This is supported by at least one commentator: Pierre Gobinet noted that it was conventional to regard the gendarmerie, especially in 'common law countries' which had none, as an antiquated alternative to conventional civilian policing. Yet he also points out that the modern gendarmerie offers specialised policing and is an important actor on the modern law enforcement scene, despite almost invariable hostility from the majority of academic commentators (Gobinet, 2008).

Positioning the EGF as a 'last resort' model for the police to impose order may appeal very much to beleaguered politicians, especially as they could claim plausibly that any enforcement actions on the streets were wholly police operations, not a (potentially lethal?) deployment of the military. In the event of such extreme disorder, however, a strategic police leader from the Mediterranean region believes that:

> 'Policing won't just be holding the ring, it'll be a full-scale militaristic response to the breakdown of law: the courts will be summary and the jails will fill. Riots will be dispersed with strong tactics and parts of Europe will look more like Egypt or Libya. [R]estoring order and peace will be the only thing.' (Interviewee M88)

We may not all share this Orwellian vision of the future, but there is no denying that the EGF is anticipating precisely such an outbreak of civil unrest and anarchy where strong riot-control tactics will be needed to restore order (della Porta et al, 2013). A Benelux region strategic leader of gendarmes noted that such an outbreak would be potentially highly disruptive:

> 'The biggest problem in our forecast for the future roles in the gendarmerie is civil unrest caused by a combining of poverty and immigration: this could be very explosive.' (Interviewee B104)

There are still internal sensitivities, of course, which this strategic police leader noted:

> 'In Europe internal security is still one of the bastions of the nation state. Due to the burden of history, it is not self-evident that a German police officer, in uniform and with a gun, [legitimately] operates on Dutch territory.' (Interviewee A26)

So much for the riot-trained, heavily equipped, formidably physical gendarme deployed to unruly city centres; what of 'clever cops'? Do they exist and what might such a police officer do? A police leader from the Nordic region was in no doubt that, across Europe, police forces needed:

> '[...] more internet police officers, more police software engineers, more police fraud experts to follow money-laundering and more experts who know how to harness science in the service of policing.' (Interviewee N96)

It was not simply those who were confident about operating in cyberspace, the same officer suggested, but:

> 'I'm sure that crime will continue to go down as we learn better prevention ways and design better living spaces and security systems in vehicles and so on; and that means that we can develop more specialist police, not only with generic police skills. We need to target precisely, like surgeons [in] a hospital, so that we can cut out crime without harming the rest of society.' (Interviewee N96)

In other words, the development of policing as a specialist 'profession', in which highly trained officers will operate with laser-accurate precision against criminality, is envisaged (Schmuckler, 2013). Some of that specialism, for example in tracking or snaring paedophiles on the internet, or online fraud investigations, is already with us, but most police specialists will have to be recruited afresh and that, in turn, will entail the police articulating exactly what skills are needed and establishing relationships with universities and other centres of higher education to recruit directly. One strategic police leader from the Central European region agreed with the broad aim of specialising, but could not resist a mischievous feminist 'slant' on such an ambition:

'So really there will be two kinds of police by ten years: the strong and not very intelligent to do gendarme duties and the clever, intellectual cops who will do investigations. Needless to speak, I believe that women will predominate in the cyber police and most police *men* will find a home in the gendarmerie.' (Interviewee C91; speaker's own emphasis)

A Mediterranean region police leader took a rather more earnest view, believing that the economic recession was an ideal time to begin recruiting "the very brightest and best" as police officers, because the jobs market was favourable. Even so, he could not resist a pessimistic conclusion that police forces will miss this chance:

'[...] we need to start recruiting clever police officers now, we are well-placed to do so, because of the economy and the difficulties people have in getting jobs. Policing is a more attractive career today than it was five or ten years ago, and this may be the same in the future. If so, we should use this opportunity to pick the very brightest and best to become police officers, especially in those two areas of international crime and crime on the Net. If we do this across Europe, and really train them well to go after criminals in a cooperative spirit, then I will have no fears for the future. The question is whether we have the will, nationally or internationally, and I am afraid that we do not. This would be an opportunity wasted.' (Interviewee M63)

A Nordic region strategic police leader broadly agreed that such recruitment should be a priority for forces across Europe because the choice was stark between either employing clever graduates or muddling on in the same old way. This was something that needed resolution over the next decade, but here too, the officer could not withhold a note of scepticism, saying that while hoping for the best, he was actively preparing for the worst. He went on:

'Policing can go one of two ways: it could be poorly resourced and not a career choice for the intelligent graduate, in which case we will preside over the most cataclysmic decline in policing status, reputation and effectiveness. This might also coincide with a progressive breakdown in law and order so that a brutalistic response to anarchy may be the only available response.

'Or, policing could be well-resourced and placed on a pan-European professional footing which will attract the highest calibre graduate to apply. That would be really exciting and forward-looking, and we would be able to develop many strategies, responses and have a "flex" of options available to deal with any contingencies. The status, reputation and effectiveness of policing would rise, so that the future of the service would be assured. I hope for the second of these, whilst actively preparing for the first.' (Interviewee N18)

A specialist finance police leader agreed, and mounted a passionate argument for such recruitment to be genuinely wide and properly professional, because criminals employ clever accountants and tax advisers to hide and move their illegal assets through a maze of hiding places. The police needed the same expertise and creativity, he argued, and "better intelligence on criminal finances" as well as work "at the strategic level to ensure that countries' finance ministries cooperate with investigations". He continued:

'If ever there was a need for a European level initiative, it is this (though of course the criminals would simply move all their assets out of Europe and beyond tracing). Policing needs to recruit more specialists in financial crime and that means people with special banking expertise and special accounting skills, but more than that we need software engineers and people with high IT skills to work on the criminal tracks. If we get them, the financial crime world will be transformed. I am pessimistic though, because there isn't the money available to recruit the very best from industry into the Financial Police and Fraud Squads and that's across Europe not just here.' (Interviewee M97)

The characteristic note of caution, almost a verbal crossing of fingers to deflect bad luck, ends his discourse, but what he says finds reflection among many of the top police leaders in Europe, who agree that policing has to move forward into a more professional, better qualified and more flexibly structured system to be able to attract and retain highly qualified people. One reflective interviewee from the Nordic region encapsulated what was simultaneously an opportunity if taken and a threat if not:

'Crimes will change; they always do, and of course the police will have new challenges. But if we recruit the right people – varying in gender, background, ethnicity, outlook and expertise – then we stand a chance of holding crime in check – even cybercrime and international crime. Criminals may be clever but they are not Superman, and we should not feel threatened by them.' (Interviewee N98)

A fellow Nordic region strategic police leader did not subscribe to the notion that the problem lay with criminals being cleverer than police officers; that, he said, is a politician's misconception. Instead, the solution lay in organising policing differently and in making profound changes in society:

'Politicians simply think that it is because the police are no good at catching clever people, but it does not work like that. The criminals are not cleverer, they have less bureaucracy and diplomacy to think about, and they are not fettered by protocols in the way I am. This does not mean that I am arguing for more powers because I am not. What I am arguing for is that all states in the EU agree on say, ten priority crimes, and then across the whole EU we try to hit those crimes hard wherever they are. [...] In the long term, we should think of legalising drugs, removing tariffs, licensing brothels and so on, to take the illegality out of commodities – as long as that does not unfairly exploit people, or enslave them. That way, if we remove criminal profit, we diminish crime.' (Interviewee N64)

Another interviewee from the Mediterranean region believed that the next five to 10 years offered an opportunity

'[...] to Europeanise all our policing, with common learning systems, common postings and common strategic approaches. After all, we face the same or very similar problems, and a riot in the suburbs of Paris is probably pretty similar to a riot in Milan, in terms of policing tactics and outcomes I mean.' (Interviewee M16)

Given that member states in Europe can scarcely agree on what constitute the top 10 cross-border crimes (as we saw with '*corpus juris criminalis*' in Chapter Six, and from Interviewee N64 above), asking for common learning, common qualifications and consequent interchangeability may be steps too far, even 10 years from now. But we cannot necessarily envisage in any detail what the conditions in Europe will be like by 2024, and one police leader's best guess is probably as good as any other's. A number of police leaders are agreed that some sort of master plan or overall strategy is required, simply so that police leaders can produce consistent responses to the demands upon them.[31] One strategic police leader echoes the views of many others when she argues that specialist police officers should deal with special problems (including gendarmeries working together to deal with social conflict), but:

> 'what would be best for all of us is a master plan for policing in the EU really to fight against the international criminals. We know we could do this, but there is no strong argument in support from the politicians and most of the EU police forces are too worried that they will lose power and prestige if they surrender their autonomies to a bigger concept. This is described as 'parish-pump politics' by the academics. Do I believe this integrated policing will happen? Not really, but it should.' (Interviewee C94)

Her note of caution suggests that, in reality, a master plan for policing in the EU is as far away as ever and that a precondition for supra-policing to work in a federal Europe would be, as she puts it, that states "surrender their autonomies"; in other words, there would have

---

[31] An EU document looking ahead (2013–24) had this to say about 'cross-border crime' in its 65th paragraph: '[The European Parliament] acknowledges that cross-border crime in the EU continues to grow, and therefore stresses the importance of sufficient funding agencies of law enforcement cooperation; believes that the current "landscape" of the various instruments, tools and channels of information exchange between European law enforcement agencies is complex and distributed, leading to inefficient use of the available instruments and inadequate democratic oversight and inadequate accountability at EU level; calls for the development of future-oriented vision on how to design and optimize the exchange of data between law enforcement authorities in the EU while guaranteeing fundamental rights, including a robust level of data protection; notes that it is necessary to increase mutual trust between law enforcement authorities in order to facilitate the exchange of information" (*European Parliament Resolution on the mid-term review of the Stockholm Programme* (2013/2024 (INI)), report prepared by Berlinguer, L., Fernando López Aguilar, J. and Casini, C. (http://tinyurl.com/l35mnme)

to be subordination of national interest to federal interest. We haven't seen that yet and the omens for such a sea change over the next 10 years are not good.

Summary of views on 'New' policing

There is a core of belief among European strategic police leaders that the police officer 'types' of the future may be moulded or dictated by social circumstances. Social unrest and a breakdown of normal societal restraints may require a strong, mobile, specialist force for intervention and the best available material for this seems to lie within the gendarmeries of Europe, who are already strategically positioning themselves to take advantage of any need for their particular brand of militarised law enforcement or 'pacification'. Simultaneously, leaders believe that now and for 10 years to come, the time is right to recruit 'clever cops', who can perform other specialist functions within policing to give it a professional edge and to damage criminality on a broad basis. Such 'clever cop' police officers will be highly qualified and, presumably, highly rewarded in order to retain them. As yet there appears to be no pan-European plan to do this, and there are no signs of political agreements or initiatives to jump-start any process to put strategic planning of this kind in place. Many officers deplore this strategic timidity, while at the same time being aware themselves of too many disappointments in the past to believe that the future will be any better, though they believe that it assuredly will be different.

Transnational organised crime

> Policing is mismatched to crime, for it is still primarily organized by geography, while crime is not. (Treverton et al, 2011, p. xvi)

The final broad theme that strategic police leaders believe will dominate the next 10 years of policing in Europe concerns police preparedness and ability to respond to the cross-border or transcendent criminality that is often called 'transnational organised crime'.[32] To an extent, this section draws on some of the comments made by interviewees to question 10 about current problems in policing, but the focus here, unlike that in Chapter Six, is on how the police will respond to transnational organised crime in the future. A Baltic region strategic police leader considers with brutal clarity the present and future threats posed by transnational organised crime and the police responses to it:

> 'Look at money-laundering, drugs, people trafficking, smuggling, internet scams, banking fraud, third-world exploitation and identity theft as examples. Its costs us billions of euros and we, the police, are limping along well behind them and hopeful only that, in their greed, [criminals] will make mistakes.' (Interviewee Ba13)

His pessimism may not be entirely justified, but many police leaders share it. They believe that they:

> 'are reactive internationally, inadequate and behind the curve. Criminals can organise themselves across borders where illegal profit is the sole motive; the police organise themselves on a local basis and are often too nationalistic to cross borders with freedom.' (Interviewee A1)

Another factor which police leaders believe contributes to their sense of impotence is apathy on the part of the wider public, to whom the threat of transnational organised crime is remote and lacks immediacy:

> 'Without doubt our biggest challenge [...] is what we can do to combat international organised crime. There are huge criminal profits being made from trafficking, drugs, the sex trade and from arms smuggling and we have a few small successes but not enough. As the economic recession increases across Europe, it will be time to say "go to war

---

[32] Indeed, it is often taught as such and is the subject of extensive academic commentary; see, for example, Edwards and Gill, 2003; Stephen Mallory's excellent *Understanding Organised Crime*, 2nd edn, 2012, Sudbury, MA: Jones and Bartlett Learning; and Reichel and Albanese, 2014. One of the pioneers of empirical research into transnational organised crime is Professor Cyrille Fijnaut of the Netherlands (see, for example, Fijnaut and Ouwerkerk, 2010); and a very good piece of analysis on the entrepreneurial criminal is by Dean et al, 2010.

against crime", but if people can't see that it is in their interest to combat it, they won't stir.' (Interviewee C48)

At the same time, the police are well aware of what they have to do to counter the seemingly inexorable rise in transnational criminality:

'[...] we don't have a good appreciation of criminal markets and criminals who are good businessmen. They are just like other entrepreneurs – they chase the profits and will not go after ventures which have no big gains. So we [police] need to be businesslike too and as clever as them in finance and exploiting opportunities to make money. Where money is, will be criminals.' (Interviewee M14)

This introduces a development that academics have been urging on the police for some time: the need for the police to understand how 'business' works (and illegal businesses follow the same general pattern as legitimate businesses; Dean et al, 2010). If the police understood business, the argument goes, they then might be able to do more about the associated factors in criminal profits,[33] including money laundering, fronting 'clean' businesses, dealing in stolen art or antiquities. What might happen if society took the major step of decriminalising some activities that currently earn criminals lots of money, such as regulating drugs or prostitution (Weitzer, 2005)? Dean et al are blunt about what profit-motivated crime means: 'Organized crime is about making money, lots of it' (Dean et al, 2010, p. 3).

Stephen Mallory expands the concept to examine the business theories which lie behind such direct venality: 'The law of supply and demand results in an enterprise that uses corruption, violence, planning, and organization [...] to control and expand the market for [...] illicit goods and services' (Mallory, 2012, p. 41). He goes on to observe that:

---

[33] The EU makes the right noises: 'We need to hit criminals where it hurts, by going after the money, and we have to get their profits back in to the legal economy, especially in these times of crisis. Law enforcement and judicial authorities must have better tools to follow the money trail. They also need greater means with which to recover a more significant proportion of criminal assets', reported a European Commission Press release (*Crime does not pay: cracking down on criminal profits*, IP/12/235 12/03/2012; http://tinyurl.com/k9yb5kc

> Enterprise theory describes organized crime activity as being well planned and executed with the primary objective of attaining profit and other goals such as power and political influence. The organized crime group involves itself in both licit and illicit activities to meet demands of willing consumers. (Mallory, 2012, p. 41)

Strategic police leaders in Europe are acutely aware of *how* criminals make profits and are cognisant of the demand for illegal supply of goods and services that drives the criminal enterprise. They seem less able to grasp what they can do about some of the global factors that lie behind criminal entrepreneurialism, yet Dean et al make it clear that to understand these concepts, you do not need to know advanced econometrics. They argue instead (Dean et al, 2010, p. 34) that simple 'push/pull' factors make criminal enterprises 'inflate' or 'deflate'. They note that a series of balloons or 'spheres' – the environment, economics, social interaction, technology and politics – all interlink and overlap. These active mixes, which Dean et al describe as 'dynamic interactivities', rise and fall depending on what is happening in the criminal business world (think of people-trafficking or cigarette smuggling) coupled with what the illegal market is demanding (Dean et al, 2010, pp. 33-35).

Interviewee M14, cited earlier, understands how the profit motive works, and believes that the future countermeasures adopted by the police must entail a denial of that profit. She offers some examples:

> 'We don't just need to work together as police, but cleverly as [in] taking profits out of the crime. This way criminals will go to something else. Look at the sex trade: licensed places which are regulated are hard for criminals. They like single girls [working] the streets – easier to control, opportunity to steal, chance for violence. None of these opportunities exists in regulated brothels, and there is better hygiene also. Art is another example: go where the crime is in art; it is forgery and theft. Take out the value/profit of the [stolen or faked] piece of art and the criminal will leave it.' (Interviewee M14)

That said, strategic police leaders do not underestimate the "horrible complexities" (Interviewee N53) that surround policing efforts to come to grips with international crime (Albrecht and Klip, 2013). Almost invariably, police forces do not work strategically but tactically, cooperating across borders on specific crimes and with specific operations, each of which, on each occasion, requires patient planning, cooperation, protocols and mutual understanding (Chapter Five). This Nordic region interviewee seemed close to despair:

> '[...] the biggest threat to all of us is international crime but the horrible complexities are in what we can do about it. Cooperation tends to be between a couple of countries for a specific operational purpose rather than a concerted or united effort to dismantle criminal networks.' (Interviewee N53)

Yet *strategic* police leaders ought to be planning and mapping "united effort[s] to dismantle criminal networks" because that is, or should be, a distinct strategic aim for them globally, not just in Europe. Interviewee N53 goes on to cite an example where police action on the ground is often nullified or frustrated:

> 'Drugs-trafficking is an example: I will mount operations with Great Britain to catch a single shipment and the organisers of it, but I know and the British know, that tomorrow someone else will have filled that temporary gap and the smuggling and distribution will go on as before. Sometimes it is very depressing, but you can only do what you can do.' (Interviewee N53)

Academic commentators agree that this phenomenon of transnational organised crime is not something the police can hope to solve on their own. Indeed, Mallory argues that: 'So far, enforcement and policies have failed to eliminate the profitability of organized crime activity' (Mallory, 2012, p. 47). And although 'the crime investigator can benefit from examining the "why" of organized crime groups, so as to better develop plans of intervention, market disruption, arrest and prosecution' (Mallory, 2012, p. 48), Mallory goes on to state flatly that: 'These organizations are too dynamic to be destroyed by law enforcement efforts alone' (p. 48).

If Mallory is right, then what may be required to defeat transnational organised crime is coordinated international activity, predicated on strong political will, mutual law enforcement intervention and consistent action by criminal justice systems. We seem a long way from attaining that.

While some may despair, others are resolute and believe that the future may hold more than merely promise of mutual cooperation against transnational organised crime. An officer from the Mediterranean region says pointedly that denying the criminal his lucrative profits is a "first step" that might have considerable effect in "chasing the operators out" and exploiting the entrepreneurial criminal's weakness:

> 'Making operating difficult for criminals is the first step, then it is working together with other police forces and then chasing the operators out of our part of the world. Europe and the US is where the money is, at the moment anyway, and that is why criminals want to operate here. There is no sex market from here to Asia – it is the other way, to get at our Euros. And that is where the criminal is weak: if we stop the profit then the crime must go down.' (Interviewee M93)

Another strategic police leader from the same region thought that there should be better protocols and "mechanisms" for denying criminals both freedom of movement and evasion of jurisdictions:

> 'We also need better mechanisms to seize profits and finance from criminals: at the moment I cannot impound the yacht of a target, so he can continue to cruise and continue to land contraband, because I have no jurisdiction in the countries he goes to.' (Interviewee M97)

Another Mediterranean region police leader gave examples of how interdiction, properly resourced and coordinated, can be effective, and that this should be the way forward for the whole of Europe, not just a few enterprising forces:

> 'I have set up with my neighbouring chiefs a system where we can make a joint arrest and whoever has jurisdiction – or the biggest claim – can have the prosecution. Since we are all talking at all levels, and we deliberately involve the prosecutors and judges, there is not a friction. And it works: we have intercepted smugglers and pirates, and we have just caught a number of drugs traffickers in a kind of "between land" between our borders; I mean, in high country where the paths are not precise.' (Interviewee M28)

One Central European region officer took this idea further, arguing for a police force above those of member states, but making it clear that he did not mean an expanded Europol, but an operational grouping that had independent coercive powers:

'I believe the major problem [...] is that there is not a [sic] EU wide law enforcement agency. I know there is Europol, but that is not the same thing as I mean. What we need is an international police in Europe, drawn from all members, with the remit to go after international criminals and the cross-border illegal business that goes on. The problem is always that individual countries will not give up a tiny bit of independence to make this happen.' (Interviewee C81)

We are back to the seemingly perpetual clash in Europe between the 'ideal of federalism' and the reality of national self-interest and protectionism (Guille, 2010a). The only thing that would break this particular *impasse* is strong EU political will, and that appears not to want to engage with transnational policing at the moment. The result is that police officers across Europe keep doing what they can, cooperate on limited operations against specific criminals, while pointing out frustratedly to enquirers what might be achieved if only Europe could act decisively as one integrated international police force.

Summary of views on transnational organised crime

Strategic police leaders in Europe are acutely aware of the threat of transnational organised crime and understand that they are able only to make a limited impact because of jurisdictional limitations, lack of coordinated effort and the absence of a transnational policing body. Some police leaders do not fully understand the nature of criminal entrepreneurialism, which lets them in for criticism from academic commentators, but even where there is knowledge of what drives a criminal enterprise, there is not always an effective means to dismantle it: there is always another criminal entrepreneur waiting in the wings to take advantage of an illegal business opportunity. The police are frustrated by budgetary constraints and occasionally by the breezy freedom from prosecution that a wily criminal can enjoy across the rest of the world, while the police forces they lead seem unable to act in joint strategies of any size or power. What is ironically certain, amid all this uncertainty and irresolution, is that transnational organised crime will continue to pose a threat to Europe; it is the one area of enterprise, both virtually and in the real world, where criminality is growing almost unimpeded.

General summary on the future of policing

The strategic police leaders in Europe who spoke to us may be only a proportion of those who could have done so, but we are confident that we have canvassed a range of opinions about the future of policing that are pretty much representative of European strategic policing concerns as a whole.

The four principal themes are:

- an explosive growth in cybercrime;
- unease at the prospect of social unrest developing perhaps from immigration and from continued economic fragility and unemployment;
- a tangible shift in the perceived need for police recruitment to move away from the conventional to the dramatically specialist (whether clever cops or stolid gendarmes);
- the protean entrepreneurialism of the transnational organised criminal and police frustration at the difficulties of dealing with them across national borders.

This suggests a police leadership that is attuned to change, but does not necessarily relish it. The elite in European policing is frustrated by what it sees as political and judicial inertia and by matters over which it has little control – including the mushrooming of the use of the internet and social messaging media. At the same time, we may need to make allowance for these characteristically doom–laden pronouncements about the collapse of society and the emergence of feral criminality, which may be a combination of special pleading and the almost innate pessimism that most police officers have about ameliorative societies, confronted as they are on a daily basis with man's inhumanity to man. It is perhaps hard to be optimistic about the future of policing, when your daily routine involves both investigation and confrontation of some heinous crimes and dealing with volumes of petty antisocial activity.

Nonetheless our interviewees do not always despair of the future, and some leaders look forward with hope (if no very great expectation) that Europe might actually solve some of its criminal justice problems, given a fair wind and some determination. But several others noted to us that they were glad that their time in policing was drawing to an end, because their ability to understand the 'brave new world' around the corner was becoming blunted, tired and redundant. It is time for others to take on the challenge, perhaps. The last word should go to an insouciant strategic leader who, asked what the future held for policing in Europe, replied:

'You must come to my lectures in 2017 to find out!' (Interviewee C50)

Maybe we should, at that.

General conclusion

What is offered in this book, for the first time we think, is rich detail of the views and attitudes of a representative range of European strategic police leaders. These officers determine the operational effectiveness of police forces across Europe, and it was timely to look at who they are, how they got there, what they do, what they want and what they believe to be the future of policing.

The strategic police leader remains an enigma, even inside policing, and for many reasons, including democratic accountability, we need to understand how this elite works and to ask whether it is properly accountable or merely self-referential. What often seems to concern the elite itself are ways and means to operate effectively across jurisdictional boundaries to interdict cross-border criminality, which is laudable but hardly strategic.

The official and political powers in the European Commission (EC) see police activity at the operational level of bilateral cooperation as an example of narrow nationalism, and would much rather encourage strategic coordination of all members' agencies on a sufficient scale to combat international criminality across Europe. But there was little in our interviewees' comments that willingly embraced this political ideal of *pan-Continental concerted police action*. In turn, this may suggest that there is something of a credibility gap between the kind of supra-national policing vision promulgated by the EC and a doggedly pragmatic determination to get the job done at the cooperative policing level.

There are also internal controversies aired by the strategic police leaders, such as:

- their scepticism about the role of Europol and Eurojust;
- their frustration at the lack of objective and systematic development programmes at the strategic level in almost every country;
- their weary, even jaundiced, view of police accountability in practice, particularly through what many saw as their 'submission' to the local mayor and to the media.

They also gave us extended commentaries on:

- cybercrime
- public order

- illegal trafficking
- transnational organised crime and criminals
- terrorism
- operational prioritisation in a time of financial austerity
- political interference.

These are all urgent topics that have engaged, and continue to preoccupy, strategic police leaders, and we should listen carefully, if dispassionately, to what they have to say. The questions whether there is a distinct species of 'police leadership' or whether generic leadership skills are merely appended to policing are also of importance, together with leaders' views on continuing development after appointment and learning opportunities in the strategic role.

It seems that patronage still plays a part in police leader selection, and there is strong emerging evidence from interviewees' testimony that succession planning across Europe continues to rely in part on potential leaders being spotted early and nurtured in a nepotistic manner by existing chiefs. This in turn raises questions about potential for 'cloning' and consequently whether ease of movement between national systems will ever be practicable. A 'face that fits' in one jurisdiction may fit very badly in another. There is no pan-European or generic police learning 'package' to nurture and develop future strategic police leaders, nor does such a concept seem to be either necessary or current in the EC.

Although there is increasing emphasis (indeed reliance) on some form of postgraduate qualification for the strategic police leader in Europe – and in most cases, such a qualification acts as a predeterminant for promotion to the elite of police command – there is no consensus on what that qualification should be (law, politics, history, forensic science, software engineering or languages?). In parallel, there is an almost equal – and somewhat contradictory – emphasis inside police forces on the experientiality of strategic leadership. The track record of a police leader is still regarded as the principal indicator of likely competence in the new role, even though a causal link between past experience and the capacity to lead has yet to be proven *a posteriori*, while rigorous analysis of what might constitute specifically police leadership skills, as opposed to generic leadership competences, is lacking.

There is modelling, and there are lists of generic strategic leadership competences galore, but currently there is no suite of skills, objectively assessed and forensically developed, that is inherent to *police* operational and strategic command, to the determination of *police* response to a situation and which a police officer *must* have, uniquely, to do the job. It might be argued that such demands are crying for the moon.

Yet the skills that strategic police leaders must possess, if they are to direct, determine, propose, explain, develop and safeguard operationally effective policing, are surely assessable? There has been no transition, and apparently no EC or CEPOL will to engender a transition, from accountable strategic command to teachable police leadership skills. But if one can develop the capacity in a senior police officer to make correct strategic operational decisions as 'Gold' that is, in charge of the strategic response to an unfolding police operation, it should not be beyond the wit of tutors and teachers to develop equivalent police leadership skills in such decision-making as impactive public order command, imaginative strategic responses to investigational pressures, efficient coordination of partners in a civil emergency or effective resolution of a terrorist incident.

Hoogewoning et al noted in 2015 the *unique features of policing*; these features (it seems to us) must be susceptible to learning and development, or no 'Gold' would ever make the right decision: such capabilities cannot be instinctive, nor can they be learned by rote. But we think they *can* be simulated, using plausible scenarios to develop effective decision-making at the strategic level, in much the same way that the computer-based simulation suite Hydra teaches such skills in the UK.[1] We need to get away from thinking only about generic leadership skills and begin to elaborate those skills that are necessary to be able to perform excellently at the strategic levels of policing.

More broadly, the European Union lacks a coherent plan for, or even consistent interest in, developing leaders in policing, even though its *political* emphasis is increasingly on cooperative strategies to counter organised crime.

---

[1] 'Hydra' is a computer-based simulation suite, originally designed to test effective senior investigating officer decisions in scenarios about homicides or serial rapes. It was developed by Dr Jonathan Crego in association with the Metropolitan Police. Professor Crego (now of the Open University) has linked with Professor Laurence Alison (University of Liverpool) to develop Hydra's wider applications. However, to our knowledge, although we are well persuaded (and have experience) of Hydra's efficacy as a teaching and learning tool, and know that it was introduced on the UK's Police Strategic Command Course in February 2014, there has been no application of it to developing police leadership skills in wider Europe. There should be. Its practical deployment as a learning tool may be seen at: http://tinyurl.com/lkdwqs2. For academic analysis and commentary, see Alison and Crego (2008) and Alison et al (2013).

- We did not detect a common pattern across Europe for strategic police leaders to follow.
- We found no consistent understanding of how to develop potential leaders.
- We discovered no attempt to ascertain whether the skills required to become a strategic police leader in one country could be transferred to the police of another.
- Damningly, we found no interest in doing any of this.[2]

National systems are entirely (and exclusively) geared towards raising people internally; they are not part of any wider plan or process. Yet thought should be given, as we suggest above, to:

- how consistent inter-European selection might be achieved;
- what such a process might look like;
- who would deliver it;
- what learning outcomes would be entailed.

Why? Because any vision that embraces effective strategic countermeasures to transnational organised crime, such as those elaborated by the EU, must depend on recognisable, exchangeable and dependable capabilities in the strategic policing response.

That response has to be simultaneously effective at both the national and international levels. It has to embrace impactive international policing on a broader front than single-issue bilateralism. How can that be done, if the selection processes and required skills for a police leader in country X are radically unlike those in country Y and both are different again from country Z? We might suggest by way of illustration – but with no disrespect to either – that police leaders in the Nordic region, replete with postgraduate qualifications in law and jurisprudence, are some distance apart from the gendarmerie generals in the Mediterranean region, with their practical command experience of international peace-keeping.[3] Can we reconcile these

---

[2]   Despite the example of the **European Diploma in Policing**, a postgraduate qualification developed by a consortium of European universities and police training schools in 2003-06, and pioneered by one of the authors. It lives on as an etiolated form in a joint Master's programme between the Dutch *Politie* and Canterbury Christ Church University in the UK.

[3]   This is not to say that 'academic' police officers cannot be practical or vice versa. It is rather that the respective regional emphases on what constitutes police leadership are at sharp variance.

differences into one consistent scheme? Is it achievable? Is it worth trying? If the answer to any of these questions is 'yes' (and the EC's sporadic pronouncements on policing at least imply that the questions are worth considering), then there should be an open, cooperative and free-ranging collaboration between police leaders, academics, trainers and developers, strategists, politicians and lawyers to create a pilot to roll out across Europe. No such collaboration seems anywhere envisaged, even by the egregiously self-regarding 'Pearls of Policing'.

Strategic police leadership in Europe is overwhelmingly a male preserve, as the data and the accounts by female officers of how they found advancement blocked to them, bear witness. The profile of a typical European strategic police leader is of a middle-aged 'pale male', in a job for life, often more civil servant than operationally active police officer – a conservative, cautious, educated, urbane, public service official. The implications of this profile for diversity within policing, for the representation of women and members of minority ethnic communities in the top strategic posts, and for the message that this sends to society as a whole about the elite in policing, should give us profound concern. There are complex barriers in European policing to a proportionate representation of women and of minority ethnic communities and there appears currently to be little political will to do anything about that, despite the EC's emollient noises and distasteful trumpeting of its modest achievements in diversity. Since the EC seems content with its mediocre standards, the police themselves should get a grip on this unsatisfactory state of affairs, as should academics and commentators on the police across Europe, because it matters significantly that EU police leadership selection systems are disadvantaging women and members of minority ethnic communities.

Not only that, but disadvantaging inhibits any real progress in policing as being representative of the rest of society as long as such thinking holds sway. It is indisputable that only a very small number of those from minority ethnic communities achieve command in the police, that fewer than half the available senior women police make the advance to strategic leadership, and that there is no systematic 'barrier analysis' in European policing. The notion that women can deal only with 'morality' crimes remains astonishingly persistent, while those from a minority ethnic origin are simply not recruited in significant enough numbers to make any kind of impact on 'pale maleness'.

The mechanisms of the EU do not help research or analysis in this field, since data about women or minority ethnic representation in policing are not routinely obtained (for a comparison, see Aebi et al, 2006). How can you know what you need to do if you cannot scope the problem in the first place? This is important to all of us, since issues of equality and diversity impact directly on the overall legitimacy of the police service in Europe. This should not simply be a stick with which to beat the opaque and aloof EC, but an issue that the supine and toothless European Parliament should take on urgently, if only as a change from squabbling about expenses.

The novelty of accountability in the former Soviet-Bloc nations was examined in some detail in our study, because of the difficulties encountered in creating a 'new' police force from the ashes of the old. The scepticism and fear that continue to be expressed by the public rightly worry the new generation of 'clean skin' chief officers, who themselves admit readily to finding problems with being answerable both to the law and to their citizens. There are some still in place who owe their positions and appointments to the old regimes, and their potential to act as a drag on (or block to) reforms was discussed, as was their relationship to their former masters in Russia and the implications that this may have both for current political 'churn' and for transnational organised crime.

In the rest of Europe, strategic police leaders have mixed feelings about the intrusion of the media into their work (some resenting it, some embracing it), while there is mistrust of political interventions to hold the police to account. This should not surprise us: there is a sense in which 'accountability' is too often given lip service in policing; oversight bodies requiring the police to justify what they do too often provoke howls of anguish from some police leaders and expressions of pained surprise from others. There seems to be a current of opinion in strategic policing that being accountable is not a priority public duty, whereas operational effectiveness is. Again, this attitude is understandable at a practical, operational level but it is not excusable at a strategic one.

Relationships with peers tended to be less fraught and competitive in the rest of Europe than in the UK, and key relationships tend to be more between chief officers and public prosecutors than between police peer groups. There is evidence to suggest that strategic police leaders prefer to develop less-competitive relationships within the criminal justice system and away from their own peer group, which in turn led us to ask what influences matter most in leaders' formulation of policing strategies. That said, one or two waspish strategic police leaders had unflattering things to say about both their peers and the professional colleagues with whom they worked.

Essentially, what the data reveal about strategic police leaders is that they are sceptical of the value of pan-European institutions and 'supra-national' organisations, preferring to conduct their day-to-day business on a bilateral basis for specific operational purposes. They argue that without a European criminal law, the '*corpus juris criminalis*' equivalent of the European Convention on Human Rights to which all EU members have to sign up, there can be no meaningful large-scale operational policing. There are very evident credibility gaps between Council of Europe strategic policy for the criminal law/strategic policing and what happens in operational practice (Ebbe, 2013).

Visions of the future

Strategic police leaders are more or less agreed on the three major challenges currently facing them:

- terrorism
- organised crime
- cybercrime.

However, they differ in the methodologies they should use, as well as differing in what should be included in the second rank of priorities.

Many seem to think that there will be a diminution in organised extremist-belief-centred terrorism over the next decade or so, but there may be a compensating rise in 'lone-wolf' terrorism: one-off attacks conducted by disaffected or deranged individuals, like Breivik or Lapshyn. But this is impressionistic, not intelligence-based.

Most agree that the major threat is transnational organised crime, and that cybercrime represents a kind of transitional phase from the real world of organised crime to the virtual criminal 'Dark Web'. Predictably, strategic police leaders are less engaged with understanding and analysing either phenomenon and more concerned with trying to control them.

Our evidence suggests that there is considerable unanimity about the threats facing Europe in the future; but also wide variations in the means that chief officers would advocate to counter those threats. The internationalism of modern policing, and the fact that no European police force can exist in isolation from others, has implications both for all British police forces – who may be forced by current political initiatives progressively to disengage from European mechanisms – and for the newly joined EU member states in terms of capability, preparedness and cooperation. At the same time, we have to allow for professional pessimism, expressed in apocalyptic terms, about ubiquitous future public order scenarios and police impotence in the face of the universality of cybercrime.

To the extent that these are projections of current unease, they may be regarded perhaps with some detachment as merely expressive of strategic police leaders' 'nightmare' visions of the future. We do not actually seem to be poised on the edge of an Orwellian abyss of disorder and rampant 'virtual' crime, whatever strategic police leaders would have us believe. We can point, less dramatically but with equal assurance, to the rapid advances made by the emergent generation of police officers who are software-savvy and highly skilled operators in cyberspace. We might indicate too the preparedness in the European Gendarmerie Force's positioning on public order. The use of 'foreign' force to resolve large-scale disturbances in national capitals may dismay us in some respects, but we can certainly envisage situations where politicians would turn to Europe's gendarmeries with some relief, and order them to restore tranquillity, and gain in stature themselves in the process.

Where the strategic police leaders have a resounding point, however, is that work in policing cyberspace and work to inhibit the international migration of the rootless and disaffected, however well coordinated within Europe, is not 'joined up'. There is no global reach or effective international coordination of effort in either of these phenomena. Realising such a dream of 'world policing' is, alas, beyond the scope of this modest book, which has now reached its own limit at the edge of the European Continent.

Bibliography

Abraham, P. (2001) The Romanian police and the challenges of transition, in A. Kadar (ed.) *Police in transition: Essays on the police forces in transition countries*, Budapest (Hungary): Central European University Press

ACPO/Skills for Justice (2003) *Twelve competences for a chief officer*, Home Office Circular 27/2003, London: Home Office

Adair, J. (1973) *The action-centred leader*, London: McGraw Hill

Aden, H. (2001) Convergence of policing policies and transnational policing in Europe, *European Journal of Crime, Criminology, Law and Criminal Justice*, 9, 99

Adlam, R. (2002) Governmental rationales in police leadership: an essay exploring some of the 'deep structure in leadership praxis', *Policing and Society*, Vol. 12, No. 1, pp. 15-36

Adlam, R. (2003) Nice people, big questions, heritage concepts, in R. Adlam and P. Villiers (eds) *Police leadership in the 21st century: Philosophy, doctrine and development*, Winchester: Waterside Press

Adlam, R. and Villiers, P. (eds) (2003) *Police leadership in the 21st century: Philosophy, doctrine and development*, Winchester: Waterside Press

Aebi, M. F., Aromaa, K., de Cavarlay, B. A., Barclay, G., Gruszczynska, B., Von Hofer, H., Hysi V. and Tavares, C. (2008) *European sourcebook of crime and criminal justice statistics*, Amsterdam: Boom Juridische Unitgevers. www3.unil.ch/wpmu/europeansourcebook/files/2012/06/Codebook_SBK_4th-ed_rev080918_r-11.pdf

Akers, R. and Sellers, C. (2004) *Criminological theories: Introduction, evaluation, and application*, 4th edn, Los Angeles, California: Roxbury Publishing Company

Albrecht, H. J., and Klip, A. (eds) (2013) *Crime, criminal law and criminal justice in Europe: A collection in honour of Prof. Em. Dr. Dr. Hc Cyrille Fijnaut*, Martinus Nijhoff Publishers

Alderson, J. (1984) *Law and disorder*, London: Hamish Hamilton

Alderson J. (2003) Police leadership, Chapter 3 in R. Adlam and P. Villiers (eds) *Police leadership in the 21st century: Philosophy, doctrine and development*, Winchester: Waterside Press, pp. 56-67

Alegre, S. and Leaf, M. (2004) Mutual recognition in European judicial cooperation: A step too far too soon? Case study—the European arrest warrant, *European Law Journal*, Vol. 10, No. 2, pp. 200-217

Alimo-Metcalfe, B. (2010) Developments in gender and leadership: introducing a new 'inclusive' model, *Gender in Management: An International Journal*, Vol. 25, No. 8, pp. 630-639

Alison, L. and Crego, J. (eds) (2008) *Policing critical incidents: Leadership and critical management*, Devon: Willan Publishing

Alison, L., van den Heuvel, C., Waring, S., Power, N., Long, A., O'Hara, T. and Crego, J. (2013) Immersive simulated learning environments for researching critical incidents: a knowledge synthesis of the literature and experiences of studying high-risk strategic decision making, *Journal of Cognitive Engineering and Decision Making*, Vol. 7, No. 3, pp. 255-272

Altus Global Alliance (2006) *Police Station Visitors' Week in Europe*. www.indem.ru/en/Cja/RegRepEu.pdf

Anderson, J., O'Dowd, L. and Wilson, T. (eds) (2003) *New borders for a changing Europe: Cross-border cooperation and governance*, London: Routledge (Frank Cass)

Anderson, M. (2011) *In thrall to political change: Police and gendarmerie in France*, Oxford: Oxford University Press

Anderson, M. and Apap, J. (2002) *Police and justice cooperation and the new European borders*, Den Haag: Kluwer Law International

Anderson, M., Den Boer, M., Cullen, P., Gilmore, W., Raab, C. and Walker, N. (1995) *Policing the European Union 'theory, law, and practice'*, Oxford: Clarendon Press

Anderson, S. and Lightfoot, D. (2002) *The language organ: Linguistics as cognitive physiology*, Cambridge: Cambridge University Press

Anderson, T. (2000) *Every officer is a leader: Transforming leadership in police justice and public safety*, Boca Raton, Florida, USA: St Lucie Press (CRC Press)

Andreas, P. and Nadelmann, E. (2006) *Policing the globe: Criminalization and crime control in international relations*, Oxford: Oxford University Press

Andreescu, A. and Malme, O. (2010) The challenge of transnational and organized crime in the Nordic countries: the case of Norway, in C. Roberson, D. Das. and J. Singer (eds) *Police without borders: The fading distinction between local and global*, New York: CRC Press (Taylor and Francis)

Andreopoulos, G. (ed.) (2012) *Policing across borders: Law enforcement cooperation for international crime*, New York: Springer Publications Ltd

Andrew, C. (2009) *Defend the realm: The authorized history of MI5*, London: Vintage

Andrew, C. and Gordievsky, O. (1990) *KGB: The inside story of its foreign operations from Lenin to Gorbachev*, London: Hodder and Stoughton

Apap, J. (2006) What future for Europol? Increasing Europol's accountability and improving Europol's operational capacity, Brussels: European Parliament, 7 September

Archbold, C. and Schulz, D. (2008) Making rank: the lingering effects of tokenism on female police officers' promotion aspirations, *Police Quarterly*, Vol. 11, No. 1, pp. 50-73

Archick, K. (2013) *European Union Enlargement*. www.hsdl.org/?searchan dcollection=limitedandfactandso=dateandsubmitted=Searchandformat andcreator=Archick%2C+Kristin

Arcudi, G. and Smith, M. (2013) The European Gendarmerie Force: a solution in search of problems?, *European Security*, Vol. 22, No. 1, pp. 1-20

Bache, I., George, S. and Bulmer, S. (eds) (2011) *Politics in the European Union*, 3rd edn, Oxford: Oxford University Press

Bäck, T. (2008) Är polisstudenter mentalt tränade för polisyrket? [Are police students mentally trained for police work?], in *Policing in Scandinavia: Proceedings from the Conference on Police Research*, Växjö, Sweden: August 2007

Backhaus, J. (ed.) (2008) *The beginnings of political economy: Johann Heinrich Gottlob von Justi*, New York: Springer

Bacon, E. and Renz, B. (2003) Return of the KGB?, *The World Today*, Vol. 59, No. 5, pp. 26-27

Bayley, D. (1999) Policing the world stage, in R. I Mawby (ed.) *Policing across the world: Issues for the twenty-first century*, London: UCL Press, pp. 3-12

Baker, T. (2011) *Effective police leadership: Moving beyond management*, New York: Looseleaf Publications

Barling, J., Slater, F. and Kellaway, E. (2000) Transformational leadership and emotional intelligence: an exploratory study, *Leadership and Organisational Development Journal*, Vol. 21, No. 3, pp. 157-161. www.emeraldinsight. com/Insight/viewPDF.jsp?contentType=ArticleandFilename=html/ Output/Published/EmeraldFullTextArticle/pdf/0220210304.pdf

Barnard-Wills, D. (2011) UK news media: discourses of surveillance, *The Sociological Quarterly*, Vol. 52, No. 4, pp. 548-567

Barnet, M. and Coleman, L. (2005) Designing police: Interpol and the study of change in international organizations, *International Studies Quarterly*, Vol. 49, No. 4, December, pp. 593-619

Baron A. and Armstrong, M. (2007) *Human capital management: Achieving added value through people*, London: Kogan Page

Barton, L. and Barton, H. (2011) Challenge, issues and change: what's the future for UK policing in the twenty-first century?, *International Journal of Public Sector Management*, Vol. 24, Issue 2, pp. 146-156

Bass, B. and Riggio, R. (2006) *Transformational leadership*, London: Routledge

Bayley, D. (2001) *Democratizing the police abroad: What to do and how to do it*, Washington: National Institute of Justice

Bayley, D. (2005) Police reform as foreign policy, *Australian and New Zealand Journal of Criminology*, Vol. 38, No. 2, pp. 206-215

Beare, M. and Murray, T. (2007) *Police and government relations: Who's calling the shots?* Toronto, Canada: University of Toronto Press

Beetham, D. (1974) *Max Weber and the theory of modern politics*, London: Allen and Unwin

Bennich-Björkman, L. (2006) Building post-communist states: political corruption and strategies of party formation in Estonia and Latvia, in S. Eliaeson (ed.) *Building democracy east of the Elbe: Essays in honor of Eduard Mokryczki*, London: Routledge

Bennich-Björkman, L. (2009) Party formation and elites in the Baltic states, *Baltic Worlds*, Vol. II: III-IV, pp. 29-36, Stockholm: Centre for Baltic and East European Studies, Södertörn University. http://balticworlds.com/the-communist-past-party-formation-and-elites-in-the-baltic-states

Bennis, W. (1989) On becoming a leader (cited in Long, M., *Leadership and performance management* (2003) in T. Newburn (ed.) *Handbook of policing*, Willan Publishing, Devon, pp. 628-654

Bennis, W. and Thomas, R. (2002) *Geeks and geezers: How era, values and defining moments shape leaders*, Boston, MA.: Harvard University Press

Benyon, J. (1994) Policing the European Union: the changing basis of co-operation on law enforcement, *International Affairs*, Vol. 70, no. 3, pp. 497–517

Benyon, J. (1996) The politics of police co-operation in the European Union, *International Journal of the Sociology of Law*, Vol. 24, No. 4, pp. 353-379

Benyon, J., Turnbull, L., Willis, A., Woodward, R. and Beck, A. (1994) *Police co-operation in Europe: An investigation*, Leicester: University of Leicester, Centre for the Study of Public Order

Berenskoetter, F. (2011) Mapping the field of UK-EU policing: a typology, *Journal of Common Market Studies*, Chichester: John Wiley & Sons

Berkowitz, L. (1972) Frustrations, comparisons, and other sources of emotion arousal as contributors to social unrest, *Journal of Social issues*, Vol. 28, No. 1, pp. 77-91

Bernstein, P. (1996) *Against the gods: The remarkable story of risk*, New York: John Wiley and Sons, Inc

Bertoalmi, F. (2012) CEPOL - Accademia Europea di Polizia [CEPOL - European Police College], *La cittadinanza europea*, Vol. 7, No. 1, pp. 117-25

Biersteker, T. and Weber, C. (eds) (1996) *State sovereignty as social construct*, Cambridge: Cambridge University Press

Bigo, D. (2000) Liaison Officers in Europe: New officers in the European security field, Ch. 3 in J. Sheptycki (ed.) *Issues in transnational policing*, pp. 67-99

Bigo, D. (2001) The Möbius Ribbon of internal and external security(ies) Chapter 4, in M. Albert, D. Jacobson and L. Josef (eds) *Identities, borders, orders: Rethinking international relations theory*, Minneapolis, MN: University of Minnesota Press, pp. 91-118

Bigo, D. and Guild, E. (eds) (2005) *Controlling frontiers: Free movement into and within Europe*, London: Ashgate Publishing Ltd

Bingöl, M. (2011) The need for gendarmeries in the years ahead, *Gendarmeries*, 183

Black, A. and Brunt, R. (2000) MI5, 1909-1945: an information management perspective, *Journal of information science*, Vol. 26, No. 3, pp. 185-197

Blair, Sir I. (2009) *Policing controversy*, London: Profile Books

Blair, Lord I. (2010) Policing: continuity, consensus and controversy, *The Political Quarterly*, Vol. 81, No. 2, April-June, pp. 167-175

Blanning, T. (ed.) (2000) *The nineteenth century*, Short Oxford History of Europe series, Oxford: Oxford University Press

Block, L. (2007) International policing in Russia: police co-operation between the European Union member states and the Russian Federation, *Policing and Society*, Vol. 17, No. 4, pp. 367-387

Block, L. (2008) Combating organized crime in Europe: practicalities of police cooperation, *Policing*, Vol. 2, No. 1, pp. 74-81

Block, L. (2011) *From politics to policing: The rationality gap in EU Council decision making*, The Hague, Netherlands: Eleven International Publishing

Body-Gendrot, S, Hough, M., Kerezsi, K., Lévy, R. and Snacken, S. (eds) (2014) *The Routledge Handbook of European Criminology*, Oxford: Abingdon

Bomberg, E., Peterson, J. and Corbett, R. (eds) (2011) *The European Union: How does it work?* Oxford: Oxford University Press

Borgonovo, J. (2007) *Spies, informers and the 'Anti-Sinn Féin Society': The intelligence war in Cork city, 1920-1921*, Dublin: Irish Academic Press

Bossard, A. (1993) *Law enforcement in Europe: Building effective cooperation*, Chicago: University of Illinois, Office of International Criminal Justice

Bottomore, T. (2006) *Elites and society*, London: Routledge

Bowers, S. (2014) British banker pleads guilty to Libor rigging: senior banker faces up to 10 years in prison as Serious Fraud Office secures first UK guilty plea in Libor rate-fixing scandal, *The Guardian*, 7 October. www.theguardian.com/business/2014/oct/07/banker-pleads-guilty-libor-rigging-rate-fixing

Bowling, B. (2010) *Policing the Caribbean: Transnational security co-operation in practice,* Clarendon Studies in Criminology, Cambridge: Cambridge University Press

Bowling, B. and Sheptycki, J. (2012) *Global policing*, London: Sage Publications

Brain, T. (2010) *A history of policing in England and Wales from 1974: A turbulent journey*, Oxford: Oxford University Press

Breda, V. (2006) A European constitution in a multinational Europe or a multinational constitution for Europe?, *European Law Journal*, Vol. 12, No. 3, May, pp. 330–344. onlinelibrary.wiley.com/doi/10.1111/j.1468-0386.2006.00320.x/full

Bridger, S. and Pine, F. (eds) (2013) *Surviving post-socialism: Local strategies and regional responses in Eastern Europe and the former Soviet Union*, London: Routledge

Brodeur, J.-P. (1983) High policing and low policing: remarks about the policing of political activities, *Social Problems*, pp. 507-520

Brodeur, J.-P. (1995) *Comparisons in policing: An international perspective*, Aldershot: Avebury Publishing

Brodeur, J.-P. (ed.) (1998) *How to recognize good policing: problems and issues*, Washington, DC: Police Executive Research Forum

Brodeur, J.-P. (2010) *The policing web*, Oxford: Oxford University Press

Broers, M., Hicks, P. and Guimera, A. (eds) (2012) *The Napoleonic empire and the new European political culture*, London: Palgrave Macmillan

Brogden, M. (1987) Emergence of the police – the colonial dimension, *British Journal of Criminology*, Vol. 27, No. 4, pp. 4-14

Browder, G. (1996) *Hitler's enforcers: The Gestapo and the SS security service in the Nazi revolution*, Oxford: Oxford University Press

Brown, A. (2007) The Gorbachev era, in R. Suny (ed.) *The Cambridge History of Russia: The twentieth century*, Cambridge: Cambridge University Press

Brown, H. (2012) The origins of the Napoleonic system of repression, in M. Broers, P. Hicks and A. Guimera (eds) *The Napoleonic Empire and the new European political culture*, London: Palgrave Macmillan, pp. 38-48

Brown, J. (1996) Integrating women into policing: a comparative European perspective, in M. Pagon (ed.) *Policing in Central and Eastern Europe. Comparing firsthand knowledge with experience from the West*, Ljubljana, Slovenia: University of Maribor Press

Brown, J. (1997) European policewomen: a comparative research perspective, *International Journal of the Sociology of Law*, Vol. 25, Issue 1, pp. 1-19

Browne, A. (2005) Brussels publishes list of first seven pan-European crimes, *The Times*, 24 November 2005

Bruggeman, W. (2002) Policing and accountability in a dynamic European context, *Policing and Society: An International Journal of Research and Policy*, Vol. 12, Issue 4, pp. 259-273

Bruggeman, W. and Den Boer, M. (2010) Ethics and policing in the emerging EU internal security architecture, *Ethics and Security*, The Hague, Eleven International Publishers, pp. 141-164

Brunger, M. (2013) Exploring the myth of the Bobby and the intrusion of the state into social space, *Revue Internationale de Sémiotique Juridique*, Vol. 26, No.1

Bryman, A., Stephens, M. and Campo, C. (2002) The importance of context: qualitative research and the study of leadership, *The Leadership Quarterly*, Vol. 7, Issue 3, Autumn, pp. 353-370

Buckley, L., McGinnis, J. and Petrunik, M. (1992) Police perceptions of education as an entitlement to promotion: an equity theory perspective, *American Journal of the Police*, Vol. 12, No.2, pp. 77-95

Burgersdijk, O. and Outram, M. (2013) Effectiveness of police leadership within the organisational context, *Pearls in policing*, privately published, text made available to the authors

Busch, N. and Givens, A. (2012) Public-private partnerships in homeland security: opportunities and challenges, *Homeland Security Affairs*, Vol. 8. www.hsaj.org/?fullarticle=8.1.18

Busuioc, M., Curtin, D. and Groenleer, M. (2011) Agency growth between autonomy and accountability: the European Police Office as a 'living institution', *Journal of European Public Policy*, Vol. 18, No. 6, pp. 848-867

Butler, R. (2006) *The Gestapo* [republished as an online book 2012], London: Amber Books

Button, M. (2012) *Private policing*, London: Routledge

Caless, B. (2011) *Policing at the top: The roles, values and attitudes of chief police officers*, Bristol: The Policy Press

Caless, B. and Tong, S. (2012) 'An appropriate space', chief officers and police accountability, *Police Practice and Research: An International Journal*, Vol. 13, No. 6, pp. 4-16

Caless, B. (ed.) with Spruce, B., Underwood, R and England S. (2014) Blackstone's *Policing for the PCSO*, 3rd edn, Oxford: Oxford University Press

Callanan, V. and Rosenberger, J. (2011) Media and public perceptions of the police: Examining the impact of race and personal experience, *Policing and Society*, Vol. 21, No. 2, pp. 167-189

Campbell, D. and Campbell, K. (2010) Soldiers as police officers/ police officers as soldiers: role evolution and revolution in the United States, *Armed Forces and Society*, January, Vol. 36, No. 2, pp. 327-350

Campbell, I. and Kodz, J. (2011) *What makes great police leadership? What research can tell us about the effectiveness of different leadership styles, competencies and behaviours. A Rapid Evidence review*, http://whatworks.college.police. uk/Research/Documents/Great_Police_Leader_REA.pdf

Cameron, F. (2004) *The future of Europe*, London: Routledge

Caparini, M. and Marenin, O. (2004) *Transforming the police in Central and Eastern Europe*, Geneva Centre for the Democratic Control of Armed Forces' Series, Munster, Germany: Munster LIT

Carson, W. (2007) Calamity or catalyst futures for community in twenty-first-century crime prevention, *British Journal of Criminology*, Vol. 47, No. 5, pp. 711-727

Casey, J. (2007) International policing, Chapter 18 in M. Mitchell and J. Casey (eds) *Police leadership and management*, Sydney, NSW: Federation Press

Casey, J. (2010) *Policing the world: The practice of international and transnational policing*, Durham: Carolina Academic Press

Castles, S., Miller, M. and Ammendola, G. (2005) *The age of migration: International population movements in the modern world*, New York: The Guilford Press

Cave, S. (2012) Forgetting Anders Breivik, *Aeon*, September. www. aeonmagazine.com/being-human/stephen-cave-anders-breivik/

CCJS (Centre for Crime and Justice Studies) (2007) *Ten years of criminal justice under Labour: An independent audit*, January, London: King's College

CEPOL (2013) *Training catalogue, courses and programmes*, Luxembourg: European Police College. www.cepol.europa.eu/fileadmin/website/ Publications/2013/Training_Catalogue_2013.pdf

Chaliand, G. (2007) *The history of terrorism: From antiquity to al Qaeda*, Berkeley: University of California Press

Chalk, K. and Burgersdijk, O. (2013) Leadership model, *Pearls in policing*, privately published: text made available to the authors

Childs, J. (2011) Barracks and conscription: civil-military relations in Europe from 1500, *EGO (European History on line)*. www.ieg-ego.eu/ en/threads/alliances-and-wars/war-as-an-agent-of-transfer/john-childs-barracks-and-conscription-civil-military-relations-in-europe-from-1500

Cole, B. (1999) Post-colonial systems, in R. I. Mawby (ed.) *Policing across the world: Issues for the twenty-first century*, pp. 88-108

Conger, J. and Fuller, R. (2003) Developing your leadership pipeline, *Harvard Business Review*, Vol. 81, No. 12, pp. 76-85

Cooke, L. and Sturges, P. (2009) Police and media relations in an era of freedom of information, *Policing and Society*, Vol. 19, No. 4, pp. 406-424

Corstens, G. (2010) *Europe and the security of the citizen*, Lecture delivered in Tilburg, 12 February (in Dutch, with literal translation). www. rechtspraak.nl/Organisatie/Hoge-Raad/OverDeHogeRaad/publicaties/ Pages/Europa-en-de-veiligheid-van-de-burger.aspx

Cottesill, K and Austin, M. (2005) *Two top cops*, Queensland, Australia: The Ninderry Press

Couldry, N., Madianou, M. and Pinchevski, A. (eds) (2013) *Ethics of media*, London: Palgrave Macmillan

Council of Europe (1993) *Police training concerning migrants and ethnic relations*, Strasburg: CE Publishing

Crank, J. and Das, D. (2011) *Policing: Toward an unknown future*, New York: Taylor and Francis

Craig, P. and de Burca, G. (eds) (2011) *The evolution of EU law*, Oxford: Oxford University Press

Crawford, A. (2002) The governance of crime and insecurity in an anxious age: the trans-European and the local in A. Crawford (ed.) *Crime and insecurity: The governance of safety in Europe*, Devon: Willan Publishing, pp. 25-51

Crosby-Hillier, K. (2012) Women and educational leadership: exploring the experiences of current and aspiring female educational administrators, *Women*, Vol. 1, No. 1 (available as a dissertation from the University of Windsor, Ontario, Canada)

Crossley, N. (2002) *Making sense of social movements*, Buckingham: Open University Press

Dabashi, H. (2012) *The Arab Spring: The end of post colonialism*, New York: Zed Books

Dalby, D. (2014) Police scandals reach crisis stage for Irish government, *New York Times*, 26 March. www.nytimes.com/2014/03/27/world/ europe/police-scandals-irish-government.html?_r=0

Dammer, H. and Albanese, J. (2013) *Comparative criminal justice systems*, 5th edn, Stamford, CN: Cengage Learning

Dardenne, S. (2005) *I choose to live*, translated by P. Dening, London: Virago Press (originally published in France as *J'avais 12 ans, j'ai pris mon vélo, et je suis partie à l'école ...* by Oh! Editions, Paris in 2004)

Das, D. and Marenin, O. (eds) (2009) *Trends in policing: Interviews with police leaders across the globe*, Boca Raton, Florida, USA: CRC Press (originally published in 2006 as *Comparative problems of policing: Interviews with nineteen police leaders from different nations*, New York: Edwin Mellen Press. www. ipes.info/docs/das%20-%20marenin.pdf

Das, D., Palmer, D. and Berlin, S. (eds) (2011) *Global environment of policing*, New York: CRC Press

Das, D. and Robinson, A. (2001) The police in Norway: a profile, *Policing: An International Journal of Police Strategies and Management*, Vol. 24, Issue 3, pp. 330-346

Das, D. and Verma, A. (1998) The armed police in the British colonial tradition: The Indian perspective, *Policing: An International Journal of Police Strategies and Management*, Vol. 21, No. 2, pp. 354-367

Davis, A. (2003) Whither mass media and power? Evidence for a critical elite theory alternative, *Media, Culture and Society*, Vol. 25, No. 5, pp. 669-690

Deacon, R. (1972) *A history of the Russian secret service,* London: Frederick Muller

Dean, G., Fahsing, I. and Gottschalk, P. (2010) *Organized crime: Policing illegal business entrepreneurialism*, Oxford: Oxford University Press

Dedman, M. (2009) *The origins and development of the European Union 1945-2008: A history of European integration*, 2nd edn, Abingdon: Routledge

Deflem, M. (1994) Law enforcement in British colonial Africa: A comparative analysis of imperial policing in Nyasaland, the Gold Coast and Kenya, *Police Studies: International Review of Police Development*, Vol. 17, No. 1, pp. 45-68

Deflem, M. (1996) International policing in nineteenth-century Europe: the police union of German states, 1851-1866, *International Criminal Justice Review*, No. 6, pp. 36-57

Deflem, M. (2002) *Policing world society: Historical foundations of international police cooperation*, Oxford: Oxford University Press

Deflem, M. (2005) A history of international police cooperation, in R. Wright and M. Miller (eds) *Encyclopedia of criminology*, New York: Routledge, pp. 795-798

Della Porta, D., Peterson, A. and Reiter, H. (eds) (2013) *The policing of transnational protest*, London: Ashgate Publishing

den Boer, M. (1999) Internationalization: a challenge to police organizations in Europe, in R. I. Mawby (ed.) *Policing across the world: Issues for the twenty-first century*, London: UCL Press, pp. 59-74

den Boer, M. (2002a) Towards an accountability regime for an emerging European policing governance, *Policing and Society*, Vol. 12, Issue 4, pp. 275-289

den Boer, M. (ed.) (2002b) *Organised crime: A catalyst in the Europeanisation of national police and prosecution agencies?* Maastricht, The Netherlands: European Institute of Public Administration

den Boer, M. (2010) Towards a governance model of police cooperation in Europe: the twist between networks and bureaucracies, in F Lemieux (ed.) *International police cooperation*, Cullompton: Willan

den Boer, M. and Fernhout, R. (2008) Police oversight mechanisms in Europe: towards a comparative overview of ombudsmen and their competencies, Paper delivered at Improving the Role of the Police in Asia and Europe conference, Delhi, 3-4 December. www.asef.org/images/docs/1270-Police_Oversight_Mechanisms_in_Europe.pdf

den Boer, M., Hillebrand, C. and Nölke, A. (2008) Legitimacy under pressure: the European web of counter-terrorism networks, *JCMS: Journal of Common Market Studies*, 46, pp. 101-124

Dennis, M. and Laporte, N. (2003) *The Stasi: Myth and reality: Themes in modern German history*, London: Longman/Pearson

Densten, I. (2003) Senior police leadership: does rank matter?, *Policing: An International Journal of Police Strategies and Management*, Vol. 26, No. 3, pp. 400-418

Denys, C. (2010) The development of police forces in urban Europe in the eighteenth century, *Journal of Urban History*, Vol. 36, No. 3, pp. 332-344 (Sage). www.sagepub.com/journalsPermissions.nav

Deutscher, G. (2010) *Through the language glass: Why the world looks different in other languages*, London: Heinemann (Random House)

Díez-Nicolás, J. (2005) Value systems of elites and publics in the Mediterranean: convergence or divergence, Madrid: ASEP and Complutense University

Dimovné, E. (2004) Hungarian police reform, *Transforming police in Central and Eastern Europe*, Münster, Germany: Lit Verlag 17, pp. 1992-96

Dixon, B. (2000) *The globalisation of democratic policing: Sector policing and zero tolerance in the new South Africa*, Institute of Criminology, University of Cape Town, Occasional Paper Series

Dixon, N. (1994) *The psychology of military incompetence*, London: Pimlico

Donnelly, D. (2013) *Municipal policing in the European Union: Comparative perspectives*, Crime Prevention and Security Management Series, London: Palgrave Macmillan

DOW, (2013) *Daily reports of the Gestapo headquarters in Vienna 1938-1945*, Dokumentationsarchiv des Osterreichischen Widerstands (DOW). http://collections.ushmm.org/search/catalog/irn41791

Drennan, J. (2003) *Police leadership and labour relations*, Ontario, Canada: National Library of Canada [rare copy in Bramshill National Police Library, Access No. 20031291 / 3DAA DRE]

Duggan, W. (2002) *Napoleon's glance: The secrets of strategy*, New York: Nation Books

Ebbe, O. (ed.) (2013) *Comparative and international criminal justice systems: Policing, judiciary, and corrections*, Boca Raton, FL: CRC Press

Edwards, A. and Gill, P. (2003) *Transnational organised crime: Perspectives on global security*, London: Routledge

Edy, J. (2006) *Troubled pasts: News and the collective memory of social unrest*, Philadelphia, PA: Temple University Press

Egan, M., Nugent, N. and Paterson, W. (eds) (2010) *Research agendas in European Union studies: Stalking the elephant*, Basingstoke: Palgrave Macmillan

Ekblom, P. (2005) How to police the future: scanning for scientific and technological innovations which generate potential threats and opportunities in crime, policing and crime reduction, *Crime Science: New approaches to preventing and detecting crime*, Devon: Willan, pp. 27-55

Ekengren, M. (2004, September) From a European security community to a secure European community – analysing EU 'functional' security: the case of EU civil protection, in The Fifth Pan-European Conference of the ECPR Standing Group on International Relations

Emsley, C. (1991) *Policing Western Europe: Politics, professionalism and public order, 1850-1940*, Westport, CT: Greenwood Publishing Group

Emsley, C. (1999) *Gendarmes and the state in nineteenth-century Europe*, Oxford: Oxford University Press

Emsley, C., (2007) *Crime, police and penal policy: European experiences 1750-1940*, Oxford: Oxford University Press

Emsley, C. (2008) Violent crime in England in 1919: post-war anxieties and press narratives, *Continuity and Change*, Vol. 23, No. 1, pp. 173-195

Emsley, C. (2009) *The great British Bobby: A history of British policing from the 18th century to the present*, London: Quercus

Entorf, H. and Spengler, H. (2002) *Crime in Europe: Causes and consequences*, Berlin: Springer

EPPHR (European Platform for Policing and Human Rights) (2001) *The recruitment and retention of police officers from minority communities*, European Platform for Policing and Human Rights, Strasburg: CE publishing

European Commission, Committee of Ministers (2010) *The European code of police ethics:* Recommendation 10. https://wcd.coe.int/ViewDoc.jsp?id=1707137

European Commission (2012) *3rd Annual report on immigration and asylum (2011)* May, p. 3. http://ec.europa.eu/home-affairs/doc_centre/immigration/docs/COM%202012%20250%20final%201_EN_ACT_part1_v5.pdf

European Commission (2013) Commission report calls for forward-looking policies on migration, IP/13/552, 17 June

European Commission (2014) What has the EU done for women?, MEMO/14/156 07/03/2014: http://europa.eu/rapid/press-release_MEMO-14-156_en.htm

EU Commission, Staff Working Document (2013) *Impact assessment on adapting the European Police Office's legal framework with the Lisbon Treaty*, Brussels, SWD (2013) 98 final. http://ec.europa.eu/governance/impact/ia_carried_out/docs/ia_2013/swd_2013_0098_en.pdf

European Union Commissioner for Human Rights (2009) *Opinion of the Commissioner for Human Rights concerning Independent and effective determination of complaints against the police*, 12 March 2009, CommDH(2009)4]. https://wcd.coe.int/ViewDoc.jsp?id=1417857

European Union Committee of the House of Lords (2008) *The Treaty of Lisbon: An impact assessment*, London: Stationery Office, p. 335 (S18 Q47)

Europol (2005) *The 2000 EU Convention on Mutual Legal Assistance (MLA) and JITs*. www.europol.europa.eu/content/page/joint-investigation-teams-989

Europol (2013) *EU Serious and organised crime threat assessment*, den Haag: European Police Office

Eurostat (2013) *Regional Yearbook*, Stat/13/143, October, Eurostat, EU. http://ec.europa.eu/eurostat/en/web/products-statistical-books/-/KS-HA-13-001

Eurostat (2014) *Regional Yearbook*, Stat/14/46, March. http://ec.europa.eu/eurostat/en/web/products-statistical-books/-/KS-HA-14-001

Evans, M. (2013) Plans to keep names of suspects secret being considered, *The Daily Telegraph*, 7 April, www.telegraph.co.uk/news/uknews/law-and-order/9977487/Plans-to-keep-names-of-suspects-secret-being-considered.html

Eyre, K. (2010) Improving global security through policing: Is ACPO effectively managing the business of international affairs?, Unpublished MSc dissertation, Cranfield University, Defence College of Management and Technology [restricted document]

Fairchild, E. (1988) *German police: Ideals and reality in the post-war years*, Springfield, IL: Charles C Thomas, Publisher

Falkner, G. (ed.) (2011) *The EU's decision traps*, Oxford: Oxford University Press

Feltes, T. (2002) Community-oriented policing in Germany: training and education, *Policing: An International Journal of Police Strategies and Management*, Vol. 25, No. 1, pp. 48-59

Feltes, T., Marquardt, U. and Schwartz, S. (2013) Policing in Germany: developments in the last 20 years, in G. Meško, C. Fields, B. Lobnikar and A. Sotlar (eds) *Handbook on policing in Central and Eastern Europe*, New York: Springer Books, pp. 93-113

Ferguson, N. (2004) A world without power, *Foreign Policy*, No. 143, Jul-Aug, pp. 32-39

Ferguson, N. (2012) *Colossus: The rise and fall of the American empire*, London: Penguin

Ferreira, E. (2011) European police cooperation in the future – reflections from the present, *CEPOL European Police Science and Research Bulletin,* Issue 5, Summer, pp. 22-29

Ferret, J. (2004) The state, policing and 'Old Continental Europe': managing the local/national tension, *Policing and Society*, Vol. 14, No. 1, pp. 49-65

Fijnaut, C. (1992) Policing Western Europe: Interpol, Trevi and Europol, *Police Studies: International Review of Police Development*, Vol. 15, No. 101

Fijnaut, C. (ed.) (2002) Special issue on police accountability in Europe, *Policing and Society: An International Journal of Research and Policy*, Vol. 12, Issue 4

Fijnaut, C. and Marx, G. (1995) *Undercover: Police surveillance in comparative perspective*, Leiden and Boston: Martinus Nijhoff Publishers

Fijnaut, C. and Ouwerkerk, J. (eds) (2010) *The future of police and judicial cooperation in the European Union*, Leiden and Boston: Martinus Nihjoff Publishers

Fijnaut, C. and Spapens, T. (2010) The Meuse-Rhine Euroregion: a laboratory for police and judicial cooperation in the European Union, in F. Lemieux (ed.) *International Police Cooperation: Emerging issues, theory and practice*, Devon: Willan Publishing, pp. 101-125

Findlay, M. J. (2008) Global terror and organised crime: symbiotic or synonymous? *Asian Journal of Criminology*, Vol. 3, No. 1, pp. 75-89

Fischer, B. (1999) *Okhrana: The Paris Operations of the Russian Imperial Police*. Washington: DIANE Publishing (a CIA imprint)

Flint, J. and Powell, R. (2012) The English city riots of 2011: 'broken britain' and the retreat into the present, *Sociological Research Online*, Vol. 17, No. 3, p. 20. www.socresonline.org.uk/17/3/20.html

Fooner, M. (1973) *Interpol: The inside story of the international crime-fighting organization*, Chicago: Henry Regnery Company

Fooner, M. (1989) *Interpol: Issues in world crime and international criminal justice*, New York: Plenum Press

Forrest, A. (2012) Policing, rural revolt and conscription in Napoleonic France, in M. Broers, P. Hicks, A. G. Ravina and A. Guimera (eds) *The Napoleonic empire and the new European political culture*, London: Palgrave Macmillan

Fosdick, R. (1969) *European police systems*, Montclair, NJ: Patterson Smith Publishers

Fouché, J. and Cole, H. (1971) *Fouché the unprincipled patriot*, London: Taylor and Francis

Fowler, A. and Pryke, J. (2003) Knowledge management in public service provision: the child support agency, *International Journal of Service Industry Management*, Vol. 14, No. 3, pp. 254-83

Frank, D., Hironaka, A. and Schofer, E. (2000) The nation-state and the natural environment over the twentieth century, *American Sociological Review*, pp. 96-116

Freeman S. and Webster, P. (2006) Cameron pledges to root out failing police officers, *The Times*, January 16: and cited in B. Caless and S. Tong (2013) 'An appropriate space': chief officers and police accountability, *Police Practice and Research*, Vol. 14, Issue 1, p. 5

Fremont-Barnes, G. (2010) *Napoleon Bonaparte: The background, strategies, tactics and battlefield experiences of the greatest commanders of history*, Oxford: Osprey Publishing

Frevel, B. and Kuschewski, P. (2009) Police organization and police reform in Germany: the case of North Rhine-Westphalia, *German Policy Studies*, Vol. 5, No. 2, pp. 49-89

Friedrichs, J. (2008) *Fighting terrorism and drugs: Europe and international police cooperation*, London: Routledge

Friehe, T. and Tabbach, A. (2013) Preventive enforcement, *International Review of Law and Economics*, Vol. 35, August, pp. 1–12

Gaines, L.K., Van Tubergen, G.N. and Paiva, M. (1984) Police officer perception of promotion as a source of motivation, *Journal of Criminal Justice*, Vol. 12, pp. 265-76

Galand, P. (2015) G4S loses its contract with the European Parliament. www.bdsmovement.net/2012/g4s-loses-its-contract-with-the-european-parliament-8901#sthash.yM8uNWiB.dpuf

Galetti, S. (2004) Italian Court Honorary Judges, in M. Gorazd, B. Lobnikar and P. Milan (eds) *Policing in Central and Eastern Europe: Dilemmas of contemporary criminal justice*, University of Maribor, Slovenja, pp. 443-52

Gallagher, D. (1998) European police cooperation: its development and impact between 1967-1997 in an Anglo-French trans-frontier setting, unpublished PhD thesis. Available as DX203150 through the British Library (Thesis Service) and The National Police Library, 0993105/3CXGAL

Gellately, R. (1988) The Gestapo and German society: political denunciation in the Gestapo case files, *The Journal of Modern History*, Vol. 60, No. 4, pp. 654-694

Gellately, R. (1991) *The Gestapo and German Society 1933-1945*, Oxford: Clarendon Press

Gerspacher, N., (2010) The France and Europol relationship: explaining shifts in cooperative behaviour, in F. Lemieux (ed.) *International Police Cooperation*, Cullompton: Willan

Gieseke, J. (2006) *Der Mielke-Konzern: Die Geschichte der Stasi, 1945-1990*, Munich: Deutsche Verlags-Anstalt

Gildea, R. (2003) *Barricades and borders: Europe 1800-1914*, 3rd edn, Oxford: Oxford University Press

Glaeser, A. (2000) *Divided in unity: Identity, Germany and the Berlin police*, Chicago: University of Chicago Press

Glamseth, R. and Gottschalk, P. (2007) Occupational culture as a determinant of knowledge sharing in police investigations, *International Journal of the Sociology of Law*, Vol. 35, No.2, pp. 96-107

Glasius, M. (2010) *Expertise in the cause of justice: Global civil society influence on the statute for an international criminal court*, Oxford: Oxford University Press

Gobinet, P. (2008) The gendarmerie alternative: is there a case for the existence of police organisations with military status in the twenty-first century European security apparatus?, *International Journal of Police Science and Management*, Vol. 10, No. 4, pp. 448–463

Gold, M. (1999) *Top cops: Profiles of women in command: Leading, succeeding, mentoring*, Chicago, USA: Brittany Publications

Goldsmith, A. and Lewis, C. (eds) (2000) *Civilian oversight of policing: Governance, democracy, and human rights*, Portland, OR: Hart Publishing

Goldsmith, A. (2005) Police reform and the problem of trust, *Theoretical Criminology*, Vol. 9, No. 4, pp. 443-470

Goleman, D. (2004) What makes a leader? *Harvard Business Review*, January, Vol. 82, No.1, pp. 82-91

Goodey, J. (2002) Whose security? Organised crime, its victims and the EU, in A. Crawford (ed.) *Crime and insecurity: The governance of safety in Europe*, Devon: Willan Publishing, pp. 135-158

Gove, M. (2005) If crime's on the up, your chief constable must explain why or be sacked, *The Times*, 15 March. www.thetimes.co.uk/tto/law/columnists/article2042724.ece

Gras, M. (2002) The legal regulation of CCTV in Europe, *Surveillance and Society*, Vol. 2, Nos. 2/3

Graziano, L., Schuck, A. and Martin, C. (2010) Police misconduct, media coverage, and public perceptions of racial profiling: an experiment, *Justice Quarterly*, Vol. 27, No. 1, pp. 52-76

Greenwood, C., (2010) Theresa May axes police performance targets, *The Independent*, June 29. www.independent.co.uk/news/uk/home-news/theresa-may-axes-police-performance-targets-2013288.html

Greenwood, P. W. and Turner, S. (2011) Juvenile crime and juvenile justice, in J. Q. Wilson and J. Petersilia (eds) *Crime and Public Policy*, New York, NY: Oxford University Press, pp. 88-129

Gritsch, M. (2005) The nation-state and economic globalization: soft geo-politics and increased state autonomy?, *Review of International Political Economy*, Vol. 12, No. 1, pp. 1-25

Grosman, B. (1975) *Police command: Decisions and discretion*, Toronto, Canada: The Macmillan Co. of Canada Ltd [a rare copy in National Police Library, Access No. 0007839 / 3DAA]

Grzymala–Busse, A. (2007) *Rebuilding Leviathan: Party Competition and state exploitation in post-communist democracies*, Cambridge: Cambridge University Press

Guatieri, C. (2007) Joint investigation teams (2007), in *ERA-Forum*, Vol. 8, No. 2, pp. 233-238. www.springerlink.com/content/t0k0846487178k22/

Guild, E. and Geyer, F. (eds) (2008) Security versus justice? Police and judicial cooperation in the European Union. Aldershot: Ashgate Publishing

Guille, L. (2010a) Police and judicial cooperation in Europe: bilateral versus multilateral cooperation, in F. Lemieux (ed.) *International police cooperation: Emerging issues, theory and practice*, Devon: Willan Publishing

Guille, L. (2010b) The proliferation of parallel tracks in police and judicial cooperation in Europe: the current 'chaos', *Policing in Europe*, 57

Gustafsson, H. (1998) The conglomerate state: a perspective on state formation in early modern Europe, *Scandinavian Journal of History*, Vol. 23, Nos. 3-4, pp. 189-213

Haberfeld, M. (2005) *Police leadership*, Upper Saddle River, NJ: Prentice Hall

Hainmueller, J. and Hiscox, M. (2007) Educated preferences: explaining attitudes toward immigration in Europe, *International Organization*, Vol. 61, No. 2, pp. 399-442

Hainsworth, P. (2008) *The extreme right in Western Europe*, London: Routledge

Halford, A. (with Barnes, T.) (1993) *No way up the greasy pole: A fight against male domination in the British police force*, London: Constable (and Trans-Atlantic Publications)

Hall, B. (1999) *Policing Europe: EU justice and home affairs co-operation*, London: Centre for European Reform

Hanak, G. and Hofinger, V. (2006) Police science and research in the European Union, *Theory and practice of police research in Europe*, 47-62

Harbeck, E. L. and Glendon, A. I. (2013) How reinforcement sensitivity and perceived risk influence young drivers' reported engagement in risky driving behaviors, *Accident Analysis and Prevention*, 54, pp. 73-80

Harlan, J. (1997) The German police: issues in the unification process, *Policing: An International Journal of Police Strategies and Management*, Vol. 20, No. 3, pp. 532-554

Harnischmacher, R. (1989) The federal gendarmerie in Austria, *International Journal of Comparative and Applied Criminal Justice*, Vol. 13, No. 1, pp. 123-134

Harris, R. (ed.) (2013) *The language myth in Western culture*, London: Routledge

Hays, K., Regoli, R. and Hewitt, J. (2007) Police chiefs, anomia, and leadership, *Police Quarterly*, Issue 10, pp. 3-22

Hebenton, B. and Thomas, T. (1995) *Policing Europe: Cooperation, conflict and control*, London: St Martin's Press

Hefferman, W. (2003) Three types of leadership, Chapter 9 in R. Adlam and P. Villiers (eds) *Police leadership in the 21st century: Philosophy, doctrine and development*, Winchester: Waterside Press

Heidensohn, F. (1992) *Women in control? The role of women in law enforcement*, Oxford: Clarendon Press

Heidensohn, F. (1997) Equally European?, *Criminal Justice Matters*, Vol. 27, Issue 1, Special issue: *Crime and Justice in Europe*

Heidensohn, F. (2003) Gender and policing, in T. Newburn (ed.) *Handbook of policing*, Devon: Willan Publishing

Heifetz, R. and Linsky, M. (2002) *Leadership on the line*, Boston, MA: Harvard Business Press

Heinz, J. and Manikas, P. (1992) Networks among elites in a local criminal justice system, *Law and Society Review*, Vol. 26, pp. 831-854

Herlihy, J. (1997) *The Royal Irish Constabulary*, Dublin: Four Courts Press

Higley, J. and Lengyel, G. (eds) (2000) *Elites after state socialism: Theories and analysis*, Lanham, MD: Rowman and Littlefield

Hill, C. and Smith, M. (eds) (2011) *International Relations and the European Union*, 2nd edn, Oxford: Oxford University Press

Hills, A. (1998) International peace support operations and CIVPOL: Should there be a permanent global gendarmerie?, *International Peacekeeping*, Vol. 5, No. 3, pp. 26-41

Harris, R. (ed.) (2013) *The language myth in Western culture*, London: Routledge

Hills, A. (2007) Police commissioners, presidents and the governance of security, *The Journal of Modern African Studies*, Vol. 45, No. 3, August, pp. 403-423

Hinton, M. (2006) *The state on the streets: Police and politics in Argentina and Brazil*, Boulder, CO: Lynne Rienner Publishers

Hinton, M. and Newburn, T. (2008) *Policing developing democracies*, Abingdon: Routledge

Hochschild, J. (2009) *Conducting intensive interviews and elite interviews*, Workshop on Interdisciplinary Standards for Systematic Qualitative Research. http://scholar.harvard.edu/jlhochschild/publications/conducting-intensive-interviews-and-elite-interviews

Hofstede, G. (1998) Masculinity and femininity: the taboo dimension of national cultures, in M. Hoppe (ed.) *Validating the masculinity/femininity dimension on elites from 19 countries*, Thousand Oaks, CA: Sage Publications, pp. 29-43

Holmqvist, C. (2005) *Private security companies: The case for regulation*, SIPRI Policy Paper No. 9, Stockholm International Peace Research Institute. http://books.sipri.org/files/PP/SIPRIPP09.pdf

Home Office (HO) (2013) Home Office circulars, www.gov.uk/government/collections/home-office-circulars-2013: accessed 27 February 2015

Hoogewoning,F., van Dijk, A. and Punch, M. (2015) *What matters in policing? Changed leadership and a comprehensive paradigm*, Bristol: Policy Press

Hoppe, M. (ed.) (1998) *Validating the masculinity/femininity dimension on elites from 19 countries*, Thousand Oaks, CA: Sage Publications

Horton, C. (1995) *Policing policy in France*, London: Policy Studies Institute

Hough, M., Jackson, J. and Bradford, B. (2013) The governance of criminal justice, legitimacy and trust, in S. Body-Gendrot, R. Lévy, M. Hough, S. Snacken and K. Kerezsi (eds) *The Routledge Handbook of European Criminology*, Oxon: Routledge

Hovens, J. and Van Elk, G. (2011) *Gendarmeries and the challenges of the 21st century*, Koninklijke Maréchaussée, Den Haag, Netherlands

Howe, s. (2000) *Ireland and empire: Colonial legacies in Irish history and culture*, OUP

Hufnagel,S., Harfield, C. and Bronitt, S. (eds) (2012) *Cross-border law enforcement: Regional law enforcement cooperation – European, Australian and Asia-Pacific perspectives*, London: Routledge

Huggins, M. and Husain, S. (2007) The political game of police reform, *International Studies Review,* Vol. 9, pp. 122–124

Hughes, V. and Love, P. E. (2004) Toward cyber-centric management of policing: back to the future with information and communication technology. *Industrial Management and Data Systems*, Vol. 104, No. 7, pp. 604-612

Hurd, D. (2007) *Robert Peel: A biography*, London: Weidenfeld and Nicolson

Ikenberry, G. (2008) The rise of China and the future of the West: can the liberal system survive?, *Foreign affairs*, Vol. 87, No. 1, pp. 23-37

Isenberg, J. (2010) *Police leadership in a democracy: Conversations with America's police chiefs*, Boca Raton, FL: CRC Press

Ivkovic, S. (2009) The Croatian police, police integrity and transition toward democratic policing, *Policing: An International Journal of Police Strategies and Management*, Vol. 32, No. 3, pp. 459-488

Jackson, J., Hough, M., Bradford, B., Hohl, K. and Kuha, J. (2012) Policing by consent: understanding the dynamics of police power and legitimacy, *European Social Survey*

Jacobs, K. (2012) Nothing succeeds like succession planning, *HR Magazine*, 19 November. www.hrmagazine.co.uk/hr/features/1075380/nothing-succeeds-succession-planning

Jenks, D., Costelloe, M. and Krebs, C. (2003) After the fall: Czech police in a post-communist era, *International Criminal Justice Review*, Vol. 13, Issue 1, pp. 90-109

Joes, A. (2006) *Resisting rebellion: The history and politics of counterinsurgency*, Kentucky: University Press of Kentucky

Johnston, L. (2000) *Policing Britain: Risk, security and governance*, Harlow: Longman Publishers

Johnston, L. (2005) *The rebirth of private policing*, London: Routledge

Johnston, L. and Stenning, P. (2010) Changes of governance and accountability for transnational private policing, in F. Lemieux (ed.) *International police co-operation: Emerging Issues, Theory and Practice*, Devon: Willan Publishing, pp. 281-297

Jolley, R. (2014) After the fall, *Index on Censorship*, June, Vol. 43, No. 2, pp. 3-5

Jones, E. (2003) *The European miracle: Environments, economies and geopolitics in the history of Europe and Asia*, Cambridge (UK): Cambridge University Press

Jones, T. (1995) *Policing and democracy in the Netherlands*, London: Policy Studies Institute

Jongman, A. (1992) Trends in international and domestic terrorism in Western Europe, 1968–1988, *Terrorism and Political Violence*, Vol. 4, No. 4, pp. 26-76

Jordan, P. and Taylor, P. (2004) *Hactivism and cyberwars: Rebels with a cause?* London: Routledge

Joubert, C. and Bevers, H. (1996) *Schengen investigated: A comparative interpretation of the Schengen provisions on international police cooperation in the light of the European Convention on Human Rights*, The Hague: Kluwer Law International

Judt, T. (2010) *Postwar: A history of Europe since 1945*, London: Vintage Books

Kääriäinen, J. (2007) Trust in the police in 16 European countries: a multilevel analysis, *European Journal of Criminology*, Vol. 4, No. 4, pp. 409-435

Kadar, A. (ed.) (2001) *Police in transition: Essays on the police forces in transition countries,* Budapest, Hungary: Central European University Press

Kakbadse, A. and Dainty, P. (1988) Police chief officers: a management development survey, *Journal of Managerial Psychology*, Vol. 3, No. 3

Kapplinghaus, J. (2006) Joint investigation teams: basic ideas, relevant legal instruments and first experiences in Europe, *134th International Training Course*. www.unafei.or.jp/english/pdf/RS_No73/No73_07VE_Kapplinghaus2.pdf

Keeble, R. and Mair, J. (2012) *The phone hacking scandal: Journalism on trial*, Bury St Edmunds, Suffolk: Abramis Academic Publishing

Kekovié, Z. and Kentera, S. (2013) Montenegrin police: current profile and future trends, in G. Meško, C. Fields, B. Lobnikar and A. Sotlar (eds) *Handbook on policing in Central and Eastern Europe*, New York: Springer Books

Keller, S. (1991) *Beyond the ruling class: Strategic elites in modern society*, New Brunswick, NJ: Transaction Books

Kelly, J. (2012) Why British police don't have guns, *BBC News Magazine*, 19 September. www.bbc.co.uk/news/magazine-19641398

Kerkkänen, P., Kuiper, N. and Martin, R. (2006) Sense of humor, physical health, and well-being at work: a three-year longitudinal study of Finnish police officers, *International Journal of Humor Research*, Vol. 17, Issue 1-2, pp. 21–35

Kešetović, Ž., Bajagić, M. and Korajlić, N. (2006) Police-media relations in the transition: from autocratic regime to democracy, in G. Meško, T. Cockroft and C. Fields (eds) *Editorial 181*, Vol. 12, No. 3, pp. 213-221

Killengreen. I. (2010) *The police in Norway*, Oslo: National Police Directorate

Kincaid, J. (2009) *Adventures in the Rifle Brigade, in the peninsula, France, and the Netherlands*, Middlesex: Echo Library

Klerks, P. (2003) The network paradigm applied to criminal organisations, Chapter 6 in Edwards and Gill (eds) *Transnational Organised Crime*, London: Routledge

Klimek, L. (2015) *European arrest warrant*, Switzerland: Springer International

Klip, A. (2002) Conditions for a European *Corpus Juris Criminalis*, in M. Faure, J. Smits and H. Schneider (eds) *Towards a European IUS Commune in Legal Education and Research*, Maastricht, pp. 109-23

Knight, A. (2003) The KGB, perestroika, and the collapse of the Soviet Union, *Journal of Cold War Studies*, Vol. 5, No.1, pp. 67-93

Knoke, D. (1993) Networks of elite structure and decision making, *Sociological Methods and Research*, Vol. 22, No. 1, pp. 23-45

Koci, A. (1996) Legitimation and culturalism: towards policing changes in the European 'post-socialist' countries, in M. Pagon (ed.) *Policing in Central and Eastern Europe: Comparing first-hand knowledge with experience from the West*, Ljubljana, Slovenia: College of Police and Security Studies

Koehler, J. (1999) *Stasi: The untold story of the East German secret police*, Boulder, CO: Westview Press

Komarek, J. (2007) European constitutionalism and the European arrest warrant: In search of the limits of 'contrapunctual principles', *Common Market Law Review*, Vol. 44, No. 1, pp. 9-40. http://elib.ukma.edu.ua/K/komarek_europ_constitutionalism.pdf

Kopeček, L. (2007) The Far Right in Europe, *Středoevropské politické studie (Central European Political Studies Review, CEPSR)* No. 4, pp. 280-293. www.ceeol.com

Kremplewski, A. (2001) The police and non-governmental organizations in Poland, in A. Kádár (ed.) *Police in transition: Essays on the police forces in transition countries*, Budapest: Central European University Press

Kuperus, H. and Rode, A. (2010) Latest trends in top public management in the European Union, *EIPAScope*, No. 1, pp. 37-43

Ladrech, R. (1994) Europeanization of domestic politics and institutions: the case of France, *Journal of Common Market Studies*, Vol. 32, No. 1, pp. 69-88

Lasswell, H., Lerner, D. and Rothwell, C. (1952) *The comparative study of elites: An introduction and bibliography*, Hoover Institute studies, Vol. 1, Stanford, CA: Stanford University Press

Law, W. (2012) Educational leadership and culture in China: dichotomies between Chinese and Anglo-American leadership traditions?, *International Journal of Educational Development*, Vol. 32, Issue 2, March 2012, pp. 273–282

Lee, M. (2005) Human trade and the criminalization of irregular migration, *International Journal of the Sociology of Law*, Vol. 33, No. 1, pp. 1-15

Lee, M. (2011) *Trafficking and global crime control*, London: Sage

Leigh-Fermor, P. (2013) *Between the woods and the water* (first published in 1986) London: John Murray

Lemieux, F. (ed.) (2010) *International police cooperation: Emerging issues, theory and practice*, Devon: Willan Publishing

Leveson, L. J. B. H. L. (2012) *An inquiry into the culture, practices and ethics of the press: Executive summary and recommendations* [Leveson Report], London: The Stationery Office

Liang, H. (1992) *The rise of the modern police and the European state system from Metternich to the Second World War*, Cambridge: Cambridge UP

Lichy, J. (2012) Policing the internet – a comparative study in France and Britain, lecture delivered at the Conference on Policing and European Studies, University of Abertay on 18 January, http:// policingandeuropeanstudies.abertay.ac.uk/?m=201201

Lieven, D. (1989) The security police, civil rights, and the fate of the Russian Empire, 1855-1917, in O. Crisp and L. Edmondson (eds) *Civil Rights in Imperial Russia*, Oxford: Clarendon Press

Loader, I. (2000) Plural policing and democratic governance, *Social and Legal Studies*, Vol. 9, No. 3, pp. 323-345

Loader, I. (2002) Governing European policing: some problems and prospects, *Policing and Society*, Vol. 12, No. 4, pp. 291-305

Loader, I. and Mulcahy, A. (2001) The power of legitimate naming: part ii: making sense of the elite police voice, *British Journal of Criminology*, Vol. 41, Issue 2, pp. 252-265

Lorincz, A.-L. (2013) The european arrest warrant as a form of international judicial cooperation in criminal matters in terms of amendments to the Romanian legislation, *European Police Science and Research Bulletin*, Issue 8, Summer, pp. 33-36

Loveday, B. (1999) Government and accountability of the police, in R. Mawby (ed.) *Policing across the world: Issues for the twenty-first century*, pp. 132-50

Luc, J. (ed.) (2002) *Gendarmerie, état et société au XIXème siècle*, Vol. 59, Paris: Publications de la Sorbonne

Lucas, G. (2014) Secrecy and privacy in the aftermath of Edward Snowden, NSA Management Directive #424: *Ethics and International Affairs*, Vol. 28, No. 1, pp. 29-38

Lutterbeck, D. (2004) Between police and military: the new security agenda and the rise of gendarmeries, *Cooperation and Conflict*, Vol. 39, No. 1, pp. 45-68

Mallory, S. (2012) *Understanding organized crime*, Sudbury, MA: Jones and Bartlett Learning

Manastire, I. (ed.) (2002) Policing in Romania, *Crime and Justice International*, Vol. 18, Issue 66

Marenin, O. and Caparini, M. (2005) Reforming the police in Central and Eastern European states, *Comparative and International Criminal Justice: Traditional and Non-traditional Systems of Law and Control*, Long Grove, IL: Waveland Press

Marenin, O. and Das, D. (2010) *Trends in Policing: Interviews with Police Leaders Across the Globe*, 3 vols., New York: Taylor and Francis, ISBN: 9781439819241 [but see Das and Marenin, 2009, above]

Marshall, G. (1978) Police accountability revisited, in D. Butler and A Halsey (eds) *Policy and Politics*, pp. 51-65

Marshall, G. (2013) Barriers to Women in Law Enforcement, unpublished MA Dissertation, Athabasca University, Alberta, Canada. http://dtpr.lib.athabascau.ca/action/download.php?filename=mais/garymarshallProject.pdf

Marx, G. (2001) Police and Democracy, in M. Amir and S. Einstein (eds) *Policing, Security and Democracy: Theory and Practice*, Vol. 2, Washington, DC: Office of International Criminal Justice. http://web.mit.edu/gtmarx/www/dempol.html

Mathiesen, T. (1999) On globalization of control: Towards an integrated surveillance system in Europe, *Plenarium*, Vol. 1, No. 4, pp. 4-34

Matthies, C., Keller, K. and Lim, N. (2012) *Identifying Barriers to Diversity in Law Enforcement Agencies*, Santa Monica, CA: Rand Corporation

Mawby, R. C. (2002) *Policing Images: Policing, Communication and Legitimacy*, Devon: Willan Publishing

Mawby, R. C. (2008) Legitimacy, in T. Newburn and P. Neyroud (eds) *Dictionary of Policing*, Devon: Willan Publishing

Mawby, R. C. (2010) Police corporate communications, crime reporting and the shaping of policing news, *Policing and Society*, Vol. 20, No. 1, pp. 124-139

Mawby, R. I. (1990) *Comparative policing issues: The British and American experience in international perspective*. Éditions Unwin Hyman

Mawby, R. I. (1999) *Policing across the World: Issues for the Twenty-first Century*, London: Routledge

Mawby, R. I. (2001) The impact of transition: A comparison of post-communist societies with earlier 'societies in transition', *Police in Transition: Essays on the Police Forces in Transition Countries*, pp. 19-35

Mawby, R. and Wright, A. (2005) *Police accountability in the United Kingdom*, Paper for the Commonwealth Human Rights Initiative. www.humanrightsinitiative.org/programs/aj/police/res_mat/police_accountability_in_uk.pdf

Mazower, M. (ed.) (2000) *After the war was over: Reconstructing the family, nation, and state in Greece, 1943-1960*, Princeton, NJ: Princeton University Press

McCann, C. and Pigeau, R. (eds) (2000) *The human in command: Exploring the modern military experience*, New York: Springer

McCarthy, Q. (2012) *Police leadership: A primer for the individual and the organization*, New York: Palgrave Macmillan

McDonald-Gibson, C. and Lichfield, J. (2014) European election results 2014: Far-right parties flourish across Europe, *The Independent*, 25 May. www.independent.co.uk/news/world/europe/european-election-results-2014-farright-parties-flourish-across-europe-in-snub-to-austerity-9434069.html

McGloin, J.-M. (2003) Shifting paradigms: policing in Northern Ireland, *Policing: An International Journal of Police Strategies and Management*, Vol. 26, No. 1, pp. 118-43

McMurray, A., Azharul, K. and Fisher, G. (2010) Perspectives on the recruitment and retention of culturally and linguistically diverse police, *Cross Cultural Management: An International Journal*, Vol. 17, Issue 2, pp. 193-210

Mendes, J. (2011) *Participation in EU rule-making*, Oxford: Oxford University Press

Merlingen, M. and Ostrauskaite, R. (2006) *European Union peacebuilding and policing: Governance and the European security and defence policy*, Abingdon, Oxon: Routledge

Meško, G. (2007) The obstacles on the path to police professionalism in Slovenia: a review of research, in G. Meško and B. Dobovšek (eds) *Policing in emerging democracies*, qv., pp.17-55

Meško, G. and Dobovšek, B. (eds) (2007) *Policing in emerging democracies: Critical reflections*, Univerza v Mariboru, Fakulteta za varnostne vede, Slovenia

Meško, G. and Klemencic, G. (2007) Rebuilding legitimacy and police professionalism in an emerging democracy: the Slovenian experience, *Legitimacy and Criminal Justice: International Perspectives,* New York: Russell Sage Foundation, pp. 84-114

Meško, G. and Maver, D. (2010) On police and policing in Slovenia: obstacles and challenges, Ch. 5 in C. Roberson, D. Das. and J. Singer (eds) *Police without borders: The fading distinction between local and global*, New York: CRC Press (Taylor and Francis)

Meško, G., Fields, C., Lobnikar, B. and Sotlar, A. (eds) (2013) *Handbook on policing in Central and Eastern Europe*, New York: Springer Books

Metcalfe, B. and Dick, G. (2002) Is the force still with her? Gender and commitment in the police, *Women in Management Review*, Vol. 17, No. 8, pp. 392-403

Metropolitan Police Authority (MPA) (2008) *Talent management and succession planning scrutiny*. http://policeauthority.org/metropolitan/scrutinies/career-dev/index.html

Michelson, R. (2013) Preparing future leaders for tomorrow: succession planning for police leadership, *The Police Chief*, June. www.policechiefmagazine.org/magazine/index.cfm?fuseaction=display_archandarticle_id=904andissue_id=62006

Middleton, J. (2007) *Beyond authority: Leadership in a changing world*, London: Palgrave Macmillan

Miller, H., Watkins, R. and Webb, D. (2009) The use of psychological testing to evaluate law enforcement leadership competencies and development, *Police Practice and Research: An International Journal*, Vol. 10, No.1, pp. 49-60

Mirčeva, S. and Rajkovčevski, R. (2013) Policing in the Republic of Macedonia, in G. Meško, C. Fields, B. Lobnikar and A. Sotlar (eds) *Handbook on policing in Central and Eastern Europe*, New York: Springer Books, pp. 143-168

Mitchell, M. and Casey, J. (eds) (2007) *Police leadership and management*, Sydney (NSW): Federation Press

Moore, A. (ed.) (2004) *Police and judicial cooperation in the European Union: FIDE 2004 national reports*, Cambridge: Cambridge University Press

Morawska, E. (2007) Trafficking into and from Eastern Europe, in M. Lee (ed.) *Human trafficking*, Devon: Willan Publishing, pp. 92-115

Morris, S. (1981) British chief constables: the Americanisation of a role?, *Political Studies,* September, Vol. 29, Issue 3, pp. 352–364

Morris, Z. (2009) The truth about interviewing elites, *Politics*, Vol. 29, No. 3, pp. 209-217

Muller, E. R. (2002) Policing and accountability in the Netherlands: A happy marriage or a stressful relationship? *Policing and Society*, Vol. 12, No. 4, pp. 249-258

Murakami Wood, D. (2009) Situating surveillance studies: Sean Hier and Josh Greenberg's *The surveillance studies reader*, and David Lyon's *Surveillance studies: An overview*, *Surveillance and Society*, Vol. 6, No. 1, pp. 52-61

Murji, K. and Neal, S. (2011) Riot: race and politics in the 2011 disorders, *Sociological Research Online*, Vol. 16, No. 4, p. 24

Murphy, S. and Drodge, E. (2004) The four l's of police leadership: a case study heuristic, in *International Journal of Police Science and Management*, Vol. 6, No. 1, March, pp. 1-15

Murschetz, V. (2010) European police cooperation in the future – legal framework of the European Union, in C. Fijnaut and J. Ouwerkerk (eds) *The future of police and judicial cooperation in the European Union*, Leiden and Boston: Martinus Nihjoff Publishers

Myazawa, S. (1992) *Policing in Japan: A study on making crime*, Albany, USA: State University of New York Press (translated by F. Bennett)

Nadelmann, E. (1993) *Cops across borders: The internationalization of US criminal law enforcement*, PA: Penn State University Press

Navarro-González, A. (2002) Relaciones Entre Las Políticas De Seguridad Interior Y Exterior De La Unidad Europea: El Caso De La Policía [Relations between the policies of inner and outer security of the European Union: the case of the police], *Ciencia Policial,* Issue 61, pp. 7-18

NCWP (National Center for Women and Policing) (2001) *Equality denied: The status of women in policing,* Los Angeles, CA: National Center for Women and Policing

Neyroud, P. (2011a) *Review of police leadership and training*, paper for the Home Secretary 2010, released April 2011, London: Home Office. www. homeoffice.gov.uk/publications/consultations/rev-police-leadership-training/report?view=Binary

Neyroud, P. (2011b) Leading policing in the 21st century: leadership, democracy, deficits and the new professionalism, *Public Money and Management*, Vol. 31, No. 5, pp. 347-354

Neyrude, P. and Vassilas, P. (2010) The politics of partnership: challenges to institution building in European policing, *Policing in Europe*, 75, quoted in Verhage, A. Terpstra, J., Deelman, P., Muylaert, E. and van Parys, P. (eds) (2010) *Policing in Europe*, Netherlands: Maklu: special edn of the *Journal of Police Studies*, Vol. 2010/3, No. 6

Ni, H. and Das, D. (2006) *Policing in Finland: The cultural basis of law enforcement*, Lewiston, NY: The Edwin Mellen Press

Nogala, D. (2001) Policing across a dimorphous border: challenge and innovation at the French-German border, *European Journal of Crime and Criminology, Law and Criminal Justice*, 9, 130

Occhipinti, J. (2003) *The politics of EU police cooperation: Toward a European FBI?* Boulder, CO: Lynne Rienner Publishers

Olsen, J. (2002) The many faces of Europeanization, *Journal of Common Market Studies*, Vol. 40, pp. 921-52

O'Neill, M. (2008) What Should egalitarians believe?, *Philosophy and Public Affairs*, Vol. 36, No. 2, pp. 121-156

O'Neill, S. and Elliot, F. (2014) Now Boris targets May over Tory Leadership, *The Times*, 11 June 2014. www.thetimes.co.uk/tto/news/politics/article4115153.ece

Organization for Security and Co-operation in Europe (2008) *OSCE Guidebook on Democratic Policing*, 2nd edn. Vienna: OSCE Publishing

Ortmeier, P. and Meese, E. (2009) *Leadership, ethics and policing: Challenges for the 21st century*, Upper Saddle River, NJ: Prentice Hall

Osse, A. and Dossett, G. (2011) *UN handbook on police accountability, oversight and integrity*, New York: United Nations. www.unodc.org/documents/justice-and-prison-reform/crimeprevention/PoliceAccountability_Oversight_and_Integrity_10-57991_Ebook.pdf

Paasi, A. (2001) Europe as a social process and discourse considerations of place, boundaries and identity, *European urban and regional studies*, Vol. 8, No. 1, pp. 7-28

Padurariu, A. (2014) The implementation of police reform in Bosnia and Herzegovina: analysing UN and EU efforts, *Stability: International Journal of Security and Development*, Vol. 3, No.1. www.stabilityjournal.org/article/view/sta.db/175

Pagon, M. (ed.) (1996) *Policing in Central and Eastern Europe. Comparing firsthand knowledge with experience from the West*, Ljubljana, Slovenia: University of Maribor Press

Pagon, M., Bojana, V. and Lobnikar, B. (1996) European systems of police education and training, Slovenia: College of Police and Security Studies. www.ncjrs.gov/policing/eur551.htm

Palmer, S. (1988) *Police and protest in England and Ireland 1780-1850*, Cambridge: Cambridge University Press

Palmiotto, M. and Unnithan, N. (2011) *Policing and society: A global approach*, New York: Delmar

Paoletti, C. (2008) *A military history of Italy*, Westport, CT: Greenwood Publishing Group

Papworth, T. and Wiharta, S. (2001) *Policing Europe: European policing? The challenge of coordination in international policing*, Workshop Report, Stockholm, 4-5 May. www.sipri.org/research/conflict/publications/Policingworkshop_report

Paret, P., Craig, A. and Gilbert, F. (1986) *Makers of modern strategy from Machiavelli to the nuclear age*, Oxford: Oxford University Press

Parris, M. and Bryson, A. (eds) (2011) *Parting shots: Undiplomatic diplomats*, London: Penguin Books

Parry, G. (2005) *Political elites*, Colchester: ECPR Press, University of Essex

Pascouau, Y. (2014) *The future of the area of freedom, security and justice: Addressing mobility, protection and effectiveness in the long run*, Brussels: European Policy Centre

Paterson, C. and Pollock, E. (2011) *Policing and criminology*, Exeter: Learning Matters

Paun, C. (2007) *Democratization and police reform*, Unpublished Master's Dissertation at the Freie Üniversität, Berlin

Pease, K. (2001) Crime futures and foresight: challenging criminal behaviour in the information age, in D. Wall (ed.) *Crime and the internet*, New York, NY: Routledge, pp.18-28

Peterson, A. and Uhnoo, S. (2012) Trials of loyalty: ethnic minority police officers as 'outsiders' within a greedy institution, *European Journal of Criminology*, Vol. 9, No. 4, pp. 354-369

Pomeranz, K. (2009) *The great divergence: China, Europe, and the making of the modern world economy*, Princeton, NJ: Princeton University Press

Ponticelli, J. and Voth, H. J. (2011) *Austerity and anarchy: Budget cuts and social unrest in Europe, 1919-2008*, available at SSRN 1899287

Prügl, E. and Thiel, M. (eds) (2009) *Diversity in the European Union*, Basingstoke: Palgrave Macmillan

Pruvost, G. (2009) A profession in process: the atypical rise of women to the high rank of police 'commissaire' in France, *Sociologie du Travail*, 51S, pp. 34-48

Punch, M. (1996) *Dirty business: Exploring corporate misconduct*, London: Sage

Punch, M. (2003) 'Rotten orchards': 'pestilence', police misconduct and system failure, *Policing and Society*, Vol. 13, No. 2, pp. 171-196

Punch, M. (2005) The Belgian Disease: Dutroux, scandal and 'system failure' in Belgium, in R. Sarre, H. J. Albrecht and D. Das (eds) *Policing corruption: International perspectives*, Lanham, MD: Lexington Books

Punch, M. and Lee, M. (2004) Policing by degrees, *Policing and Society*, Vol. 14, No. 3, pp. 233-249: and an expanded version (2006) *Policing by degrees*, Groningen, Netherlands: Hondsrug Press

Punch, M., van der Vijver, K. and Zoomer, O. (2002) Dutch 'COP': developing community policing in the Netherlands, *Policing: An International Journal of Police Strategies and Management*, Vol. 25, No. 1, pp. 60-79

Radaelli, C. (2006) Europeanization: solution or problem?, in M. Cini and E Bourne (eds) *Palgrave advances in European Studies*, Basingstoke: Palgrave Macmillan, pp. 56-76

Radaelli, C. M. (2012) Europeanization: the challenge of establishing causality, in T. Exadaktylos and C. Radaelli (eds) *Research design in European studies: Establishing causality in Europeanization*, 1-16, London: Palgrave Macmillan

Rapport, M. (2012) The Napoleonic civil code: The Belgian case, in M. Broers, P. Hicks and A. Guimera (eds) *The Napoleonic empire and the new European political culture*, London: Palgrave Macmillan

Rawlinson, P. (2010) *From fear to fraternity: A Russian tale of crime, economy and modernity*, London: Pluto Press

Reichel, P. and Albanese, J. (eds) (2014) *The handbook of transnational crime and justice*, 2nd edn, Thousand Oaks, CA: Sage Publications Inc

Reicherts, M. (2014) EU Commissioner for Justice statement on Human Rights, 18 July

Reiner, R. (1991) *Chief constables: Bobbies, bosses, barons or bureaucrats?* Oxford: Oxford University Press

Reiner, R. (1997) Media made criminality: the representation of crime in the mass media, in M. Maguire, R. Morgan and R. Reiner (eds) *Oxford Handbook of Criminology*, 2nd edn, Oxford: Clarendon Press

reiner, r. (2003) policing and the media, in t. newburn, *handbook of policing*, Devon: Willan Press, pp. 259-281

Reiner, R. (2010) *The politics of the police*, 4th edn, Oxford: Oxford University Press

Reinke, H. (2009) German policing, in A. Wakefield and J. Fleming (eds) *The Sage dictionary of policing*, London: Sage Publications, pp.146-147

Reiter, H. and Fillieule, O. (2013) Formalizing the informal: the EU approach to transnational protest policing, in D. della Porta, A. Peterson and H. Reiter (eds) *The policing of transnational protest*, London: Ashgate Publishing

Reith, C. (1956) *A new study of police history*, London: Oliver and Boyd

Resetnikova, A. (2006) Women in policing in a transforming organization: the case of the Estonian police, *The Journal of Power Institutions in Post-Soviet Societies*, Vol. 4, No. 5: (unpaginated). http://pipss.revues.org/502

Reynolds, E. (1998) *Before the Bobbies: The night watch and police reform in metropolitan London, 1720-1830*, Stanford, CA: Stanford University Press and Macmillan Ltd

Rhodes, R., Hart, P. and Noordegraaf, M. (2007) *Observing government elites: Up close and personal*, London: Palgrave-Macmillan

Rice, G. (2010) Reflections on interviewing elites, *Area*, Vol. 42, No. 1, pp. 70-75

Rigakos, G. and Papanicolaou, G. (2003) The political economy of Greek policing: between neo-liberalism and the sovereign state, *Policing and Society: An International Journal of Research and Policy*, Vol. 13, Issue 3, pp. 271-304

Rijken, C. and Vermeulen, G. (2006) *Joint investigation teams in the European Union: From theory to practice*, The Hague: TMC Asser Press

Rix, A., Faye J., Maguire, M. and Morton, S. (2009) *Improving public confidence in the police: A review of the evidence*, Home Office Research Report No. 28, December, London: Home Office

Roberson, C., Das, D. and Singer, J. (eds) (2010) *Police without borders: The fading distinction between local and global*, New York: CRC Press (Taylor and Francis)

Rolph, C. (1962) Report of the Royal Commission on the Police, *British Journal of Criminology*, Vol. 3, pp. 177-179

Rosenberg, S. (2011) Anders Breivik Trial: a ten week ordeal, *BBC*. www.bbc.co.uk/news/magazine-18558319

Rowe, P. (2002) *Control over armed forces exercised by the European Court of Human Rights*, Geneva Centre for the Democratic Control of Armed Forces. Working paper series, No. 56

Ruggiero, V. (2014) Organised and transnational crime in Europe, in S. Body-Gendrot, M. Hough, R. Levy, K. Kerezsi and S. Snacken (eds) *The Routledge handbook of European criminology*, Chapter 9, pp. 154-167

Sandford, D. (2014) Ukraine crisis: Vladimir Putin visits annexed Crimea, *BBC News Europe*, 9 May. www.bbc.co.uk/news/world-europe-27344029

Santiago, M. (2000) *Europol and police cooperation in Europe*, Lewiston, New York: The Edwin Mellen Press

Savage, S., Chapman, S. and Cope, S. (2000) *Policing and the power of persuasion: The changing role of the Association of Chief Police Officers*, London: Blackstone Press

Savage, M. and Williams, K. (2008) *Remembering elites*, Oxford: Wiley-Blackwell

Scarborough, K., Van Tubergen, G., Gaines, L. and Whitlow, S. (1999) An examination of police officers' motivation to participate in the promotional process, *Police Quarterly*, Vol. 2 No. 3, pp. 302-20

Schafer, J. (2010) Effective leaders and leadership in policing: traits, assessment, development and expansion, *Policing: An International Journal of Police Strategies and Management*, Vol. 33, Issue 4, pp. 644-663

Schalken, T. and Pronk, M. (2002) On joint investigation teams, Europol and supervision of their joint actions, Vol. 10, No. 1, *European Journal on Crime Criminal Law and Criminal Justice*, 70-79, http://heinonline.org/HOL/LandingPage?collection=journalsandhandle=hein.journals/eccc10anddiv=12andid=andpage=

Schmeidel, J. (2008) *Stasi: Shield and sword of the party*, New York: Routledge

Schmidt, V. (2004) Democratic challenges for the EU as 'regional state,' *EUSA Review*, 17, pp. 4-5

Schmuckler, E. (2013) Strategic planning, in M. Kurke and E. Scrivner (eds) *Police psychology into the 21st century*, Hove, Sussex: Psychology Press

Schneider, C. L. (2008) Police power and race riots in Paris, *Politics and Society*, Vol. 36, No. 1, pp. 133-159

Schulz, D. (2003) Women police chiefs: a statistical profile, *Police Quarterly*, Vol. 6 No. 3, pp. 330-45

Schulz, D. (2004) *Breaking the brass ceiling: Women Police chiefs and their paths to the top*, Westport, CT: Praeger Publishing

Scott, J. (ed.) (1990) *The sociology of elites*, 3 vols, Aldershot: Edgar

Seba, I. and Rowley, J. (2010) Knowledge management in UK police forces, *Journal of Knowledge Management*, Vol. 14, Issue 4, pp. 611- 626

Shah, G. (2002) *Top cops: Biographies of world's top policemen*, 3 vols, New Delhi: Cosmo

Shaw, M. (2002) Crime, police and public in transitional societies, *Transformation: Critical perspectives on Southern Africa*, Vol. 49, No.1, pp. 1–24

Shelley, L. (1999) Post-socialist policing: limitations on institutional change, in Rob Mawby (ed.) *Policing across the world*, London: Routledge

Sheptycki, J. (1995) Transnational policing and the makings of a postmodern state, *British Journal of Criminology,* Vol. 35, No. 4, pp. 613-635

Sheptycki, J. (ed.) (2000) *Issues in transnational policing*, London: Routledge

Sheptycki, J. (2002) Accountability across the policing field: towards a general cartography of accountability for post-modern policing, *Policing and Society*, Vol. 12, No. 4, pp. 323-338

Sheptycki, J. and Wardak, A. (eds) (2005) *Transnational and comparative criminology*, Routledge-Cavendish

Siegel, D. (2014) *Mobile banditry: East and Central European itinerant criminal groups in the Netherlands*, The Hague: Eleven International Publishing

Silverman, D. (2005) *Doing qualitative research*, 2nd edn, London: Sage Publications

Silvestri, M. (2003) *Women in charge: Policing, gender and leadership*, Devon: Willan Publishing

Silvestri, M. (2006) 'Doing time': Becoming a police leader, *International Journal of Police Science and Management*, Vol. 8, No. 4, pp. 266-281

Silvestri, M. (2007) 'Doing' police leadership: enter the 'new smart macho', *Policing and Society*, Vol. 17, No. 1, March, pp. 38-58

Silvestri, M., Tong, S. and Brown, J. (2013) Gender and police leadership: time for a paradigm shift?, *International Journal of Police Science and Management*, Vol. 15, No. 1, pp. 61-73

Sinclair, G. and Williams, C. (2007) 'Home and away': the cross-fertilisation between 'colonial' and 'British' policing, 1921–85, *Journal of Imperial and Commonwealth History*, Vol. 35, No. 2, pp. 221-238

Slaughter, A.-M. (2009) *A new world order*, Princeton, NJ: Princeton University Press

Smith, A. (2013) Europe and an inter-dependent world: Uneven geo-economic and geo-political developments, *European Urban and Regional Studies*, Vol. 20, No. 1, pp. 3-13

Smith, G. (2009) Citizen oversight of independent police services: bifurcated accountability, regulation creep, and lesson learning, *Regulation and Governance*, Vol. 3, No. 4, pp. 421-441

Soeters, J., Hofstede, G. and Van Twuyver, M. (1995) Culture's consequences and the police: cross-border cooperation between police forces in Germany, Belgium and the Netherlands, *Policing and Society: An International Journal*, Vol. 5, No. 1, pp. 1-14

Sommer, P. (2004) The future for the policing of cybercrime, *Computer Fraud and Security*, Vol. 1, pp. 8-12

Sørensen, E. and Torfing, J. (2003) Network politics, political capital, and democracy, *International Journal of Public Administration*, Vol. 26, No. 6, pp. 609-634

Stead, P. (1983) *The police of France*, London: Collier Macmillan Publishers

Stefanescu, M. (2001) Governance in Romania, in A. Kadar (ed.) *Police in transition: Essays on the police forces in transition countries*, Budapest, Hungary: Central European University Press

Stevens, J. (Lord) (2013) *Policing for a better Britain: Report of the Independent Police Commission* (Labour Party funded), http://independentpolicecommission.org.uk/uploads/37d80308-be23-9684-054d-e4958bb9d518.pdf

Stone, C. (2007) Tracing police accountability in theory and practice from Philadelphia to Abuja and Sao Paulo, *Theoretical Criminology*, Vol. 11, No. 2, pp. 245-259

Storey, J. (2005) What next for strategic-level leadership research?, *Leadership*, Vol. 1, No. 1, pp. 89-104

Suman, K. (1998) Self-evaluations of police performance: an analysis of the relationship between police officers' education level and job performance, *Policing: An International Journal of Police Strategies and Management*, Vol. 21, Issue 4, pp. 632-647

Sun, I. and Wasileski, G. (2010) Gender differences in occupational attitudes among Slovak police, *International Criminal Justice Review*, September, Vol. 20, No. 3, pp. 248-264

Symonds, T. (2014) Child abuse image investigation leads to 660 arrests, *BBC News*, 26 July. www.bbc.co.uk/news/uk-28326128

Tabur, L. (2013) Policing in Estonia: from police force to police service, in G. Meško, C. Fields, B. Lobnikar and A. Sotlar (eds) *Handbook on Policing in Central and Eastern Europe*, New York: Springer Books, pp. 81-91

Tak, J. (2005) The relationship between public prosecutors and the police in the member states of the Council of Europe, *Council of Europe, Conference of Public Prosecutors of Europe*, 6th Session, May

Tang, Y. and Zhong, L. (2013) Toward a demystification of egalitarianism, *Philosophical Forum*, Vol. 44, No. 2, pp. 149-163

Thoral, M.-C. (2012) Small state, big society: the involvement of citizens in local government in nineteenth-century France, in M. Broers, P. Hicks and A. Guimera (eds) *The Napoleonic empire and the new European political culture*, London: Palgrave Macmillan

Tiffany, D. and Tiffany, P. (1973) Social unrest: powerlessness and/or self-direction?, *American Psychologist*, Vol. 28, No. 2, pp. 151-154

Timoney, J. (2010) *Beat cop to top cop: A tale of three cities*, Philadelphia, PA: University of Pennsylvania Press

Tobias, J. (1975) Police and the public in the United Kingdom, *Police Forces in History,* London: Sage Publications

Tonry, M. and Bijleveld, C. (2007) Crime, criminal justice, and criminology in the Netherlands, *Crime and Justice*, Vol. 35, No.1, pp. 1-30

Treverton, G., Wollman, M., Wilke, E. and Lai, D. (2011) *Moving toward the future of policing*, Santa Monica, CA: The Rand Corporation Monographs. www.rand.org/content/dam/rand/pubs/monographs/2011/RAND_MG1102.sum.pdf

Tsifakis, N. (2012) *Contracting out to private military and security companies*, Brussels: Centre for European Studies. http://martenscentre.eu/sites/default/files/publication-files/contracting_out_private_military_and_security_companies.pdf

Tupman, B. and Tupman, A. (1999) *Policing in Europe: Uniform in diversity*, Exeter: Intellect Books (European Studies Series)

Urban, M. (2003) *Rifles: Six years with Wellington's legendary sharpshooters*, London: Faber

van Buuren, J. (2012) Runaway bureaucracy? The European Police Chiefs Task Force, *Policing: A Journal of Policy and Practice*, Vol. 6, Issue 3, pp. 281-290

van der Burg, M. and Lok, M. (2012) The Dutch case: the Kingdom of Holland and the imperial departments, in M. Broers, P. Hicks and A. Guimerá, (eds.) *The Napoleonic empire and the new European political culture*, London: Palgrave

van der Lippe, T., Graumans, A. and Sevenhuijsen, S. (2004) Gender policies and the position of women in the police force in European countries, *Journal of European Social Policy*, Vol. 14, No. 4, pp. 391-405

Van Dijk, T. (1993) *Elite discourse and racism*, Thousand Oaks, CA: Sage Publications van Ewijk, A. (2011) Diversity within police forces in Europe: a case for the comprehensive view, *Policing*, November, pp. 1-17. www.upf.edu/gritim/_pdf/diversity_within_police_forces_europe_vanewijk.pdf

van Sluis, A., Marks, P. and Bekkers, V. (2011) Nodal policing in the Netherlands: strategic and normative considerations on an evolving practice, *Policing*, Vol. 5, No. 4, pp. 365-371

van Steden, R. and Sarre, R. (2007) The growth of private security: trends in the European Union, *Security Journal*, Vol. 20, No. 4, pp. 222-235

Vast, A. and Kuitert, J. (2009) Eurojust and the European Judicial Network, *NTER (Dutch Journal of European Law)* pp. 298-305

Vegh, S. (2002) Hacktivists or cyberterrorists? The changing media discourse on hacking, *First Monday*, Vol. 7, No. 10. http://ojs-prod-lib.cc.uic.edu/ojs/index.php/fm/article/view/998

Verbitz, M. (2004) New Russia (in an old trap), *Perspective*, Vol. 14, No. 3, pp. 1-12, Boston University

Verhage, A. Terpstra, J., Deelman, P., Muylaert, E. and van Parys, P. (eds) (2010) *Policing in Europe*, Netherlands: Maklu: special edn of the *Journal of Police Studies*, Vol. 2010/3, No. 6

Videtic, J. (2000) Policing democracy: the Slovenian experience, *Challenges of policing democracies: A world perspective*, pp. 343-352

Vinnicombe, S. (2000) The position of women in management in Europe, in M. Davidson and R. Burke (eds) *Women in management: Current research issues*, Vol. 2, pp. 9-25

Vinton, K., (1998) Nepotism: an interdisciplinary model, *Family Business Review*, Vol. 1, No. 4, pp. 297-303

Waddington, P. A. (1999) *Policing citizens: Authority and rights*, London: Psychology Press

Wainwright, R. (2013) Serious and organised crime threat assessment, Europol, www.europol.europa.eu/content/eu-serious-and-organised-crime-threat-assessment-socta

Walker, N. (1993) The accountability of European policing institutions, *European Journal on Criminal Policy and Research,* Vol. 1, No. 4, pp. 34-52

Walker, S. (2005) *The new world of police accountability*, Thousand Oaks, CA: Sage

Wall, D. (1998) *The chief constables of England and Wales: The socio-legal history of a criminal justice elite*, Aldershot: Ashgate

Wall, D. (ed.) (2001) *Crime and the internet*, New York, NY: Routledge

Wallace, H., Pollack, M. and Young, A. (eds) (2010) *Policy making in the European union*, 6th edn, Oxford: Oxford University Press

Wallace, W. (1994) Rescue or retreat? The nation state in Western europe, 1945–93, *Political Studies*, Vol. 42, s.1, pp. 52-76

Walsh, D. and Conway, V. (2011) Police governance and accountability: overview of current issues, *Crime, Law and Social Change*, Vol. 55, Nos. 2-3, pp. 61-86

Walsh, D., Conway, V. and Walker, N. (2002) Policing and the supranational, *Policing and Society,* Vol. 12, No. 4, pp. 307-321

Waters, I., Hardy N., Delgado, D. and Dahlmann, S. (2007) Ethnic minorities and the challenge of police recruitment, *The Police Journal*, Vol. 80, pp. 191-216

Watson, T. and Hickman, M. (2012) *Dial M for Murdoch*, London: Penguin

Weber, R. (2001) Police organisation and accountability, in A. Kadar (ed.) *Police in Transition, Essays on the police forces in transition countries*, Budapest, Hungary: Central European University Press

Weiss, T. (2012) *Blurring border between the police and the military in the EU: The new research agenda*, paper presented at Policing and European Studies conference, University of Abertay, 18 January, http://policingandeuropeanstudies.abertay.ac.uk/?m=201201

Weitzer, R. (2005) New directions in research on prostitution, *Crime, Law and Social Change*, Vol. 43, Nos.4-5, pp. 211-235

Welch, C., Marschan-Piekkari, R., Penttinen, H. and Tahvanainen, M. (2002) Interviewing elites in international organizations: a balancing act for the researcher, *International Business Review*, Vol. 11, No. 5, pp. 611-628

Whetstone, T. and Wilson, D. (1999) Dilemmas confronting female police officer promotional candidates: glass ceiling, disenfranchisement or satisfaction?, *International Journal of Police Science and Management*, Vol. 2, No. 2, pp. 128-43

West, J. (2011) *Karama! Journeys through the Arab Spring*, London: Heron Books

Williams, C. (2012) *Researching power, elites and leadership*, London: Sage Publications

Williams, M. (2010) Cybercrime, in F. Brookman, M. Maguire, H. Pierpoint and T. Bennett (eds) *Handbook on Crime*, Devon: Willan Publishing, pp.191-213

Winsor, T. (2012) *Independent Review of police officer and staff remuneration and conditions*, Cm 8325, London: The Stationery Office. www.gov.uk/government/uploads/system/uploads/attachment_data/file/250812/8325_i.pdf

Wintle, M. (1996) Policing the liberal state in the Netherlands: The historical context of the current reorganization of the Dutch police, *Policing and Society: An International Journal*, Vol. 6, No. 3, pp. 181-197

Wolcott, H. (2009) *Writing up Qualitative Research*, 3rd edn, Thousand Oaks, CA: Sage Publications Inc

Wolfe, N. (1992) *Policing a socialist society: The German Democratic Republic*, Westport, CN: Greenwood Press

Woollons, N. (1991) Europe: a short history of policing, *Law and Order*, Vol. 39, No. 4

Wright, A. (2001) Policing a diversity of cultures: community policing in transforming societies, *Policing in transition*, Budapest: CEU Press, pp. 157-175

Wright, A., Alison, L. and Crego, J. (2008) The current state of police leadership research, in L. Alison and J. Crego (eds) *Policing critical incidents: Leadership and critical management*, ibid

Wyngaert, van den C. (2004) Eurojust and European public prosecutor in the *Corpus Juris* model: water and fire?, in N. Walker (ed.) *Europe's area of freedom, security and justice*, XIII/2, 201-239, Collected Courses of the Academy of European Law, Oxford: Oxford University Press

Yar, M. (2013) *Cybercrime and society*, 2nd edn, London: Sage Publications

Ziemke, E. (1975) *The US Army in the occupation of Germany, 1944-1946*, Washington, DC: Center of Military History

Zott, H. (2002) Grundlagen internationaler Zusammenarbeit in der Kriminalitätskontrolle im Rahmen der Europäischen Union [Fundamentals of international cooperation in crime control within the European Union], *Schriftenreihe der Polizei-Führungsakademie: Mobilität und Kriminalität – Die Straße als Tatort,* [Short title: *Schriftenreihe der PFA*], Vol. 4, No. 4, pp. 103-116

Zuckerman, F. (1996) *The Tsarist secret police in Russian society, 1880-1917*, New York: New York University Press

Index

Note: References to tables are in *italics*. References to footnotes give the page number followed by the note number (eg. 59n4)